Crooked Cats

'*Crooked Cats* brings together a tapestry of material on the societal and environmental setting of big cat–human encounters in a changing world. Rich in insight yet easily accessible to all, a book not to be missed.'

– Dr Mahesh Rangarajan, Ashoka University

'In this captivating book, Mathur offers a sensitive examination of ordinary ethical struggle with cruelties and injustices spawned by human domination of the earth. She writes gripping stories of big cats, mostly from within the villages and towns of Himalayan north India, to bridge the different ways in which the global climate crisis has been imagined, understood, and explained. This is precisely the bridge that must be crossed to reach solutions that are locally meaningful and globally just.'

– K. Sivaramakrishnan, Yale University

'At a time when scholarship is highlighting the phenomenon of extinction, Mathur offers an important intervention that redirects attention from this accelerating absence by focusing instead on imaginatively constituted interactions between humans and animals under threat. Introducing many innovative, intriguing, and witty concepts, *Crooked Cats* is a distinctive contribution to the ongoing and ever-evolving conversation about human–animal conflict and coexistence.'

– Kath Weston, University of Virginia

Crooked Cats

Beastly Encounters in the Anthropocene

NAYANIKA MATHUR

HarperCollins *Publishers* India

First published in the USA by the University of Chicago Press Ltd in 2021
University of Chicago Press,
1427 E. 60th St., Chicago, IL 60637

First published in India by HarperCollins *Publishers* 2022
4th Floor, Tower A, Building No. 10, Phase II, DLF Cyber City,
Gurugram, Haryana – 122002
www.harpercollins.co.in

2 4 6 8 10 9 7 5 3 1

P-ISBN: 978-93-5489-587-6
E-ISBN: 978-93-5489-393-3

Printed and bound at
Thomson Press (India) Ltd

To Tapsi

छोटी बहन

CONTENTS

PREFACE

Living With That Which Might Kill You

As 2022 begins we are being told that we must learn to live with the novel coronavirus. This book, too, is about living with a nonhuman that may—or may not—kill you. It is concerned with what such a living-with entails and what it might teach us about the planet we currently inhabit. Two years into the pandemic we are still struggling to come to terms with the losses endured, to somehow make sense of it all. This book, too, wrestles with finding a language—and a storyline—that can adequately express what it is to live with potentially predatory big cats in your midst and, perhaps most importantly, why this story needs to be told afresh in this moment of planetary crisis.

But I get ahead of myself in this recounting of striking similarities between the questions—intellectual, political, literary, existential—opened up by the pandemic and the beasts that haunt this book.

Let us take a step back in time to March 2020 when the Covid-19 pandemic really began to feel terrifyingly real. "Apologies for the apocalypse" signed off an email as my university went into a lockdown. In more muted terms, other messages noted that this was an "extraordinary time." Most struggled to find an analogous moment in living memory. Strangely enough, for me that period of quarantine—in which I was putting the final touches to this book—was eerily reminiscent of the very period in my life that led to the birth of *Crooked Cats* in the first place.

"Stay home, stay safe!" we were told in the UK as the pandemic silently swept through the world. Going even further back in time, this was precisely the only protection that was at hand over three months in 2006–2007 when a leopard haunted the small Himalayan town of Gopeshwar in the north Indian state of Uttarakhand. Then, I had been living in Gopeshwar for my doctoral fieldwork. The leopard—or *bagh,* as it is known in Hindi—was a crooked cat, or what are popularly known as "man-eaters." She spread what was widely described as "a reign of terror" in the town and surrounding villages, and killed and ate seven humans before she was herself hunted down. During this period, it was hard for us to leave our houses other than in big groups and in broad daylight. Before dusk fell, we would scurry home and firmly lock the doors, not daring to step out till the next day. At night we shivered with fright in our beds, hearing—or imagining we were hearing—her beastly roar echo through the small Himalayan town. Our lives were at risk, quite literally, if we left our homes—a feeling that reverberated through the early lockdowns around the world.

I laughed inwardly when I read these lines from the diary of an Italian editor under lockdown in Florence: "We live as if a predator roams outside. And no one knows when it will tire of the hunt and move on."[1] The similarities between the first European lockdown and the reign of terror of the big cat in the Indian Himalaya were not just a spatial incarceration and the unknowability of how long the situation might persist for, critical as those aspects are. The resemblance was also in some features of this moment in the world that lie at the heart of this project: a dawning awareness of the intricate entanglements between spheres that are often kept apart, especially human–nonhuman relationships and planetary health, and the ways in which a slight change in one affects the other. Consider the videos of starving monkeys in Thailand and India and deer in Japan that were supposedly behaving oddly—fighting among one another or traveling to metro stations and crowded traffic-filled streets in pursuance of food—due to a drop in human tourists. Obversely, in some quarters, narratives of a resurgent nature came to dominate, with a celebration of, for instance, the return of fish to Venetian canals or dolphins to the shores of Mumbai. Such "digital ecological encounters" (Turnbull, Searle, and W. Adams 2020) led to a problematic mode of storytelling regarding the pandemic. In lieu of the "nature is healing/returning" account, the pandemic should actually push us to more clearly see how inextricably entangled human and nonhuman lives are (N. Mathur 2020).

More than two years in we are still racked with uncertainty over the pandemic. Even questions of the origin of Covid-19 linger on—and probably always will do so (Lynteris 2020).[2] What does it mean to say Covid is now endemic? How—if ever—will this pandemic end? What will the next variant look like and for how long can the current vaccines offer a defence? We all seek answers to these and so many other questions and cannot really find crystal-clear responses. The many questions that the pandemic has opened up, which may or may not be answered with time, mimic the foundationally questioning nature of *Crooked Cats*. This book, too, is as much about asking new questions as it is about answering them with certainty. It works through the complexities and unresolvable unknowing associated with managing and living with big cats that have gone rogue and are, inexplicably, turning on humans.

What is becoming apparent with the pandemic is the profound difference that political systems, state forms, and leadership styles are making to the management of the pandemic.[3] Different political, economic, and social systems are producing distinct results in the handling of seemingly the same virus. Some governance regimes have proven to be markedly more successful, and some have shown themselves to be abject failures. India, especially during the devastating second wave of 2021, is placed firmly in the latter category. In the pages that follow, there is an overarching interest in human-designed, historically-molded political systems and the critical role they play in regulating crooked cats—what I term "the government of big cats." This form of nonhuman governance is akin to, but also departs in some vital ways from, governmental regimes directed at humans. Hitherto, the governance of nonhuman animals has been kept somewhat apart from the study of the Anthropocene as well as from multispecies ethnography.

Finally, what does the Anthropocene have to do with the pandemic? Everything, if certain voices are to be believed. The pandemic is directly linked to habitat loss, which is forcing animals into a "repeated, intimate contact" with humans "that allows the microbes that live in their bodies to cross over into ours, transforming benign animal microbes into deadly human pathogens."[4] The real story of the pandemic, according to some voices, is not that of the novel coronavirus jumping from an animal into humans, but that of the ecological collapse and the modern models of agribusiness with regard to industrial meat production that are increasing zoonotic diseases. Contemporary capitalist forms and the destruction of habitats are coming together to create this pandemic. Many of these connections aren't easy to trace out, even more than two years in, but they are absolutely vital to understand.

To clear my head, I have taken to long walks in Oxford.

I often begin by walking to my college, which sits on the Cherwell River. Oftentimes the river is in flood, with the waters rising to drown out the harbor where the punts are otherwise tethered, and the fields around it. It doesn't, quite yet, threaten the college buildings, but the flooding reminds me of the images I saw—in utter horror—in June 2013 of the divine disaster, the *daiviya apada*, in Uttarakhand, where the river Ganges, in a ferocious flood, ripped through the mountains, killing thousands and causing destruction of an unimaginable form. It was as if the rage of the river would destroy everything it touched. Eating, as an act and as an analogy, is found in this book: being eaten by animals, like the big cats that animate this book; the eating of money, used to signify corruption and the greed for political power above all else, in India; the earth itself opening up and swallowing living beings as revenge for the harms visited upon her. Disasters of such a form, that we can now with greater certainty term "climate disasters", are becoming commonplace in Uttarakhand. Take what is popularly known as the Chamoli disaster that occurred in February 2021, the very region in which this book was birthed. A core proposition of this book is that the tales of crooked cats are intimately linked to the climate disasters or *apadas* that we now see regularly taking place all over South Asia.

Walking away from the college, I approach a spot I go to often when I am stuck with the writing. I only head here after it is dark and the streets are abandoned, and my only real companions are the friendly foxes that live in this leafy neighborhood too. There is a house that has a tiger peeping out of the front window. The tiger is a giant stuffed one, and I can spot it only when the light in this room, which appears to my prying eyes to be a small study, is on. The first time I noticed this big cat, I had been cycling past it late in the night and nearly fell off my bike in shock. The tiger in the Oxford window reminds me of something I had felt all those years back in Gopeshwar: the fact that there is a big cat, somewhere in the town, that is watching you closely. There are beastly eyes trained on you all the time, but it is only rarely that you spot them yourself as a human. What does it mean to inhabit such a world? Especially now, when the numbers of these nonhuman animals are dwindling worldwide. What would it mean for these eyes to vanish altogether, but, more pertinently for this moment in history, how does one capture this living-beside in a text?

As I walk on from the tiger window, I come, once again, to the river—this time in a disciplined form as a canal—and walk alongside it, glancing at the water levels and the boats and the ducks, into Jericho, where alongside the gleaming Blavatnik School of Government that is so controversially named after its Russian oligarch donor, a vast, empty piece of land stands. On this spot the new Schwarzman Centre for the Humanities is going to come up through Stephen Schwarzman's £150 million donation to Oxford—described by the university as the "largest donation since the Renaissance."[5] Contemplating that large clearing, I muse that the line between the climate crisis and this to-be building is, actually, a direct one. Stephen A. Schwarzman is a US financier who is also the cofounder and chairman of Blackstone, which is considered a major contributor to the global housing crisis and the deforestation of the Amazon.[6] In the case of big cats dying out as a species or behaving in an odd manner, the relationship between habitat destruction, global warming, and capitalism is, to my mind, similarly clear. But somehow, just as Oxford University turns its face away from the truth of the Schwarzman Centre, so too there continues to be a reluctance to understand big cats within such a planetary, climatic framing.

Farther down the road heading toward the town center stand the grand premises of Oxford University Press (OUP). Inside the OUP head office are stored the archives of Jim Corbett, a prominent colonial hunter-conservationist-writer whose work and legacy are central to the story of this book. I continue on to the Ashmolean Museum, where lions from ancient Egypt sit beside Mughal miniature paintings depicting tiger hunting, past the Oxford India Institute (OII) next to the Bod (as the Bodleian Library is referred to) with the elephant wind vane at the top. The OII was built directly by money gathered from India when she was under British colonial rule. Probably the most Orientalized wind vane in the world—in the shape of an elephant—is located on the roof of the OII. This building with "Oxford India Institute" emblazoned on it was, however, mysteriously emptied of its Indianists and taken over by the university in what appears to be a land grab a few years back. I hold the seminars for my climate-crisis research network in the OII, as the funder for this network is now based in the same building. Every time I walk past the wooden doors with ornate Kashmiri engravings in the OII or see some of the Indian art on the walls, I am reminded anew of the imperial histories that the wealth and privilege of Oxford rest on. On the road parallel to the OII—just past the Radcliffe Camera and All Souls College—stands the statue of Cecil Rhodes, in the very heart of Oxford. The imperial relationship between my two homes of India and Britain plays out in the pages that follow, where the colonial power's history of governing and knowing big cats and controlling the "jungliness" (wildness) of India is intimately bound up with the present in complicated ways.

I often end up at the anthropology museum named the Pitt Rivers Museum (PRM). Despite my familiarity with this space, given that I often attend seminars here, I still respond viscerally to it. Walking past the natural history museum with its dinosaur skeletons, one arrives at the PRM, where Naga masks from India and other exotica sit side by side. The love of alterity that remains at the beating heart of anthropology as a discipline is up on spectacular display here (Chua and N. Mathur 2018). I am, however, conscious of my colleagues' and students' efforts to reckon with these uncomfortable pasts and decolonize these sites and, indeed, the university.[7] These ongoing moves mirror my own struggles with anthropology as a discipline and with an academic life largely spent in overwhelmingly white academic institutions of the United Kingdom, as well as with the teaching of South Asian studies in what once used to be the center of empire.

My perambulations around Oxford not only reveal the material-affective conditions of production of my scholarship but also reflect many concerns of this book. It is an attempt to make connections between the past, the present, and the perceived future through a focus on an inscrutable subject—crooked cats—and the deployment of methodological tools gained from a discipline that I simultaneously value and find uncomfortable. As I repeat often in this work, there is no certainty to my arguments, no overarching theory or method that I deploy, and no forensic clarity on the question of living with big cats. The Anthropocene frames this work as it allows me to mold it to my desire; it is as yet an open and broad enough concept that is amenable to politicization and can—if deployed correctly—open up discussions of the deep damage visited by humans on this planet. It also allows me to make the connections I feel urgently need to be made, and to move away from the purity of one discipline or even subfield like multispecies ethnography. With no established canon on the Anthropocene quite yet, my ambition is to bend the concept to my will in order to draw attention to both the fragility and the vitality of the relationship between humans and big cats in India.

Nayanika Mathur
April 2022

INTRODUCTION

The Beastly Tale of the Leopard of Gopeshwar

This book has emerged from the life and death of one particular big cat (*bagh*)—the leopard of Gopeshwar. This was the first crooked cat I came to intimately know: to sense, feel, and fear. She arrived one winter morning in a town called Gopeshwar in the Indian Himalaya and was hunted down three months later. I never, mercifully, saw her until after she was gone. But I felt her presence almost constantly: through her pugmarks; the corpses and injuries left behind; the dogs and other animals that vanished; her beastly *chinghaad*—scream-like roar—that she would let out in the middle of the night; gossip, rumor, jokes; the taste of fear; and the hair that stood up on the back of my neck. So overwhelming was her presence that I began to maintain a bagh diary, which sat alongside my personal diary and my fieldwork notes.

None of us ever knew beyond a modicum of doubt why the leopard of Gopeshwar (*Gopeshwar-wallah bagh*), as she was called, went off the straight and narrow path and became crooked (*tedha*) by attacking and eating humans. However, everyone was certain that human actions had something to do with her abnormal behavior. We were all terrified of her but were also, contradictorily, somewhat in awe of her. When she was finally killed, we celebrated and felt overwhelming relief but also shed a silent tear. Her corpse was paraded on the front of a forest department jeep with a red mark (*tilak*) on her forehead. The hunter, resplendent in his *shikari* (hunting) gear, and several police and forest department officials, also dressed in their khakis, stood behind with more than a touch of triumph (figure 0.1). Those three months of living with a fearsome beast evoked such a jumble of conflicting emotions and left so many unanswered questions hanging in the air that this book, somehow, had to be written.

There are, I was told, two types of big cats. There are those that are *seedha-saadha* (straightforward/simple) and are as scared of humans as we are of

0.1. Hunter posing with a "man-eater" he has killed and agents of the state. Credit: Lakhpat Singh Rawat

them, if not more. Such bagh—the vast majority of leopards, tigers, and lions, in fact—know how to live with humans and are careful to avoid any unpleasant encounters with them. The problem lies with the other type of bagh, those that have gone off the straight and narrow path to become *tedha* (crooked). Popularly known as "man-eaters" (*adamkhor*), these big cats actively prey on humans. Their crookedness leads them to disrupt the peaceful coexistence that otherwise prevails between humans and big cats.

What makes a big cat crooked? How do we humans come to recognize and intimately know a crooked cat? How does one live beside such beasts? And what might they have to do with the climate crisis and life in the Anthropocene or, even more perplexingly, with disciplinary boundaries, methodologies, and the question of how academic writing intervenes in the world?

These are some of the questions that emerge directly from the beastly tale of the leopard of Gopeshwar. There is no resolution forthcoming in this book inspired by a particular big cat, no forensic clarity on why big cats become crooked and make prey of humans, no attempted prescription on how we can fix this unique problem of lions, tigers, and leopards that devour humans in India. What lies ahead, instead, are tales of multispecies encounters that seek to ask new questions emerging from an ethnographic grounding in India, while a planet in crisis looms large in the background.

†

Early on in my research on crooked cats I met a young man at a tea stall (*dhaba*) in a small town in the central Indian Himalaya. Shuddering slightly at the remembrance, he recounted a beastly tale to me. Two years ago he had been walking home from a friend's house when a leopard suddenly appeared out of nowhere and dug its teeth into his right arm. As it was early evening and he was in a busy part of town, other people came running up to defend him and managed to yank the leopard off his body. In doing so, a large chunk of his arm was ripped off and had to be subsequently amputated in its entirety. All through our conversation, he kept gesturing with his left hand to the prominent absence on the right side of his body:

> Do you know why that leopard attacked me? Because he has no food left for himself anymore up here in the mountains. Everything here is dying: the forests, the rivers, the soil, the animals. The only living beings left are us humans and even we won't last here for much longer at the rate things are going. And the reason for all of this is that they [the Indian state and elites from the plains] come here to cut down our trees, to steal our minerals and water. They rob us of all that rightfully belongs to the mountains. Our rivers are dammed to generate power for the air conditioners in their own houses in the cities of the plains when most of our villages remain unelectrified . . . they drive around in their big cars but they don't even bother to build roads for us up here. Their industries spew out all this filth which comes up here to ruin our environment. . . . We are being eaten up alive by leopards and tigers but even then they remain more concerned with saving the life of big cats than our human life. I don't blame the *adamkhor bagh* [man-eating big cats] but I do blame our *sarkar* [state] that is nothing but a *kaghazi bagh* [paper tiger] . . . the real truth is this has been happening for ages and ages [*arzon se*]—even from the time of the *angrez* [British], but it is only becoming worse and worse now with the current state of Indian democracy [*loktantra*].[1]

I was to hear similar narratives across the Himalaya. When I would ask residents of the mountains about crooked cats, they would refer to human actors and historically shaped political structures. The presence of an exploitative state that is only interested in furthering the interests of its own narrow coterie of powerful and wealthy people, all living in the distant plains of India, was particularly stressed. This state (*sarkar*) does not care if human lives are being brutally lost and is interested only in the exploitation and expropriation of the rich natural resources of the mountains. Mere lip service is paid to the need to conserve big cats. And those who are genuine about the need to preserve the lives of big cats tend to do so without according the same worth to human lives. Capital was ever-present in these accounts—in the form of polluting, fume-spitting, resource-draining big businesses and the lopsided fruits of such industries that benefit a thin sliver of the population. Empire, too, was never absent, with references made to the British Raj, and the postcolonial Indian state was oftentimes accused of practicing a form of "internal colonialism." Metaphors of death, destruction, predation, endings, and being swallowed/eaten alive were omnipresent, as was a sense of deep time.

A sympathetic stance toward crooked cats was discernible—once they had been killed or captured, that is—with elaborate theories propounded to explain why they do what they do. Rich accounts of individual, named big cats—alive and dead—were also narrated. The real beast of the tale, in the majority of the tellings, was not the offending leopard or tiger but rather certain types of humans. The centrality of human action and the role of politics, history, the British Raj, capital, ecology, the landscape, forests and the destruction of them, the rage of the rivers, gods like Shiva, other animals like dogs and bears, government documents, the state (*sarkar*), political parties, charismatic individuals (human and big cat alike), reincarnation, social media, myth, surveillance regimes, and many other—often surprising—features were brought up to explain the presence and actions of crooked cats. These accounts show a sharp understanding of history, capitalism, modern politics, animal behavior, sociology, and the ecological breakdown. They rippled with anger, beauty, humor, fear, deep historical sensibilities, ecological consciousness, vivid imaginations, literary sensibilities, and sharp political analyses. I weave these stories together to claim they are powerful depictions of life in the Anthropocene. Paying careful attention to the connections they trace, their logics and poetics, and the regimes of governance and intimacies they emerge from allows us to productively deploy the concept of the Anthropocene.

In *Crooked Cats*, I locate beastly tales—stories that are populated by human and nonhuman beasts of all types and their intricate entanglements—at the very center of a series of cascading questions. First, and quite simply, how does one understand the phenomenon of crooked cats in India today? Leading on from this, how might the beastly tales of crooked cats deepen our understanding of the causes, consequences, and conceptualization of the climate crisis? And, finally, how do they open out the debates on the Anthropocene? I hope to show that beastly tales illuminate the Anthropocene in three critical ways: as method, as a way of reframing human-nonhuman relations on the planet, and as a political tool indicating the urgency of academic engagement.

A few clarifications are in order at the very outset. "Anthropocene" is a term coined by geologists to signify the epoch subsequent to the Holocene in which human actions are shaping the planet so profoundly that they are now acting as a geological force (Crutzen 2006). This is the age we are currently living in, though debates about precisely when it began continue to rage.[2] Climate change[3] is now widely accepted to be anthropogenic in nature—it is caused by humans. The distinction between climate change and the Anthropocene is nicely set out by Julia Adeney Thomas (2019), where she describes the Anthropocene as a multidimensional predicament that needs to be navigated through by the deployment of new ways of thinking. Climate change is a product of the Anthropocene but is not fully encapsulated by it, and it would be dangerous to conflate the two (also see Yusoff 2018, 40).[4] I use "climate change" and "the climate crisis" interchangeably to refer to the very same sets of phenomena ranging from extreme events to extinction to water shortages to the destruction of resources like forests to biodiversity degradation to the melting of glaciers—all of which are linked to and demonstrate the impact of anthropogenic climate change.[5] I utilize the Anthropocene throughout this book to refer to the critical requirement of finding new ways of thinking and doing academic labor.[6] I work from the premise that the Anthropocene signifies a political and ethical imperative to act on the world with a new urgency (Tsing, Mathews, and Bubandt 2019).[7] To do so requires the weaving together of stories and elements of social, ecological, biological, historical, and political life that have been hitherto kept apart. This is not the same challenge as the one that the long-standing issue of interdisciplinarity posed but is a somewhat different animal, so to say, due to the need to write in a new geological epoch and its potentially apocalyptic effects for life—human and otherwise—on Earth (de la Cadena and Blaser 2018).

Human-animal relationships the world over are being profoundly shaped and changed by the ecological breakdown.[8] Many of the central themes of this book—the bewildering rise in attacks on humans by cats; the changing behavior of crooked cats that is being captured on phones and surveillance cameras and is evidenced in acts such as their increasing entry into urban, heavily populated sites; imminent species extinction, with the tiger in a particularly vulnerable position; human anger at and struggles with conservationism—are intimately linked to a changing planet. In that sense, the climate crisis enters empirically as a fact that can no longer be turned away from and is in urgent need of acknowledgment. There is, of course, a very long history to crooked cats in India (Hughes 2013; Corbett 1991a; Rangarajan 2005; Anderson 2002). The very images and narratives of man-eating tigers and their hunting down were central to British colonial representations of India (Pandian 2001; Brittlebank 1995; Hussain 2012). An extremely rich tradition of studying the environment and wildlife of India has produced some wonderful work on the relationships between humans and big cats, including a full-length monograph set in the Sundarbans (Jalais 2011).[9] Building on this literature, I suggest that the time has come to locate climate change squarely in the middle of discussions on human-animal relations and to ask how we might come to resee and comprehend them in the light of the Anthropocene.[10]

To do so requires a transformation in how we narrate the story of human-animal relationships as well as the plotline and who—or what—the main protagonists are. This new form of storytelling also requires what we can perhaps call an agonistic stance toward the boundedness of both disciplines and their subfields such as, say, environmental anthropology or wildlife history or more-than-human geography. The concept of the Anthropocene, if exploited to its full potential, requires the opening up of a new way of working within and across disciplines. It entails a questioning of long-standing modes of describing the world—in this specific case, of describing relationships between humans and big cats in India. As Latour states in his polemic on politics in the new climatic regime, an answer to the despondent question of what is to be done is, "First of all, *generate alternative descriptions*" (2018, 94; italics in the original).

My descriptions of the relations between humans and big cats and the depredations of crooked cats emerge from almost fifteen years of research, largely undertaken in the central Indian Himalaya and in the city of Mumbai. I have been researching crooked cats ever since my first beastly encounter with the Gopeshwar leopard in the winter of 2006. Aside from two extended stints (2006–2008 and 2015–2016), my fieldwork has consisted of shorter trips to different parts of India in between academic terms and over the summer vacation. One fine morning during the 2006–2008 period when I was doing my doctoral research on bureaucracy, paperwork, and the state, the leopard of Gopeshwar of the introduction title "returned" (*vaapis aa gaya*), as everyone described her arrival. This big cat had a walk-on part in *Paper Tiger*, the book that resulted from this research, most strikingly in the conceiving of the book title and in the final chapter on bureaucratic temporalities and the failures of law (N. Mathur 2016). In 2015, I returned for an extended fieldwork stint in Uttarakhand, the north Indian state where Gopeshwar is located. This time I was based out of the capital city of Dehradun. Within weeks of my arrival, a young woman was killed and devoured by a leopard just down the road from where I was residing, in an uncanny mirroring of precisely what had happened almost a decade back in Gopeshwar. This time, instead of being in a small, "remote" Himalayan town, the attack was located in the sprawling capital city of the state in the plains and within the bounds of the Forest Research Institute, an institution that was central to the birth of scientific forestry in India in the nineteenth century. Dehradun reverberated with the shock of this killing, there was a proliferation of bagh talk, and, once again, I was pulled back into the world of crooked cats.

The nature of my primary research as well as the Anthropocene framing gets reflected in the lineaments of *Crooked Cats*. The long time span has allowed me to track certain marked differences, such as the entrance of big cats into particular areas and their mysterious disappearances from others, the changes in their behavior that are most volubly commented on, and the effects of the widespread penetration of smartphones and new technologies in recent times. The episodic nature of some of my research—sometimes conducted during repeat short, sharp trips to Mumbai, for instance, or during several wanderings off to Rajasthan or while hanging out in the Delhi zoo—is also evident. Key individual big cats from significant moments in time bookend this work: the leopard of Gopeshwar, who began this story, and the tigress Avni, who shot to global prominence just as I was putting my pen down. Every chapter is speculative in nature, offering several possible theories, case studies, and informed musings. *Crooked Cats* sits uneasily with the production of an overarching and authoritative explanatory narrative that is oftentimes expected of academic writing. This unease is partly a reflection of the temporality and form of my research but is primarily, I believe, derived from the topic under consideration. Crooked cats are discussed through recourse to speculation, through guesswork, through the proffering of theories, through analyses of cases, through gesturing to historical examples, and by leaning on biographical details (of humans and big cats alike). The methodological impulse of the Anthropocene, too, is one of fluid movement across different bodies of knowledge. I have, thus, consulted scientific and conservationist journals as well as state manuals, books of history, animal behavior, human geography, anthropology, political theory, fiction, colonial diaries, and popular culture. My methods range from long-term participant observation in a bounded site to free-ranging interviews to discourse analysis to the study of WhatsApp messages, social media, news items, and images. My interlocutors, similarly, are a motley bunch, including but not restricted to hunters, families of victims, the injured, conservationists, forest guards, bureaucrats, journalists, wildlife wallahs of all stripes, taxi drivers, schoolchildren, college students, biologists, photographers, people who regularly see a tiger or leopard near their house, and even the odd poacher.

Almost all my interlocutors, ranging from conservationists to residents of the Himalaya to hunters, claim there is a massive spike in the unusual actions and "visits" of big cats in recent times. To chart this out statistically is difficult due to the unreliability or absence of data for all of India over the *longue durée*. Mapping this out also involves relying on a particular form of knowledge—the quantitative or the statistical—as a mode of persuasion. An ambition of this book is to instead rely on what I term "beastly tales" to do this labor of convincing for us. I take very seriously the universal claim among my interlocutors that big cats are acting in ways that are increasingly considered out of character. In northern India in the Himalayan state of Uttarakhand, which has the highest number of attacks on humans by leopards and tigers in India, this claim is widely accepted. In this scenario, from among a raft of possible, overlapping explanations, I posit climate change as a central factor.

There are several theories on the existence of crooked cats as well as speculations on why they are acting thus, which I explore in this work (see chapter 1). It is difficult—and, as I ultimately argue, unnecessary—to separate out these various theories to claim that there is a singular explanation for why animals are considered to be becoming more violent than before. There are many unknowns in the story of crooked cats. In fact, this book was birthed out of the uncertainty that characterizes the presence and spread of crooked cats.[11] Uncertainty around crooked cats is what leads to the dense proliferation of beastly tales of the form showcased in this book. There is a long history to the existence and study of what are popularly termed "maneaters" (big cats that have become habituated to eating humans and actively seek them out) by a variety of disciplines ranging from the behavioral sciences to zoology to history. Yet, these cats remain largely unknowable and unpredictable. Despite the absence of firm knowledge, the state and conservationists have to behave as if they are certain and in accordance with unbending rule books. This acting with certainty in the face of something that remains relatively unknown is a conundrum that lies at the very heart of what I term "the government of big cats." As Kelly et al. note, "ignorance and uncertainty never describe a generic absence of knowledge, but always refer to highly specific forms of *unknowing*" (2020, 2; italics in the original). This book depicts several forms of unknowing around crooked cats and the means through which concerned humans attempt to arrive at greater certainty. So when I refer to uncertainty and unknowns, it isn't to depict my interlocutors as ignorant or somehow lacking. Rather, it is to highlight the tentative, affective, and situational knowledges that are in operation. It is also to highlight how formal institutions of governance and conservation refuse to acknowledge the fact that they, in truth, function through such uncertain knowledge practices yet demand—and, more often than not, work to *actively manufacture*—legible fixed knowns.

There may be many unknowns around why cats go crooked, but it is now indisputable that anthropogenic climate change is central to species extinction. It is widely accepted that we are now living through what has been termed the sixth mass extinction. A synthesis of published studies argues that if climate changes proceed as expected, one in six species could face extinction (Urban 2015). In May 2019, the global assessment report released by the Intergovernmental Science-Policy Platform on Biodiversity and Ecosystem Services noted that "around 1 million species already face extinction, many within decades, unless action is taken to reduce the intensity of drivers of biodiversity loss."[12] I don't rehearse the conservationist policy discourse, but briefly put, the blame for what is referred to as human-animal conflict falls on growing human populations, encroachment by humans on animal land, competition over resources, and generalized biodiversity depletion arising from anthropogenic climate change (see Pooley et al. 2017).[13] The World Wildlife Fund (n.d.), for instance, tells the story of conflict between humans and big cats as one of direct competition between increasing populations of humans and their livestock and a decreasing number of vulnerable big cats.[14]

The COVID-19 pandemic has brought a new animal—the pangolin—into prominence for reasons that strongly resemble the core concerns of this work. Pangolins are famously the most trafficked mammals on Earth and are on the verge of extinction. There is a strong suspicion—note it is a mere suspicion that will be hard to prove even though it is very highly possible—that the COVID-19 pandemic started when the novel coronavirus "jumped" from a pangolin (or was it a bat? or some other animal?) to a human. While we may never be able to definitively identify the source of the COVID-19 pandemic, it is undeniable that the human destruction of wildlife is in turn grievously hurting humans, often in ways that aren't entirely transparent or immediately obvious, such as with the spread of zoonotic diseases. When my interlocutors in the Himalaya say that big cats are attacking humans because of the historical injustices of our *human* actions and what we are inflicting on the cats, their statements aren't just a reference to karmic retribution. Rather, these are astute observations that bring the damage of the Anthropocene to light.

Climate Translations

On the one hand, then, there is a gathering scientific and conservationist consensus that establishes climate change and its effects quite centrally as a factor affecting human-animal relations, especially but not limited to extinction and species endangerment. It is important to not disregard this emergent body of knowledge, which had not been at hand in this form for many of the earlier studies on why humans and big cats have come to clash.[15] At the same time, it remains crucial to not let such legitimized "scientific" works entirely dictate how we understand the question of human-animal relations in a rapidly changing world. *Crooked Cats* attempts precisely this delicate balancing act. The task as I see it is not to somehow "add the science" onto the ethnography but rather to think about what happens to history, ethnography, politics, and literature when climate science is written into the humanities and social sciences.[16] What happens when in lieu of being led by the science or through a reliance on numbers and graphs, we enfold these different ways of comprehending the world one into the other? Additionally, we need to recognize that seemingly scientific accounts are themselves derivatives of the stories we choose to tell about the world.[17] As Ursula Heise has argued, biodiversity, endangered species, and extinction are "primarily cultural issues, questions of what we value and what stories we tell, and only secondarily issues of science" (2016, 5). The story around changing human-animal relations and the increase in what is problematically termed "conflict" has taken a particular form, with the natural sciences, policy, and conservationist voices taking a lead in it (Pooley et al. 2017; Redpath, Bhatia, and Young 2015).[18] The ambition of *Crooked Cats* is to present a somewhat different story through the medium of beastly tales via an engagement with knowledge practices that are often kept separate from one another and through a foregrounding of long-term ethnography from the global south. What happens to our understandings of not just relations between humans and big cats but also, perhaps more critically, imminent species extinction, the climate crisis, and the Anthropocene when we center voices, processes, and narratives that are often ignored in these weighty discussions on the future of life on Earth?

Let us once again consider the snippet from the interview with the person who lost a limb to a big cat. It is my claim that he—as well as the other interlocutors whose accounts form the core of this book—is referring to the Anthropocene and factors that are contributing to the climate crisis, just *not in the very same register*. While the narratives emanating from victims and their families might not actually utilize the term "climate change," all the practices that they speak of are the ones that contribute to anthropogenic climate change. When discussing crooked cats, Himalayan residents speak of history, capitalism, inequality, power, retribution, neglect, violence toward both humans and nonhuman animals, exploitation of biodiversity, deep time, and even nonhuman migration and capture. These accounts of human-animal relationships don't speak in the abstract—like an article in the top journals *Science* or *Nature* might—but work through more embodied and impassioned rhetorical styles. Differences in tone and content shouldn't, however, blind us to these narratives' overlapping claims. Just as critical work on climate change shows us how the local is folded into the global, so too do the alternative stories in the Indian Himalaya draw our attention to inequality and active marginalization, albeit within the nation-state of India. Furthermore, the utilization of metaphors of death, destruction, and endings in these localized narratives bears strong affinity to more mainstream narratives on catastrophic climate change—for instance, the sort presented in recent cli-fi (climate fiction) works such as Barbara Kingsolver's *Flight Behaviour* (2012), Mark Martin's *I'm with the Bears* (2011), and Amitav Ghosh's *Gun Island* (2019).

The beastly tales I relate here initially perplexed me for one reason. When a crooked cat was in the vicinity, most people wanted him or her killed or captured at the earliest. Oftentimes a preference was expressed for the death of the crooked cat, which would assuage collective anger but also ensure the cat wouldn't eventually escape and return to once again haunt the area with an even greater vengeance. At the very same time, a sympathetic stance toward the big cat was professed. The cat was often referred to as a *bechara* (poor thing) or *bekasoor* (innocent). I argue that these two contradicting narratives on crooked cats can coexist because the people who live in close proximity to them are conscious that the crookedness is not the doing of the individual feline but rather emerges from longer-term structures and human actions. In the heat of the terrified moment, they wish to do away with the individual but are aware that the blame lies on the doorstep of "us" humans.[19] Of course, the category of humans is parsed out carefully—there are several specified types of humans who are singled out as responsible for this horrific state of affairs. There is no undifferentiated "we" of humankind invoked here; rather, there is a clear understanding of power and social stratification along lines of caste, class, gender, age, location, and race. Climate change, as has been well argued by now, is notoriously hard to pin down to just one thing, to clearly see, and to articulate coherently, and there is great difficulty too in making the complex interconnections across time and scale that then allow it to be brought into visibility (Hulme 2009; Latour 2018; Morton 2013). It is also hard to clearly identify who all are responsible for this crisis given the gesturing to vastly depersonalized systems like "capitalism" or "consumerism." A central claim of this book is that the stories of crooked cats recounted here do this intellectual work of pulling together disparate elements that allow us to experience—and fathom—the climate crisis in a unique way. But this requires a receptiveness to the message in the beastly tales, a willingness to trace the connections that explain our current planetary predicament *through* the peculiar phenomena of big cats that make prey of humans in India.

I argue we need to pay careful attention to these stories—beastly tales—and appreciate their powerful political and ecological imaginaries.[20] Taken together, they ground the Anthropocene within localized politics and ecosystems and can serve to relay the voices, imaginaries, and opinions of those people, such as the residents of the Indian Himalaya described here, who are already coping with the damaging consequences of climate change.[21] One need not, after all, be able to use the (English-language) category of climate change or speak the same expert language of environmental change and damage or even subscribe to the universalism of science to *know* that climate change is an overwhelming threat.[22] Crucially, these stories are not just about the Himalaya or big cats or even India—the relations they trace, the scales they shift, and the present and futures they reflect are indicative of a planetary predicament. As Tsing, Mathews, and Bubandt put it, this isn't just a story about how things are changing in the place where I did my fieldwork. It is not enough for anthropologists to stop here, for we all know the world is heating up, changing, melting, collapsing. Rather, "how are we to understand this radical difference when it happens both site specifically and on a planetary scale?" (Tsing, Mathews, and Bubandt 2019, 187). This, then, is not just a story about the increasing crookedness and endangerment of big cats in India. It is, of course, that. But it is also a collection of beastly tales from the Anthropocene that open up a fresh perspective on the planetary predicament.

In short, not only are there new studies—from a variety of disciplinary angles—emerging that show connections between the climate crisis and the dramatic changes in human-animal relations (Cassidy 2012), but also, and more pertinently for this work, there are many ways of telling, and hearing, the story of a planet in crisis. Exploring the changing relations between crooked cats and humans in India is but one way of narrating this most beastly of tales. This book is an attempt to take on the task of what I have elsewhere described as "climate translation" (N. Mathur 2017). Etymologically, translation "evokes an act of moving or carrying across from one place or position to another, or of changing from one state of things to another" (Buden et al. 2009, 196). Benjamin (1996) in his seminal essay "The Task of the Translator" makes the point that this act of translation is not about literality or a fidelity to words. Rather, it is about capturing something of the essence of the original in the translation. As he describes it, it is about aiming for an echo that resonates in some way with the original: "aiming at that single spot where the echo is able to give, in its own language, the reverberation of the work in the alien one" (1996, 258–59). Following Benjamin, I propose that the task of the climate translator lies in the transference of stories reflective of people's relationships with the world across domains that are normally kept separate—such as those of science and myth or quotidian chatter and conservationist discourse or emotions and law.[23]

Climate translations become important for several reasons, including their potential to bring an alertness to climate change—a phenomenon that somehow still remains possible to disregard or unsee. The disregarding of climate change results from many factors. It can come from a sense of overfamiliarity, given that, as Forrester and Smith have pointed out, "there have always been ideas of an uncertain, unknowable 'Nature' capable of destroying cities and hastening the onset of the apocalypse" (2018, 1). As Forrester and Smith go on to note, these analogies are generally strained but are politically effective in the dismissal of climate change concerns. It is noteworthy that even those who aren't explicitly climate skeptics or denialists can be seen disregarding or downplaying it as an overwhelming factor of contemporary lives. And perhaps these are the most complex forms of unseeing the crisis that is staring us in the face—a perplexing refusal to make connections that are increasingly apparent from a variety of distinct sources.[24] Amitav Ghosh (2016) has aptly termed this "the great derangement" in his vital book by the same name. As he points out, the incapacity to write about climate change is also a crisis of the imagination and a failing of culture.[25]

The Anthropocene and Its Discontents

Spurred by a growing concern about climate change, the idea of the Anthropocene has generated a fast and furious debate in the social sciences and the humanities. Chua and Fair (2019) have outlined distinct ways in which anthropologists have engaged with the Anthropocene, "both as a set of phenomena (e.g. climate change, mass extinction) and as a politically and morally loaded concept."[26] Powerful as the concept of the Anthropocene is, some trenchant criticisms of it exist; in fact, it has already spun out a veritable "industry of critiques" (Hetherington 2019, 3).[27] Given the Euro-American academic marketplace, with its dizzying number of "turns" and production of increasingly abstruse concepts, I, too, was somewhat skeptical of the Anthropocene when it initially burst onto the scene with, as Howe and Pandian (2016) put it, "astonishing speed, dislodging familiar terms like *nature* and *environment* from their customary preeminence as signs of the world beyond ourselves" (see N. Mathur 2015). Yet, as I worked and reworked the tricky subject of crooked cats in India, I found myself increasingly drawn to the Anthropocene. A particular conceptualization of the Anthropocene opened up a methodological flexibility, a gesturing to several disparate phenomena simultaneously, even as it allowed for an escape from moribund discussions on "interdisciplinarity" and "applied anthropology versus activist anthropology."[28]

Zoe Todd (2015) observes that she initially mistrusted the term "the Anthropocene" due to its overwhelming whiteness. Kathryn Yusoff, in her critique of the structural whiteness of the Anthropocene, succinctly terms one telling of the Anthropocene the "white man's overburden" (2018, 28). Both Yusoff and Todd, however, go on to suggest the Anthropocene narrative can be critically remade through a refusal of its whiteness. Todd (2015) makes a call for "indigenizing the Anthropocene" through a thoughtful review of the concept, its criticisms, and the ways in which it can be deployed by scholars, including artists. She argues that through joyful and critical indigenous thought and praxis, the hegemonic tendencies of a universalizing paradigm like the Anthropocene can—and should—be resisted. Yusoff powerfully demonstrates the colonial geology of the Anthropocene, proposes a "Black Anthropocene," and "launches a call for a different kind of world making" (2018, 12). I find myself in agreement with many of the critiques of the Anthropocene that have thus far been propounded—particularly those that center the need to ground colonialism and capitalism more centrally and question the Eurocentrism and whiteness of the literature around the term as well as those that note the dangers of anthropocentrism. Much like that of Tsing, Mathews, and Bubandt, my approach to the Anthropocene is one of "critical and curious engagement rather than either celebration or rejection" (2019, 187).

As stated in a personal communication, Amanda Power uses the Anthropocene in her rewriting of medieval history as an accusation—an accusation of what has been in the past that has allowed for this terrible planetary present. For Jedediah Purdy, the main point of what he terms the "Anthropocene condition" is that "the contrast between what is nature and what is not no longer makes sense" (2015, 15). The Anthropocene not only unsettles the nature/culture divide but also makes clearer the connections and deep entanglements between humans and nonhumans (Latour 2014).[29] Simultaneously, it challenges social scientists on how we produce knowledge, what it means to write from outside the established and safe spaces of a traditional discipline, and how we account for climate change in our work. I take inspiration from recent books emerging from anthropology and fiction alike that shift scales, (re)tell stories, and draw out connections between elements that have, for too long, been kept separate, and thus demonstrate the potential of the Anthropocene (Tsing 2015; Haraway 2016; Ghosh 2016, 2019; Powers 2018). *Crooked Cats* is an attempt to fill out the concept of "the Anthropocene," to mold it such that these humble beastly tales can come together to illuminate something as big and apocalyptic as the climate crisis and animals as elusive and endangered as tigers or leopards as well as their relationships with humans in India.

Beastly Tales

The humanities and social sciences are beginning to move toward new forms of thinking and disciplinary reorientations in the face of the climate crisis.[30] Central to these attempts is the question of method that writing about the Anthropocene has opened up. Storytelling has become a favored mode of responding to this.[31] Of course, humans have always told stories as a way of making sense of life, and in fact, as Maggio (2014) has observed, anthropologists have always been storytellers. Yet, stories, narratives, and storytelling are being re-marshaled in climate change research in a variety of ways (Moezzi, Janda, and Rotmann 2017).[32] The new literature on the Anthropocene and the sorts of methodological and ethical choices it is making exemplifies the point that Donna Haraway has made, drawing from Marilyn Strathern: "It matters what matters we use to think other matters with; it matters what stories we tell to tell other stories with . . . it matters what stories make worlds, what worlds make stories" (2016, 12). Living in an era of climate change demands new ways of storytelling. It compels us to see stories not as "mere stories" but as much more powerful tools to retell the world from. As Haraway notes, the earth is already intensely storied, but we need to have the imagination to see those tales and the capacity to retell them even as we exercise caution in which ones get told and which don't.

From the multispecies feminist Donna Haraway to the climate scientist Mike Hulme to Marxist geographer Jason Moore to the novelist Amitav Ghosh to humanities scholars Ursula Heise and Elizabeth DeLoughrey to the environmental writer Elizabeth Rush, there have been calls to rethink climate change, extinction narratives, and multispecies entanglements through a focus on stories and narratives.

In this book, I take on the methodological challenge of writing and relating stories that illuminate interspecies entanglements and what it is to live life in the Anthropocene by centering both big cats and human lives and accounts. I work through beastly tales to describe what it means to share space with nonhuman animals, to think more carefully about our interspecies entanglements and how we might come to consider them beyond received ideas of conflict/coexistence or simply through the lens of preservation and narratives of extinction, and even to think about what we might be able to "do" in the face of the direness of the climate crisis. Stories of the form that are described in this book can be considered as a form of translation between nature and culture, natural science and the social sciences, human and nonhuman, empire and the postcolonial, us and them, the local and the global, and the contemporary, the past, and the future; they are a type of climate translation.

I term the stories that this book is built on "beastly tales," for they are about beasts of all forms: tigers, lions, leopards, humans, the state, capitalists, bureaucrats, hunters, poachers, bears, dogs, monkeys, gods, and demons. This phrasing is also a play on the question, *Who is the real beast in the Anthropocene?*

Is it the crooked cats or is it certain types of humans, such as big industrialists who build destructive dams or polluting factories and exploit the labor of the poor? Or is the beast the gods or mother nature, who is furious at the state of the planet? These various types of beasts and complex assemblages of things, humans, and nonhumans have together brought us to the state of a climate emergency. *Crooked Cats* is a tale, as it is but one way of narrating the Anthropocene, one that is no doubt guided by my idiosyncratic understanding of what the real story is. Animals have always been a particularly effective mode of relating the world, perhaps especially when they act as protagonists in the story.[33] Finally, the phrase "beastly tales" is borrowed, with immense gratitude, from the writer Vikram Seth (1999), who has an utterly delightful collection of poems entitled *Beastly Tales, from Here and There*. Seth's book contains ten animal tales—all in verse form—taken from around the world, including India, China, Greece, Ukraine, and the mythical Land of Gup. All ten are morality tales resting on unlikely animal relationships, such as between a crocodile and a monkey or an elephant and a tragopan.[34] The relationships that are part of *Crooked Cats*—such as between paperwork and statecraft, between surveillance cameras and emotion, between space and evidence, and between history, ethnography, and fiction—are somewhat more mundane but can also, I hope, be similarly illustrative.

With that, let us return to the scene of Gopeshwar and the bagh who set this work in motion in the winter of 2006.

For the time the crooked cat co-resided with us, she unleashed what is best described as a reign of terror. Terror refers now to quite a different global situation, and the word "terrorist" does not normally conjure up images of a big cat. These charismatic nonhuman animals are, conversely, believed to be in need of protection from the destructive habits of human beings. I write of the "terror of the bagh" (*bagh ka atank*), despite its colonial antecedents, because the word *atank* (terror) is very apt to describe the situation that prevailed over the town.[35] Additionally, it demonstrates the agentive side of the big cat, who is capable of acting as the ruling sovereign in an area and has the power to strike terror in human hearts. The phrase "reign of terror of the big cat" demonstrates that this situation is not the normal course of things as, ordinarily, it is humans who rule, terrorize, destroy, or prey upon the Himalaya and its other living beings. There has been a rich debate on the agency of nonhuman animals,[36] which is now being resolved in favor of working from the assumption that, in fact, animals are highly intelligent (de Waal 2016; Montgomery 2015); have subjectivities (Saha 2018), cultural lives (Whitehead and Rendell 2015), and memories (Rangarajan 2013); and were central to the shaping of colonial power (Deb Roy 2020); they labor (Barua 2017, 2018), grieve (King 2014), and even spy (N. Mathur 2019; Shell 2015). Animal agency and emotion are foundational premises of this work, and ethnography is utilized to enrich these understandings of what it is to be an animal that has gone off its normal path in life and embraced a crookedness that severely impacts humans.[37]

The Government of Big Cats

The phenomenon of man-eating leopards, lions, and tigers has a long history in India. Crucially, government accounts have consistently noted the unreliability of the statistics they have been collecting. For instance, the *Himalayan Gazetteer*, which is where some of the earliest records for the Himalaya have emerged, admits, "This return is avowedly imperfect, as it only includes the deaths reported to the authorities and the animals killed for which rewards have been claimed" (Atkinson [1881] 2002, 16). Presently too, the construction of state statistics remains unreliable for a variety of reasons, including underreporting of incidences, especially when they occur in distant mountain villages; the painfully convoluted documentary regimes associated with the production of state statistics in India; and the flat refusal of officials to accept certain cases as such a recognition would lead to claims of monetary compensation from the state (N. Mathur 2016). What this results in is the generation of watered-down statistics, something that officials readily acknowledged when off the record. In the course of the year I spent in Gopeshwar, for instance, there were only three deaths by a man-eating leopard that were officially declared, even though unofficially there was talk of at least seven deaths and many more injuries, some of which were grievous.

Statistics on deaths aside, there is constant speculation in all quarters on the reason or reasons why big cats become man-eaters in the first place. The colonial *Gazetteer*, for instance, describes the hill tiger as a "quarrelsome creature" and the leopard as "very common all over the hills and in parts very destructive" (Atkinson [1881] 2002, 16). It does not, however, specify the reasons for this destructive nature of the leopard. Generally, it is believed that big cats turn on humans—an otherwise alien prey—when they are unable to hunt their normal food due to old age or injuries (Corbett 2007). Indeed, this has been the standard explanation for man-eaters for the longest time among colonial and postcolonial officials as well as big-cat conservationists. *Crooked Cats* offers alternative theories, derived from long-term ethnographic immersion rather than colonial sources or staunchly conservationist perspectives, to understand beastly encounters between humans and big cats in India.

Below are some of my notes from my yellowing bagh diary that illuminate how the narrative arc of this book has been shaped by the life and death of this individual leopard. Every chapter of this book, as outlined below, emerges from that originary beastly tale.

†

*In a press conference that was organized in the district magistrate's office, all the journalists accused the state [*sarkar*] of shipping leopards from the plains up here to hunt down the mountain persons. The forest department, in particular, was attacked, and even though the foresters vehemently denied any such state policies or actions, the local journalists were not convinced. Repeatedly, everyone says this bagh is* badtameez *[misbehaved] and not a local. They have actually been* *brought here by an external agency. This agency is the evil Indian state that is operated primarily by the plains people [*maidani*], who have no regard for the lives of the mountain people [*paharis*]. To prop up their argument of the nonlocal origin of the bagh, they said that "this bagh has no manners, unlike our local ones, for he dares to walk on Mandir Marg [Temple Street—the street on which a ninth-century temple called the Gopinath Temple, from which Gopeshwar derives its name, is situated] in broad daylight"; "he is rushing to people to shake hands with them"; "unlike local leopards this one is not frightened by humans, rather he actively seeks their company, which is a sure indication of his past interaction with humans." "This just cannot be a local bagh for he is not acting like our pahari bagh do." Similarly, my office mate accused me directly, saying that "you people from the plains come here to the wild and set these animals free without thinking of the impact this has on our lives."*

†

This book opens with the central question, Why and how do some big cats turn on humans as prey? What makes a specific leopard or tiger into, as they are popularly known, "man-eaters" or, as I prefer to term it, "crooked"? Most big cats, it is widely agreed, are not thus inclined. Chapter 1 works through a range of explanatory narratives offered for the very existence of man-eaters to distinguish three broad forms: political, biological, and climatic. The state, with its policies of management, conservation, and regulation, figures prominently in all explanations. For instance, there is a powerful argument that it is, in fact, the capture and relocation of big cats by the Indian government that have exacerbated the incidence of attacks on humans (Athreya 2006). Conservationists tend to blame the encroachment of humans into wild spaces or the feeble attempts made to preserve these increasingly endangered species as the reasons underlying conflict (Saberwal et al. 1994; Mukherjee and Mishra 2001). A more conspiratorial version of these arguments exists in the Himalaya, where many mountain persons are convinced that man-eaters have been sent to their homes in the mountains by a rapacious Indian state that wishes to finish them off (N. Mathur 2015). What is noteworthy here is that human–big cat relations are seen as a derivative of human-human relations. The former are not about the leopard or the tiger per se but rather about human structures and discriminatory or violent policies.

A second order of explanations pins the blame on biology and genes. For instance, if the parents of a big cat—especially the mother—are or were used to human flesh, then it is assumed the cubs will become "automatic man-eaters." Hunting as well as the visualization of what is prey is considered both cultural (as in it is actively learned from a parent or from the wider pride of lions, for instance) and genetic (in terms of being innate). Some explanations discuss human eating as the exhibition of an unusual genetic or biological flaw that suddenly makes itself manifest in a particular animal. A third form of explanation that is gaining wider acceptance makes direct links between climate change and interspecies discord, as I spelled out above.

There is, then, no widely agreed-on theory that might comprehensively explain this crooked behavior among individuals of the species. Each of the explanations detailed in this chapter remains disputed, with some falling into the realm of pure fantasy. The uncertainty over why big cats become man-eaters creates a genuine governance problem: How do you prevent or guard against a phenomenon—crooked cats—when you don't know why it happens in the first place? This lack of understanding of some big cats' predatory behavior has important social and political effects, which the remainder of this book explores in vivid detail.

†

The hunter who has been called in from Gairsain and some of the locals who are unafraid of leopards have been tracking the pugmarks of the bagh. They are convinced that this is a relatively young female. Two cubs have been spotted playing in the sun a few days back, and we are all fairly certain they belong to her. It is, I am told, quite understandable for a leopardess that is unable to find normal prey to turn on humans, especially if she also has babies to feed. Yet, everyone continues to refer to her as a him. The hunters kill a leopard and we are delighted, but only momentarily for an analysis of the pugmarks shows that this is probably the wrong cat. It isn't the man-eater but a bekasoor *[an innocent] bagh. We are all despondent, but the hunters tell me ruefully that they can never know till after the killing if they have, indeed, got the right one. Overnight, the corpse of the leopard vanishes and there is no paper trail left. It is as if this never happened. Officials are nervous, for they gesture to the stipulation on the hard-won hunting permit that stipulates that the leopard must be "ID'd" before it is hunted.*

†

Chapter 2 asks a question that bedevils hunters and aggravates conservationists—namely, in a landscape in which several big cats coexist, most of which are not man-eaters, how is the crooked cat identified? How is certain knowledge of the guilt of a specific big cat arrived at anterior to its killing? The chapter constitutes a deep ethnographic study of the various methods through which hunters, bureaucrats, locals, scientists, conservationists, and other actors identify a specific, individual man-eater. These methods range from bureaucratic ID'ing to scientific camera-trap images, fecal analysis, and DNA tests to the practices of the colonial cultures of *shikar* (the hunt). I contrast statist injunctions to the lived, embodied, visceral practices that are actually operationalized in the hunt. I show the criticality of correct identification of a man-eater subsequent to the passage of the Wildlife Protection Act of 1972, which made any killing of a tiger, lion, or leopard that has not been declared a man-eater into a criminal offense. The question I ask here is, What difference has the legal protection of big cats and the creation of a new state document—the hunting permit—that regulates killing effected in the project of managing man-eaters? I explore the vexed twin issues of correctly identifying a particular big cat as a man-eater and the state's response to its own accidental—and illegal—killing of an innocent big cat. I describe the complicated game of retrospective erasure that needs to be played—involving the disappearance of various matter ranging from the body of the big cat to photographs to the silencing of accomplices and members of media—in order to paper over the illegal death of an innocent big cat. I stress the point that all *shikaris* (hunters) make, which is the inherent impossibility of ever being able to incontrovertibly identify a big cat prior to killing it. Yet, given the transnational drive of preserving big cats and in the context of India's own conservationist legal regime, the hunting permit and associated documents that claim correct identification remain on, often as impediments to swift action and always as a necessary fiction of the reasoned government of big cats.

†

Three jalooses*—processions—have already arrived at the DM's office to protest against the bagh. One of them was particularly efficacious in getting its appeals heard. I shift base to the DM's office to see the official records on the many leopards that have haunted Gopeshwar. This is the most astonishing archive of letters, petitions, memos, newspaper cuttings, telegrams, and statistics. The petitions are overwhelming in quantity and make for deeply emotional reading. There is, in short, a huge leopard archive in the Gopeshwar office that is much at odds with what the conservationist literature argues. In this archive not only is there not much of a preservationist sympathy, but more importantly it shows the big cat to be peculiarly and powerfully agentive. It also demonstrates the fraught nature of the government of big cats with the constant to-ing and fro-ing and the visceral anger at the state* *for valuing the lives of big cats above human lives. Again and again I see the same question pop up in petitions: "Whose life does sarkar [the state] care most for? The big cat's or a human's?"*

†

In chapter 4, the final chapter on the government of big cats, I consider an assortment of petitions that were successful in their demands for the capture or killing of big cats in the north Indian Himalayan state of Uttarakhand. Within the wider project of the government of big cats, this chapter is interested in understanding both the role of petitions and, more importantly, how certain petitions attain efficacy. This efficaciousness is rare given the context of a stringent legal regime that is geared almost exclusively toward the protection of endangered big cats as well as the hegemonic position occupied by wildlife conservationism. Not only is it difficult to petition against charismatic and cosseted big cats, but also it isn't an easy task for *any* petition to be heard and acquiesced to in contemporary India. In the process of attending to the rarity of several efficacious petitions, this chapter makes a case for expanding our conceptualization of what, in practice, a petition is. It does so by outlining the changing forms of efficacious petitions, which can range from a telephone call to a register entry to a message on a smartphone to the more traditional paper-based petitions. Beyond discussing the petition's ever-changing medium, this chapter demonstrates the criticality of folding petitioning into a wider process that involves planning, performance, perseverance, repetition, and the capacity to elicit visceral responses. I argue that this reimagining of petitions and processes of claim making is made possible through closer attention to the specificity of relations between humans and big cats. Several calls have been made to "bring the animal back in" or to acknowledge the role of animal lives in our human worlds. This chapter constitutes an example of the value of such a move, whereby the centering of tigers and leopards allows humans to rethink their own tools of government and methods of claim making.

The government of big cats is aimed at enfolding microprocesses of the state and bureaucratic everydayness—ranging from petitions to identification practices to the execution of conservationist law and government guidelines—into the conversation on the Anthropocene and climate change. Even in some otherwise strong writings on the climate crisis we see that such banal bureaucratic practices and things—as well as the state form—are neglected or treated as somehow irrelevant to the discussion. The focus is on issues like ecological collapse, with, for instance, the impacts of flooding or the devastation of a cyclone considered as somehow distinct from grumbles about corruption, bureaucratic inertia, and state violence.[38] *Crooked Cats* argues for the untenability of such a separation of domains ("the climatic" from "the political" or the state); it demonstrates that the endangerment/extinction of vulnerable species like tigers, lions, and leopards cannot be divorced from serious considerations of the state; politics at local, regional, national, and international levels; and their corresponding governance regimes. As Jobson has correctly noted in his review of sociocultural anthropology in 2019, "The Anthropocene marks a crisis not only of climate but of the state form" (2020, 263). The governance of big cats depicts the inextricability of these twin crises—of the climate and the state.

Beastly Intimacy

We know the address of the bagh, said the forest department official to me: his specivic address is the BSNL telephone tower that was constructed right on top of the mountain on which Gopeshwar is located. This area around the tower is quite heavily forested and is giving him the hiding place he needs. Last year, the story goes, a leopard did walk on Temple Road in the busy bazaar area at noon and settled himself down for a nap in the sun on someone's terrace right in the center of town. There is constant imagery of Gopeshwar as a town where one finds leopards walking around with an insouciance that would be admirable were they not such a dire threat to everyone who lives here. Again and again, we are told of big cats coming into spaces they should not be present in.

†

There was a visible obsession with tracking the urban perambulations of the leopard in Gopeshwar. Where is he and when? Where did he go and why? Why was he spotted at this particular spot at this time? How does he know this is where X lives or this is where Y works? How utterly cheeky of him to turn up at this spot in town, but well done on bowing his head outside the Shiva temple. I make an argument in chapter 6 for centering space, particularly urban spaces, as a key to intimate human understandings of big cats. Where, when, and how big cats appear as well as how they behave in that particular space become a central modality through which we (humans) come to comprehend them. But space is not just an empty container, as legions of geographers, urban anthropologists, and sociologists have long argued. Rather, space is formed through its history, politics, built forms, and emplaced quotidian practices. These spaces are reshaped by both human and nonhuman practices. Humans can, quite quickly, find their relationships with big cats changing—for the better or for the worse.

These human-nonhuman co-dwellings are not static but fluid due to a complex concatenation of causes that we can, again, only intelligently guess at. A comparison of three very different cities in India—Dehradun, Shimla, and Mumbai—illuminates this claim and allows us to think of space itself as a form of evidence in our quest to understand the inscrutable and, depending on where you are positioned, charismatic or terrifying big cats.

In chapter 6, I discuss how potentially dangerous and seemingly out-of-place animals elicit different responses due to the urban spaces they appear in. I foreground the ecological histories and lived geographies of the three cities I researched. When leopards or tigers walk into these spaces, they are encountering a complex past and expanding urban futures. I outline three distinct narratives on living with leopards that have come to dominate in each of the cities. Bloody encounters between leopards and humans have taken place in Dehradun and Mumbai, whereas, thus far, there have been no such reported incidents in Shimla. In Mumbai there has been an active engagement between the forest department and various individuals who came together to devise means of peaceful coexistence. In Shimla, there has been either a studious ignoring of the leopards or feeble efforts to trap and relocate leopards. In Dehradun, the only response to the presence of leopards has been to immediately hunt them down. What accounts for these widely varying approaches to the very same phenomenon, living with big cats in urban India?

†

All stories related to the bagh's shenanigans reached me within hours of them happening and were merely corroborated the next morning in the local Hindi newspapers. I would hear them either through people in the office or through my very friendly and inquisitive neighbors or through shopkeepers, taxi drivers, or bus conductors, or I would just overhear the conversations as people stood huddled up on the streets loudly discussing the bagh. My favorite and most spicy source (my "informants," as we would put it in anthro-speak) remains the two small boys aged twelve and thirteen whom I teach English to in the evenings. We would begin every session with them regaling me with vivid and bloody and, needless to say, highly exaggerated stories of the bagh. These stories often included dire predictions of the bagh knowing about the didi *[elder sister] from Delhi who is sure to make a very delicious meal for him. The bagh has become very central to our tuitions now. For instance, when they knock on my door and I ask who it is, I am nearly always answered with a growl or a hoarse voice saying "the bagh has come for you." I threaten them with inviting the bagh to our sessions if they don't do their homework and solemnly tell them that the bagh eats children who can't recite "Jack and*

Jill" perfectly to him. They respond in kind by growling outside my window late at night, then giggling loudly just so I don't really get a fright, and running away. The next day, they will innocently tell me that someone told them that the bagh had come looking for didi yesterday night.

In the morning, the siren awakens us. At evening, the nagar palika dhol *[town municipal drum] goes around town describing his movements and attacks and warning us all to be cautious.*

I am riding back from Joshimath in a shared taxi when the driver, who appears drunk, points to a wandering goat on the road and tells me "yeh to bagh hai; wohin Gopeshwar-wallah bagh" [this is a leopard, that same one from Gopeshwar]. He laughs uproariously, as if something very funny has been said. Jokes and humor mix with horror stories in our daily life under the reign of terror of the big cat.

†

In chapter 7, I ask, How do we see big cats and what role does emotion play in this seeing? I focus on the practice of laying camera traps in tandem with the expansion of closed-circuit television (CCTV) and on the use of digital photography and smartphones to circulate images of tigers and leopards in order to argue that these new technologies are leading us to resee big cats in critical and hitherto under-studied ways. Believed by many to constitute the future of conservation, these new technologies for entrapping animals are proliferating, unleashing a range of emotions—from shock and horror to spine chills to laughter and even tears. These emotive responses to new visuals of big cats are often overlooked in the technocratic desire to know more about our nonhuman counterparts. What also remains unremarked on is how new forms of secretive and elite knowledge are being created, raising troubling ethical questions of who comes to know what and who doesn't about our feline friends and sometime enemies. The moral question of whether we should share novel bits of information revealed by camera-trapping exercises or by access to security cameras should push us to reconsider the ethics and politics of both conservationism and amateur wildlife photography in new and unexpected ways. New legal questions related to copyrights to and ownership of these images and knowledges are also beginning to be opened up, as is the question of the legal personhood of nonhumans ranging from rivers to animals such as tigers and fish. These questions of law cannot be unlinked from the ways in which we are now coming to see nonhumans and, especially, from the range of emotions these images elicit. In this chapter, I outline the ethical and legal questions in tandem with a description of the new forms of beastly intimacies that the entrapment of big cats is allowing for.[39]

The government of big cats and beastly intimacy are, of course, inseparable. This entanglement of governmental rationalities and affect is sharply brought into evidence in the brief tales of named individual tigers and leopards that are scattered throughout this book. In chapter 3 we consider the question of the cuteness of tigers through a feline biography of Vijay, a white tiger who lives in the Delhi zoo, to think more situationally about how such ascriptions come to be applied. What allows one tiger to be distinguished from the others? And why are some cuter or more charismatic than the others? In chapter 5 we ponder the differences between fact and fiction through accounts of the man-eating leopard of Rudraprayag and the tiger Shere Khan. The former was written about in a book that is part memoir, part shikar diary by the colonial hunter Jim Corbett, while the latter is the villain of Rudyard Kipling's well-known novel *The Jungle Book*. Individual animal lives are, *Crooked Cats* underlines, important to consider.[40] How do specific big cats come to be known, named, loved/hated, remembered, and memorialized, and how do they acquire powerful afterlives and fame?

†

Vimla, my neighbor, rounds up all the dogs on the street every evening, and we divide them up between us for the night. As she is rounding them up, she says to them in Hindi that they better hurry up and come inside or the bagh will eat them up. Obediently, they trot over to the group of us who have volunteered to give them shelter in our homes for the night. Sheroo, that magnificent dog who lives on the street and doesn't really belong to anyone, always comes to me and won't let anyone else accompany him. We have fast become best friends. Thankfully, I haven't yet encountered the Gopeshwar-wallah bagh, but I have seen her half-consumed, dead prey and her pugmark imprints outside my room, in the mud. Not being able to see her yet feeling her constant presence makes her seem even more terrifying. How beastly is this intimacy.

When I do finally see the adamkhor, she is but a corpse. In death she appears small, innocent, and strangely vulnerable. It is a peculiarly painful sight to behold. All of us silently assembled around her dead body are at a loss for words to describe the form of grief we are collectively feeling. I almost cannot believe this is the same beast we were all living in mortal fear of for so long.

†

In lieu of a conclusion to this beastly enterprise, I end with three brief tales. The first is a short life history of a tigress called Avni who lived in central India and became very famous for her crookedness in 2018. Avni's life and death exemplify the core concerns of *Crooked Cats*. The fact that the climate crisis was never really written into her prominent public life hints at the silences and lookings away that this work wishes to bring into question. The second is centered on bears that are said to be going "mad," the disappearance of a major glacier, and a divine disaster in the Himalaya. The bears, the melting glacier, and the divine disaster are said to serve as precursors of the coming apocalypse. The climate crisis is here already, with the most vulnerable struggling to survive it. We might be stumbling over our words, but it is untrue to state we cannot develop a lexicon for these troubled times of ours that we can, perhaps helpfully, term "the Anthropocene" (Howe and Pandian 2020). Narratives and events that can illustrate the planetary crisis and the very localized ones—of that starving tiger that turns on humans in the village in central India, for instance—are very much to hand. It is just that we haven't been listening to certain voices that have been, for long and in vain, exclaiming at the predations—not by big cats but by the *anthropos*, the human. The final tale involves our most loyal of companion species and proves that amid all the uncertainties and fears of our times, there remain moments when we *just know* and are held together by interspecies love and extraordinary acts of kinship. All encounters in the Anthropocene need not, after all, be beastly. If only humans were willing to change their crooked ways.

ONE

Crooked Becomings

Four months after the end of the reign of terror of the crooked cat of Gopeshwar, another leopard took up residence in our small Himalayan town. At certain times of the day we would hear—or think we had heard—his roar, his pugmarks, and tracks were spied on the wet muddy ground, and stories of sightings of him proliferated. The previous leopard—who had turned out to be crooked—had announced his arrival in dramatic style with an attack in broad daylight. This one, mercifully, had not attacked humans, though his presence was signaled by the sudden disappearance of two pet dogs and the bloody sight of a half-eaten goat on the road. In an unnerving mimicry of the cold winter months when all we had done was discuss our new nonhuman town resident, frenetic speculations on the nature of this leopard started. He was referred to, quite simply, as the new leopard (*naya bagh*). We waited in dread-filled anticipation before we could affix "*adamkhor*" (man-eating) to his name even as we spent hour upon hour discussing whether or not he, too, was a man-eater.[1] With the *naya bagh* had come the now-familiar bagh chatter and that indescribably spooky sense of beastly haunting.

Residents of the Indian Himalaya are good at distinguishing different kinds of big cats from one another: *seedha bagh* (straightforward/simple big cat) from *tedha bagh* (twisted/crooked big cat); *adamkhor* (man-eater) from *bekasoor* (innocent).[2] Due to habitat destruction and the increasing rates of urbanization, humans are now sharing increasingly constricted spaces with big cats. This feature of the contemporary makes the distinguishing of a seedha bagh from a tedha bagh a vital skill. The seedha bagh is normal and simple in that the cat takes care to avoid humans and will not target humans even if one were to accidentally bump into the cat in the jungle. The tedha bagh, on the other hand, is an altogether different story, and we need to maintain the strictest of vigilance vis-à-vis this type of cat. Given the relatively healthy population of big cats in the Himalaya, residents of this region have come to acquire certain anticipatory and speculative skills in connection to the character of an individual—often named—big cat. The simplicity or crookedness of a known—through name, size, look, temperament, sound, behavior, or some other distinguishing feature—big cat needs to be calculated. In this chapter, I discuss how such judgments are derived and outline the diverse theories that circulate and serve to explain the very reasons for the crookedness of certain big cats.

In the public imagination, big cats are on the verge of extinction and live in demarcated "wild spaces" such as national parks or wildlife sanctuaries. The fact that humans share space with all three big cats in India—lions, tigers, and leopards—might appear somewhat improbable. But, in reality, big cats in India live in proximity to humans, and, in fact, a notable feature of the past decade has been the increasing entry of big cats—tigers and leopards—into densely populated urban spaces. In rural areas as well as within wildlife parks, large human populations co-reside with them.[3] For complex, historical reasons, laid out comprehensively by Divyabhanusinh (2008), lions are now to be found only in the Gir region of Gujarat in western India. Tigers are certainly highly endangered, though they are more widely spread out around India. Both of these big-cat species come in close contact with humans, and the feature of becoming an adamkhor persists too, especially among tigers.[4] The crookedness of leopards is a particularly prominent concern, given their healthy numbers and capacity to conceal themselves. In the Himalaya as well as in Mumbai, where I have conducted research, sightings of leopards (*Panthera pardus*, or the ordinary leopard) are commonplace. A leopard census undertaken in India in 2015 gave an estimate of approximately twelve thousand to fourteen thousand leopards in India currently.[5] This figure has been disputed by several experts who claim that the number might actually be higher, even though the future of this species is looking bleak given high levels of poaching.[6] Another recent study based on genetic data analysis argues that there was a possibly human-induced 75 to 90 percent leopard-population decline across India between 120 and 200 years ago (Bhatt et al. 2020). The leopard census pins the number of leopards in Uttarakhand at a suspiciously precise figure of 703. Another study by Uttarakhand's forest department in 2008 gave the more believable figure of 2,335 leopards in the state (Sondhi et al. 2016). Dubiety of the exact number aside, the fact remains that there is a relatively large population of big cats in the state at this point, with frequent sightings

1.1. Etching of a leopard.
Credit: The Wellcome Collection

and encounters. The density of leopards in Mumbai, which is higher and better studied, has been put at thirty-one in the one hundred and forty square kilometers of the Sanjay Gandhi National Park (Surve 2015).

Just as the Hindi language doesn't distinguish between leopard, tiger, and lion by referring to all three as *bagh*, theories of man-eatingness remain the same for all. There are similar accounts for why tigers in the Sundarbans (the mangrove forests lying on the India and Bangladesh border), lions in the Gir Forest of the state of Gujarat, and leopards in the Himalaya become man-eaters. Having said that, there is no one dominant or even uniform set of modalities for distinguishing crooked cats. Rather, various indicators and theories proliferate. In these diverse theories on the making of man-eaters, big cats do not appear just as passive objects that humans impose their cultural, political, and social beliefs on. Instead, we see big cats as active agents with their own biological features, temperaments, histories, political leanings, memories, social structures, kinship patterns, desires, emotional lives, and individual psyches (figure 1.1).

Is There Such a Thing as a Man-Eater?

One of the most curious things about crooked cats is that most big cats are not, in fact, thus inclined. Big cats that actively seek out humans to consume are generally the exception, as it is believed that, as Boomgaard puts it, all big cats have "a natural, ingrained respect, fear, mistrust, or aversion of human beings" (2001, 66). While many of my interlocutors in the Himalaya disagree that tigers and leopards respect humans, they do also largely believe that normal big cats—the seedha bagh that constitute the vast majority of big cats—tend to avoid humans. Due to their keen senses of smell and hearing, tigers and leopards know when a human is approaching and will normally hide or move away as an act of avoidance. Only in rare circumstances do big cats actively seek out humans as prey; intentionality and repeat action are what make a big cat a legitimate man-eater. Man-eaters retain a minority status, but it is statistically impossible to say what that may be. That hasn't prevented some writers from making guesses, with estimates ranging from three or four man-eaters per one thousand tigers to approximately ten per one thousand tigers (Hodges-Hill 1992, 20). Marginally better statistics are available for deaths of humans by man-eaters in colonial India. Over the period 1882–1904 an annual average of 1,206 humans died due to tigers and leopards in India (Boomgaard 2001). This is easily the largest number of human casualties from big cats in the world, even when compared to numbers from Southeast Asia and Africa. However, even these figures are dubious, for a whole range of reasons related to the government of big cats and the bureaucratic practices of the Indian state (N. Mathur 2016). The unreliability of the statistics led the colonial British state to stop publishing annual figures on death by wild animals in the 1920s, even though numbers continue—to date—to be collected on a sporadic, unreliable basis by provincial states.

The one fact that we can, however, authoritatively establish through government records, independent studies, anecdotal and media accounts, and my own ethnographic research is that crooked cats *do* continue to exist, and the human casualties and injuries caused by them are significant. In the small state of Uttarakhand, "over 200" humans were killed by man-eating tigers and leopards over 2000–2015, and 140 big cats (leopards and tigers) were officially declared man-eaters in the same period.[7] It is curious to read works that say either man-eating big cats no longer haunt South Asia or there is no such thing as a man-eater.[8] Such pooh-poohing of the reality of man-eaters stems from a somewhat peculiar combination of the end of colonial practices—which were responsible for the celebrity acquired by certain named man-eaters, *because* they were hunted by the white man; unrelenting data collection by what Nicholas Dirks (2001) has famously described as "an ethnographic state"; hunting diaries and accounts by white colonial officials; the fictionalization of India into jungle stories; the projection of Pax Britannica as bringing order to an uncivilized land animaled with fierce man-eaters—coupled with the rise of conservationist impulses that declare big cats to be mere victims of human depredations. Conservationists argue that big cats are charismatic, innocent, beautiful, and even "cute," and at all costs they must be protected and conserved; there is nationalistic pride in the population of tigers; and a fiercely conservationist legal regime from the 1970s lumped together lions, tigers, and leopards as similarly protected animals. The one thing that unites both colonial and conservationist positions on the absence of man-eaters is their strikingly similar skepticism of native claims. In the archives, it is common to see constant questioning of whether a particular tiger or leopard is or isn't a man-eater. This querying isn't a product of the contemporary concern with the dwindling population of big cats. Rather, in the colonial period this was a straightforward questioning of the intelligence of natives and their basic capacity to distinguish good big cat from bad big cat. In the Himalaya, local elites, especially state officials and big-cat enthusiasts, continue to ridicule the opinions of the mountain persons to this day. In tussles between the innocence of big cats and that of humans, almost always the big cat wins out. Explaining the actions of crooked cats becomes particularly difficult as there remains no coherent explanation for *why they exist* in the first place.[9] Furthermore, the actions of some of the big cats as well as the possible reasons why they have gone crooked appear so implausible that this opens up the space to doubt their very existence.

What are the dominant theories on why and how a big cat turns to eating humans? While some of the theories might appear far-fetched at first look, I suggest they merit closer examination. Upon doing so, we can discern close overlaps between these supposedly improbable hypotheses that often border on overt conspiracy theories and the more legitimately "scientific" studies. This focus on diverse knowledge practices regarding the making of crooked cats suggests that it is hard to neatly delineate local/indigenous/native knowledge as separate from the more legitimized, seemingly scientific and rational forms of knowledge (see Agrawal 1995). In lieu of a dichotomy, which is often assumed in much of the conservationist literature, perhaps we would be better served by thinking in terms of multiple domains of knowledge and by carefully noting how they overlap and intersect. Furthermore, what we have here is a scenario where the knowledges and theories arise from nonhuman sources. In other words, what lies ahead in these pages is not just what different types of humans ("natives," "scientists," "bureaucrats," "tiger lovers") are telling us about big cats. Big cats themselves loom large, for this story is not just about what we learn by studying them from afar. It is also drawn from what we learn by living in their very midst, sometimes at an uncomfortably close range.

Unafraid of Humans

The *naya bagh* of Gopeshwar was considered suspect by the town residents due to one specific behavioral trait that is believed to be symptomatic of a man-eater: he seemed unafraid of humans. Instead of shunning humans, he appeared to be unperturbed by them and almost seemed to be seeking them out, given his appearance in busy parts of town in broad daylight. If he had been a "normal leopard," he would have taken pains to hide himself away from humans. This lack of fear signals immediately to mountain persons that the leopard is potentially dangerous.

One late evening I was out taking a walk. Out of the chilly Himalayan dusk an elderly man appeared, making me jump with fright. Noting my reaction, he nodded his head and said, "Yes, it could have been the naya bagh instead of me." He proceeded to scold me for walking alone and at a time when not many others were out and about. Did I not know that a suspicious-looking big cat had been lurking around town? Did I, furthermore, not remember the antics of the recently killed man-eater? Did I not recall that big cats prefer the taste of the sweeter blood of women? It is for this reason, he firmly told me, that most of the victims of man-eaters are women or children and not men. Having lived through the reign of several man-eaters, the experienced mountain person (*pahari*) that he was, he "just knew" (*bas pataa hai*) when another one was watching us. "I can feel his eyes boring into my back as I go about my daily chores. He is watching and waiting. Are you not feeling his eyes upon you even as we speak?" Shamefacedly, I admitted that I was not. My road acquaintance surmised that my lack of awareness of the man-eater's presence arose from my non-Himalayan upbringing: "This is because you are a maidani [person from the plains] and not a pahari like me. If you were, you would also feel the gaze of the big cat."

I never met this person again. In fact, I often wonder now if, in the feverish state of dreading another crooked cat's arrival, I did not dream him up. Whether he was real or not, the details of that conversation were often repeated to me by other paharis. They too "just knew" when there was a man-eater in the area and when there was a normal leopard—that is, the type that is scared of humans and keeps a healthy distance from them. They too could often feel him gazing at them, watching them, lurking someplace close by. To be a real inhabitant of the mountains—to be a pahari—means to (*just*) know how to share space with all sorts of nonhumans, especially big cats that might wish to devour you.

But it was not just the paharis who could feel the prick of a predatory feline gaze on their backs. Official documents, too, echoed this suspicion of big cats that appeared to lack a fear of humans and would actively mingle with them. This official belief comes across strongly in those documents that seek to establish the dangerousness of a big cat and are requesting permits to hunt or capture these highly protected animals. These official documents—letters and petitions—utilize such fearlessness as an indication of the tiger or leopard becoming "habituated" to stalking and killing humans and not just out of a "chance encounter" (cf. Margulies 2019). For instance, in July 2006 there was a leopard that was haunting Gopeshwar, but he had only killed some poultry thus far. He was being sighted with a worrying frequency in human habitations. On July 28, his behavior took a distinct turn for the worse. One evening around 8 p.m., four women were walking together in a group in the middle of the town, engaged deep in conversation, when, all of a sudden, the bagh appeared and attacked them. Two of the women sustained severe injuries, and one of them eventually died due to them. This event was described by the divisional forest officer to the chief wildlife warden in a letter in which he claimed that this bagh is "very dangerous" (*atyanta khatarnak*) and is exhibiting "aberrant behaviour" (an English term used in an otherwise entirely Hindi-language letter): "This sort of behaviour is increasing the possibility of destruction of life in the near future due to which it is imperative to immediately discipline the concerned leopard. In order to regulate the concerned leopard and seeing the failure of the present efforts to do so, I request you to utilise Clause 11 of the Wildlife Protection Act of 1972 on a priority basis and give me the permission to do the required work at my level to get him killed."[10]

The lack of fear of humans is considered aberrant for several reasons, not all of which are related. In the first place, it confirms a long-held popular belief that big cats are "naturally" scared of humans. Officials, in particular, hold onto this idea that a leopard is not normally comfortable in the vicinity of humans, and they use lack of fear as official evidence for the declaration of a big cat as a man-eater. Across the board, big cats that are unafraid of humans are considered "aberrant" and "unnatural," but the reasons for their lack of fear vary dramatically.

The Alien Cat

One of the most popular explanations for why certain (potentially man-eating) big cats are unafraid of humans is rooted in the idea that those cats lack indigeneity. This non-indigene theory was memorably brought home to me one day during the peak of the reign of terror of the Gopeshwar leopard. We were all scurrying home before darkness enveloped the town and increased the cover for the bagh. A journalist who works with a prominent local newspaper came up to me and held out his hand in the gesture of a handshake. As he was reeking of alcohol and it is not a normal cultural practice to shake hands (especially with a man if one is a woman) in this part of India, I did not return the gesture. On this, he said in appreciative tones, "Very good." He proceeded to tell me that if a big yellow cat with polka dots does precisely this (gives out a paw to shake my hand), then I will know it's the adamkhor (man-eater) from the zoo in the plains and I should do just what I did right now—that is, not return the handshake. In the zoo the leopard has gotten used to seeing humans and therefore thinks nothing of shaking hands with them and has probably, according to the journalist, been taught the "trick" of handshaking much like pet dogs are.

The journalist, in his inebriated state, was that day narrating to me the most popular theory of why there are so many man-eaters in the Himalaya: because they are alien to the mountains and their true provenance is located in the plains. When leopards grow old in their zoos in the plains, the plains persons send them up to the mountains to die. Or when zoos get overcrowded with leopards, then, too, they ship them up to the mountains. As these zoo leopards are used to being provided with meals and some are, in any case, too old to hunt wild animals, they turn on the easiest prey of all—humans. As more and more rescue and rehabilitation centers for big cats are set up in India, the issue of overcrowding has extended to these spaces as well.

The belief that captured or zoo-accustomed big cats are sent up from the plains to the mountains has to be understood in the context of a historical mountain-plains animosity that dominates the politics of this impoverished borderland region. A movement for statehood that allowed for the creation of a distinct Himalayan state of Uttarakhand in 2000 had voiced a long-held and much fretted-over perception that the postcolonial nation-state has systematically neglected this region (Mawdsley 1997). The neglect is coupled with an active exploitation of this region's rich natural resources—such as water, timber, minerals, and herbs—that has been going on from the colonial period right through to the present. The release of old leopards and tigers from zoos into what the plains persons merely consider "jungle," with no heed paid, as usual, to the perils this poses for its inhabitants, is considered just another item in a long list of actions by the plains people that combine abuse and neglect of the mountain people.

At times people would thunder away at this history of neglect-cum-exploitation that is mirrored in the big cats that are sent up. At other times they would half-jokingly say that they know this *maidani bagh* (leopard from the plains) misses the company of humans, but he really need not impose himself so aggressively onto the paharis, though in doing so he is merely following the historical precedent established by his fellow *maidanis* (plains people). During the winter of my time in Gopeshwar, the man-eating leopard that was "visiting us," as his arrival was popularly described, came out and sunned himself on a ledge near the bazaar at noon in full sight of the gawking Gopeshwar-ites. Sometimes he would be seen strolling through the main roads of the town, walking around the busy town temple and, generally, appearing to seek out human company instead of—as "normal" leopards would do—shunning or shying away from humans. This leopard's "abnormal" lack of fear of humans and "cheekiness" left everyone in town absolutely convinced that he hailed directly from a zoo in the plains.

Mannerless and rude (*badtameez*) and cunning (*chatur*) were the adjectives used most often to describe the leopard. When the maidani and zoo origins of the Gopeshwar man-eater were directly discussed, he was described as possessing no manners and absolutely no fear of humans. This inhabitant of zoos in the plains positively reveled in the attention of humans and was therefore making efforts to seek them out. The overwhelming identity of being a pahari that I described above is not restricted to humans but extends to nonhuman animals as well. Thus, the *Gopeshwar-wallah bagh*, or the man-eating leopard of Gopeshwar, was clearly not a pahari; he was certainly from the plains (*maidan*), and that explained his lack of civility and rudeness (*badtameez bagh*). Just like his fellow maidanis, the big cat felt superior to the paharis, and this was reflected in his predatory, rude, and obnoxious behavior. In a parallel observation, Jalais (2011) documents the widespread belief that tigers in the Sundarbans forests in West Bengal turned against lower-class and lower-caste Bengali refugees as the tigers somehow knew that the state had granted the cats greater citizenship rights and entitlements to living in Bengal than it had to the unwanted refugees from Bangladesh. The Sundarbans tigers in Jalais's study had become "vengeful," "self-important," and "the very embodiment of arrogance" (2011, 152) due to the protection they are accorded by the state. Tigers treated the Sundarbans islanders as "tiger food" as the government had "endowed their tigers with the arrogance of knowing their species are superior" (172).

Were the man-eaters in Uttarakhand in fact from zoos or from rescue centers in the plains? Is it true that they have been sent up to the mountains or released into what is widely considered merely a "jungle" or "wilderness" (but is in fact densely peopled)? In my interviews with forest officials this theory of big cats being sent up to murder the mountain people has been entirely ridiculed as a bogus conspiracy theory. I have, however, met and interviewed several eyewitnesses who swear they have seen leopards and tigers being released in the mountains by the forest department. In all probability, there is a de facto practice of translocation of big cats underway in the Himalaya. There are several contributing factors. Firstly, there is a very real issue of overcrowding of leopards in zoos and in the rehabilitation centers that are set up for the putatively crooked ones. Due to space and budgetary constraints many of the captured leopards are, in practice, released back into jungles. Secondly, the forest departments in the Himalayan states of Uttarakhand and Himachal Pradesh are open about the commonplace practice of capturing troublesome tigers and leopards in cages and taking them away for time in "rehab" in rescue centers. These modes of entrapment are, as I discuss in more detail later in the book, only increasing in recent years due to stark differences in the behavior and presence of big cats in this time of the climate emergency. The big cats are not legally meant to remain in these centers for more than thirty days unless there is "proof" that they are, in the words of the Wildlife Protection Act, 1972, clause 11(1)(a), "dangerous to human life." Often, these leopards have to be released back into the very region that they were captured from, or some distance away in a "jungle" or in a landscape that is considered more naturally suitable for big cats.

Translocating Big Cats

Reliable statistics on the capture and relocation of big cats are difficult to come by in India for several reasons. In the first place, they are not stringently maintained by the state; there are no legal injunctions or historical precedence or customary behavior that enjoins officials to diligently note and file the number of big cats captured, from where, and where they were released back. The federal nature of governance in India further complicates this issue, as different states maintain varying sorts of records related to wildlife. Hence, the form of record keeping in Uttarakhand is vastly different from even that found in the neighboring Himalayan state of Himachal Pradesh when it comes to translocation practices. Secondly, many captures and relocations of tigers, leopards, and lions in India are now done under the radar in order to keep wildlife conservationists off officials' backs, as well as to avoid having to adhere to the strict wildlife laws and regulations. Given the secrecy that is increasingly shrouding even the state's own interventions in the lives and futures of big cats, it is becoming extremely difficult to obtain officially sanctioned accounts, interviews, or records. Making matters worse, translocation of "problem leopards" is now so common that different wings of the forest department undertake it on a regular basis and in an ad hoc manner without finding it necessary to inform other levels, far less document it.[11] Thus, I would often speak to a divisional forest officer who would be genuinely in the dark about a specific individual cat that one of his or her own underlings might have tranquilized or caged. The frequent occurrence of these "problem animals," as they are often referred to, has led to an odd form of decentralization of power whereby leopards can be trapped and released at will, or so it seems.

During the legislative assembly elections in Uttarakhand in 2012, many leopards were captured and taken away from bigger towns so that the incumbent political party would not be blamed for such sightings. Sighting these big cats in a town or other such spaces that are considered nonbeastly is widely considered a damning failure of governance. To avoid electoral backlashes, state governments issue surreptitious orders to ensure that all leopards are safely locked away till the last vote has been cast. As I was doing fieldwork in the Himalaya at that time, I heard this firsthand from the men who were setting up the traps and relocating the captured leopards. Nowhere was this documented nor were official orders given to this effect. Similarly, during my fieldwork in the neighboring Himalayan state of Himachal Pradesh, there were several cases of capture and translocation reported, and many were documented in the forms of emails and petitions.

But why might translocation of big cats lead to or aggravate interspecies violence?

There is ample evidence from around the world to indicate that increased human-animal conflict can be the fallout of translocation.[12] Translocation is a process that involves capturing a perceived "problem animal" alive in the area of conflict and transporting it to another area where the animal is duly released. This method has gained in popularity since the 1960s due to its nonlethal character. In India, it is particularly attractive given how difficult it is to legally kill the three highly protected big cats. Translocation of big cats in India gained momentum, according to my interviews, in the mid-1980s, but its success or desirability remains questionable. As Linnell et al. (1997) have noted, there is very poor monitoring of post-release translocated carnivores and sparse studies on the effects of translocation in reducing conflict. One of the first studies was undertaken in Kenya in 1979 by Hamilton (1981), where over a period of eleven years a total of 108 leopards had been released into Meru National Park. They had been trapped elsewhere, up to two hundred kilometers away, due to the trouble they were causing farmers. Hamilton radio-collared eight leopards, which he monitored for between one week and eighteen months. He found that all eight of the leopards left the park and attempted to return to their original spaces. On the African continent, especially in Kenya, where many of the translocation of carnivora studies have been undertaken (e.g., Cobb 1981), the human population density is much lower than it is in India. Thus, the conflict or "nuisance value" that is noted is normally between big cats and livestock. In India, the same space is shared between a high number of both humans and leopards, with the latter attacking not just livestock and domesticated pets but also humans.

Athreya et al. (2011) argue that when there is increased translocation of big cats, the level of conflict goes up in the region of the release area. They arrive at this conclusion through a quantitative data analysis of state records for the state of Maharashtra. They show that, in the absence of relocation, serious human-leopard conflict is absent, even in high-human-density landscapes. From their research in an area called Junnar in Maharashtra, they note that "prior to the large-scale translocation program, an average of four leopard attacks on humans occurred each year between 1993 and 2001. After the translocation program was initiated, the average increased substantially to 17 attacks" (Athreya et al. 2011, 133). Another important study was undertaken in Mumbai in the Sanjay Gandhi National Park (SGNP). It traces two peaks in conflict in SGNP and nearby Thane areas and claims that the large peak over 2002–2004 is a direct outcome of the large-scale capture and release of leopards in and around this area:

> The attacks on humans peaked at a smaller level between 1997–1998 when a total of 24 attacks on people were reported and a much larger peak between 2002–2004 when a total of 84 attacks on people were reported. The average number of leopard attacks on humans (if both injuries and deaths are considered) are seven per year between 1986 and 2010 but in the two years between 1997–1998, the average was 12 attacks on humans per year, and in the three years between 2002 and 2004, it was an average of 28 attacks per year. Between 2005 and 2010, the average number of leopard attacks on people was 2 per year. (Mumbaikars for SGNP 2014, 11)

This study exhibits very clear correlation between the trapping and relocation of leopards and the spurt in attacks on humans. Carnivore biology provides several reasons that help explain why translocation fails as a mechanism for managing conflict and how it can in fact lead to increased levels of conflict. In the first place, once certain individuals of a carnivore species like leopards or tigers are removed from a site, the territory left vacant is speedily occupied by younger subadults or other immigrants. Athreya et al.'s (2011) study clearly shows this for western Maharashtra, where, following the removal of a leopard from a site, livestock attacks are still reported and more leopards continue to be trapped from the same area. A study in Utah, in the United States, similarly shows that once the territory occupied by twelve mountain lions was vacated (as they were trapped or killed following livestock attacks), it came to be speedily reoccupied by seventeen different and younger individual lions (Linnell et al. 1997). In other words, relocation of a big cat from its territory has not caused the space to become devoid of the feline presence. Rather, newer "migrants" are quick to take up the same space.

Additionally, the research in Africa and South Asia establishes the strong homing instinct of big cats that leads them to return from the release site to their original territory. As they try to find their way home, these large cats encounter difficult and unfamiliar geographical features, such as water bodies, deserts, and mountains. Most critically, they run into human-populated areas, thus increasing the chances of encounters between humans and big cats and the spreading of conflict to hitherto unaffected sites. Even when they do manage to return home, they often face disruptions in the kin and social structures of yore.

The trapping and relocating of big cats is a fraught enterprise. In India, all animals are trapped and kept caged by the local forest department, which, in most cases and certainly in my experience, possesses neither the resources nor the expertise to maintain an animal in captivity. The rough trapping experience, poor transportation facilities, and abysmal conditions of the cages in most of the rescue centers lead to injury, stress, and the deterioration of the animal's health prior to its release (Karanth and Gopal 2005). This might explain why relocated leopards tend to have much higher mortality rates (Hamilton 1981). As I touch on in the next chapter, it is very hard to correctly identify an individual leopard. The snares, cages, and traps that are laid to capture the putatively problematic big cats cannot be perfectly targeted at the individuals in question. Thus, many times "innocent leopards" (*bekasoor bagh*) get captured, caged, and translocated. This disruptive and often very harmful process leads to the needless creation of new crooked cats.

Despite the obvious limitations of translocation as a mode of dealing with conflict between humans and big cats in India, this method is only gathering traction, as it opens up the space for bureaucratic maneuvering and makes for a quick short-term solution to the vexed issue of "problem animals." There is also the growing issue of sightings of big cats in urban areas—particularly through CCTVs, the use of which is spreading rapidly in private and public spaces alike—and the demand by the urban citizens that the big cat be immediately captured and taken back to its putative home in a jungle or a wildlife park (see chapter 6). Thus, translocation seems set to increase in the near future. This will only add more substance to the "alien cat" theory that residents of the Himalaya have for long raised.

Conspiracy to Murder

A variant of the released-from-the-zoo explanation for man-eaters also has some traction in Uttarakhand. In this version, the alien leopards have not merely been released from zoos or rescue centers and neglectfully sent up to the mountains. Rather, these man-eaters have been sent up with an actively malign intent, to kill and destroy the paharis. The conspiratorial element in this explanation is explicit. As I mention above, it needs to be understood in the context of a long-standing historical sense that the plains people have exploited the Himalaya. A very similar discourse is present in the neighboring Himalayan state of Himachal Pradesh, where several people told me, straight out, that the man-eaters are objects of extermination controlled by the state. Similarly, many residents around the Sanjay Gandhi National Park in Mumbai believe that in the evenings the park authorities "open the gates" and the leopards come out of the park to hunt and eat whatever they can find—from pet dogs to humans. In studies of human-animal conflict around the world, such an intentionality behind the appearance of dangerous animals is often assumed, with, most often, the state being accused of conspiracy to murder.[13]

There is a much longer history to consider around who the targets of man-eaters are. A popular belief during the period of European imperial domination in Asia was that man-eating tigers kill only Asians and not Europeans. This belief appeared as early as 1662 and continued on till the twentieth century.[14] In colonial India, while there were many white Europeans who were killed by man-eating big cats, the number of natives killed is much higher for obvious reasons, including the much larger native population and their increased exposure to tigers, leopards, and lions in daily life. But it is not just between the white man and the natives that big cats have discriminated. Man-eaters, across time and space, are believed to actively seek out certain categories of person to prey on even while they leave others untouched. The ones who are most likely to be targeted tend to belong to minority or vulnerable communities—refugees, lower castes, mountain persons, adivasis, the poor, women. As I show in this book and as Jalais (2011) has also demonstrated for the Sundarbans, there are complex political and socioeconomic reasons that make certain humans more likely to be victimized by crooked cats. These reasons run along axes of class, caste, gender, race, age, location, and nationality. Thus, crooked cats and their depredations allow for a bloodied mirroring of the wider inequalities of the world.

It is not just the type of person but also the posture or position of the human at the time of the attack that is considered important. In the Sundarbans it is believed that tigers only attack humans when they cannot see the human's face. Because of this, people were advised to wear masks on the backs of their heads when they went out of their homes, as a protective measure (Jalais 2011; Ghosh 2016). Another belief is that tigers will only attack stooping figures or those who are not in an upright manner. I have been told in different parts of India that if I accidentally encounter a tiger or leopard, then I must make sure to stand straight so that I loom large over the big cat and, hopefully, intimidate it. But I have also been told, perhaps most memorably by my Nani (maternal grandmother), that if I ever bump into a *sher* (tiger/lion), then I should lie flat on my back and play dead, as, apparently, my Nana (maternal grandfather) once did in Rajasthan when a tiger walked into his room. As is the norm with most quandaries related to big cats, there are contradicting answers to a long-standing question: What should you do if you encounter a tiger in India?

In Mumbai, many of the attacks by leopards took place when a person was squatting in a field or in their toilet. Many a wildlife conservationist has told me that it was only these humans who were attacked, which my own interviews with victims entirely contradict. But the conservationists claim that when the big cats attack squatting human figures, they are doing so out of confusion, for they think the human is a dog or a goat and hence regular game. The large number of female victims in the Himalaya is also often ascribed to women's "weakness" as a gender as well as their relatively lower body weight that lets leopards carry them with ease. In addition, women are believed to have "sweeter blood" that big cats like. While body weight might have a role to play and not the gendered constructs of weakness and sweetness, the most likely explanation is that women and children are much more likely to be targeted due to the social roles they have and the positions they occupy: fetching water from springs and wood and grass from the jungle, tending to the homesteads, feeding livestock, having to go squat behind rocks and shrubs farther away from humans due to the widespread absence of sanitation facilities, and so on.

Retributive Justice

But big cats do not just target women or refugees or brown people. They can also narrow their victims down on the basis of other criteria. Between 2012 and 2014 there was a crooked cat in Pithoragarh District in Uttarakhand that appeared to kill only inebriated men. The cat killed six men in 2012 and five men in 2013, all of whom had consumed large amounts of alcohol. The man-eater turned out to be a leopardess and was hunted down in the end after two years. She had been rather selective in her killing for she wasn't active all the time but would periodically appear in villages in the Didihat block and specifically target drunk men. The belief was that this leopardess's kin—her "husband" or a parent or a child—had been killed by a drunk man and, hence, this was her seeking revenge. Many other such stories proliferate, especially some that include elements of the Hindu belief in reincarnation. In these accounts, a specific tiger or leopard suffered some distress at the hands of a human, or one of their family members did, and thus, when the big cat is reborn in a new life, it deliberately seeks revenge on that human or on those who are related to the human in some manner. Govindrajan (2015) discusses stories that view man-eaters as sent by the deities that the humans have angered. These leopards and tigers actively choose to spread reigns of terror because the gods have not been properly propitiated or humans have done something—like taking away land on which a temple once stood—that has offended them.

In addition to specific stories of retribution or reincarnation, there is also a widespread consensus that the more you hunt or hurt a species—be it big cats or snakes or monkeys or, indeed, humans—the more you will suffer from vengeful acts, either in this life or the next.[15] Notions of retribution and reincarnation cannot be disentangled from Hindu cosmology given that the Himalaya is heavily populated with Hindus. However, as Rashkow (2015) has argued through a study of Hindu opposition to the hunting of animals in colonial India, this protection of wildlife extends beyond religious beliefs to encompass forms of what can be termed "cultural conservation." He finds numerous examples of active resistance to the killing of animals in colonial India and reads them as instantiations of an environmental consciousness.[16]

In the Himalaya, I am often told that the large amount of killing and poaching of leopards and tigers has made them—as a species *and* as individuals with particular biographies—angry with humans. Thus, the many crooked cats that exist are nothing but the kin of the hunted, mutilated, and poached big cats, who are seeking revenge on humans. This revenge is extracted by making prey of humans in the very same way that humans predated their ancestors or relatives. Interestingly, studies of North American cougars have indicated that the hunting of them leads to an increase in conflict between humans and big cats. Journalist Noah Sudarsky describes it as a sort of "biological backlash."[17] The ethnobiologist Joao Pedro Galhano Alves (1999b) notes that the Van Gujjar community in the Sariska Tiger Reserve in India did not report trouble with tigers and explains it thus: "If the tigers almost never attack people in the region it is because we don't kill the tiger and so the tiger doesn't kill. We respect the tiger and it respects us" (cited in Greenough 2012, 186).[18] This is a generalized belief in the Himalaya too—the more you kill and hunt tigers and leopards, the more they will retaliate in kind. In India, statistical studies that draw direct links between levels of hunting and levels of conflict have yet to be undertaken, to my knowledge. It is, however, strongly indicative that the highest numbers of man-eaters are in those regions where there is the greatest level of hunting. Most powerfully, this trend was mapped by the BBC Two documentary "Leopards: 21st Century Cats."[19] In the documentary, we are taken on a ride through high-conflict and low-conflict areas of India. There is some wonderful footage of a leopard eating its kill quite peacefully near humans whom he is well aware of. There is also coverage of a region of Rajasthan called Jawai where several leopards come out to a temple with a priest and display no aggression toward either this human or each other or, indeed, the other villagers in the vicinity. This peaceful coexistence is contrasted with the atmosphere in high-conflict regions—most markedly Uttarakhand—to question the very different relationship between humans and big cats there. The documentary locates the answer in the unprecedented levels of hunting that are allowed in Uttarakhand in stark contrast to the rest of the country. In doing so, it displays a discernible overlap between what putatively "scientific" studies throw up and what long-term human residents of regions with big-cat populations tell us. They all tell us that higher levels of hunting or violence toward a species lead to problems in its relationship with humans. Extending this argument to the global scale, we are now realizing that the climate crisis itself is an outcome of the forms of harm humans have collectively inflicted on the nonhuman world over the *longue durée*.

Feline Histories

In an interview I undertook with a woman who was viciously attacked by a leopard in the Himalaya, the conversation moved beyond Hindu notions of reincarnation to speak about individualized revenge. This woman, whom I call Vimla, claimed a particular leopard had scratched and bitten her grievously *not* because it was a man-eater and wanted to consume her. Rather, it was seeking to extract revenge, because when this leopard was a small cub, Vimla had accidentally injured him. She had been tending to her little farm and cutting weeds off with a scythe. This cub was sitting in the long grasses, unbeknownst to her, and caught an edge of the sharp instrument on his hind leg. At that time she was too scared to tend to the cub's injury as his mother might have been lurking nearby. So she abandoned the injured cub and ran home. A few years later she noticed that this leopard, which limped a little as if its hind leg was not fully formed, would come and watch her from a distance. If he came too close, then she would run home or mock threaten him with her farming instruments. This leopard never stalked anyone else in the same manner. She knew that it was the same leopard and one day he would wreak his revenge on her. And, indeed, one evening as she went out of her home, she was suddenly attacked and injured. The leopard ran off without killing her—though he easily could have—and has never been seen since or attacked any other human in the vicinity.

Vimla not only recited a tale of the capacity of a big cat to identify human individuals and vice versa, she also pointed out the capacity that non-human animals have to remember and target humans. In a beautiful essay, the wildlife historian Mahesh Rangarajan (2013) tackles the related question of whether lions have history by studying a century of human-lion relations in Gujarat. He is of the opinion that it might be "going too far to endow lions with historical consciousness," but he does believe they have what he describes as a "memory of memories" (2013, 109). He notes lions have coexisted with humans in relative harmony, other than two periods of breakdowns in this otherwise equable relationship. During 1901–1904 and 1987–1988, there was a large number of attacks on humans by lions, or the spread of what Rangarajan, after Boomgaard, terms "lion plagues." Boomgaard had originally spoken of tiger plagues in Southeast Asia as sudden outbursts of man-eating tigers stimulated by a sharp increase in human or animal corpses—due to epidemics, epizootics, famines, and wars—or a lack of game and cattle caused by droughts, famines, forest fires, and so on. Rangarajan, similarly, attributes increases in conflict to the drought in Gujarat, depletion of game animals, presence of human corpses, and conflict over cattle kills between lions and the humans who were competing for the cattle hide. Corbett, too, has argued that in the 1920s Himalayas there was a surge in man-eating leopards—what we can perhaps call a "leopard plague"—due to the noncremation of dead bodies after a cholera pandemic (Corbett 1991b). One of the many theories on why the two maneless lions in Tsavo in present-day Kenya became man-eaters also considers the long-term practice of abandoning enslaved persons in the region. It has been suggested that lions learned to eat humans over time due to the slave trade, during which large numbers of humans traveled in the slave trains. When these humans died, their bodies were left by the railway tracks. This allowed for the development of a taste for human blood among these crooked lions (Caputo 2002).

Lion, tiger, and leopard plague arguments, thus, are centered on the availability of human bodies—either due to natural reasons, such as droughts or epidemics, or due to political reasons, such as the slave trade—and, very interestingly, the *learning* of big cats to consider humans prey.[20] Alternatively, certain researchers ascribe the turn to man-eating to the absence of alternate prey (Packer, Scheel, and Pusey 1990), a situation that can be caused by droughts or floods or, as I discuss in detail below, anthropogenic climate change and species extinction. Almost all studies stress the fact that it takes big cats some time to start considering humans—alive or dead—as something to be consumed. This process of learning to become a man-eater has been studied in various ways: through a focus on adaptive behavior, memory, history, or—as my interlocutors in the Himalaya stress—capacity for retribution.[21] The desire to seek retribution can emerge from any number of reasons.[22] It can be directed against humans as a species for their land grabs, depletion of resources, poaching, hunting, and wanton destruction of habitat. Equally, nonhuman animals seek retributive justice from specific individuals for their very particular actions, whatever those may be.

Shere Khan of *The Jungle Book*

No work has done more to globally popularize the memory and retributive capacities of big cats than Rudyard Kipling's iconic *Jungle Book* stories. The original Kipling tale has undergone several transformations as it has moved to film, animation, new book editions, TV series, and folklore. Several Walt Disney versions of *The Jungle Book* coexist with wildly popular Japanese anime renditions and the Indian government's official Hindi-language version that was aired on national television. All these recent iterations tend to ever-so-slightly shift the blame for why Shere Khan the tiger (and villain of the piece) wishes to kill Mowgli (the human "cub" who was reared by a pack of wolves) onto humans. Thus, Shere Khan seeks out Mowgli because of what his parents or humans did to the tiger. While the exact nature of the complaint with humans varies in each iteration—the tiger was burnt or grievously hurt by humans or Mowgli's parent or because of what humans did to Shere Khan's ancestors—there is a displacement onto humans to account for this most famous of man-eaters.

In Kipling's original version, published in 1894 under the title "Mowgli's Brothers," Mother Wolf says that Shere Khan was named Lungri (the lame one) at birth by his mother. His deformity meant he could only hunt cattle and not the speedier prey tigers normally seek out. Just as Father Wolf and Mother Wolf are disparagingly discussing how Shere Khan is now going to hunt man because there "were not enough beetles and frogs in the tanks" (Kipling 2018, 15), Mowgli the baby boy crawls into their cave. Hot on his heels comes the tiger, who demands the wolves return his "quarry" to him. Mother Wolf refuses to do so, and she insults the tiger, who, she claims, has no dominion over this part of the jungle. In this version, Mowgli becomes the object of Shere Khan's revenge fantasy because of the tiger's fall out with the wolves. Shere Khan's feet are burning because he leapt onto the woodcutters' fire (hence, his lifelong fear of fire, or "the red flower," as it is termed), but Mowgli's parents did not hurt him personally, for they had run away and, in the ensuing chaos, lost their baby boy. In other words, the anger is caused by tiger-wolf rivalry and animosity and not due to the preexistence of a "man-eater." In Kipling's own words tigers tend to stay away from man-killing as it contravenes the "Law of the Jungle":

> The Law of the Jungle, which never orders anything without a reason, forbids every beast to eat Man. . . . The real reason for this is that man-killing means, sooner or later, the arrival of white men on elephants, with guns, and hundreds of brown men with gongs and rockets and torches. Then everybody in the jungle suffers. The reason the beasts give among themselves is that Man is the weakest and most defenseless of all living things and it is unsportsmanlike to touch him. They say too—and it is true—that man-eaters become mangy, and lose their teeth. (Kipling 2018, 15–16)

Originally published in 1894, Kipling's story presents several justifications for not just why big cats don't become man-eaters but also, from the big cats' perspectives, why they shouldn't. For one, the white hunter would get them and—in the process—hurt others too. It was considered a duty of state by British colonial officials to hunt man-eaters down, but it is, of course, entirely incorrect that the "brown" hunters were incapable of killing big cats or didn't also protect people from the reigns of terror unleashed by man-eaters. In Kipling's tale, imperial ideologies of racial superiority fuse with British mores of sportsmanship wherein one attacks only one's equal. Finally, humans don't provide good nourishment and make big cats grow

Table 1.1 Official Accounts from the Chief Wildlife Warden on the Number of Human Deaths Caused by Leopards in Uttarakhand, 2004–2006

Year	Oct.–Jan. (Winter)	Feb.–May (Spring/Summer)	June–Sept. (Monsoon)	Total Deaths
2004	19 (56%)	4 (22%)	4 (22%)	27
2005	10 (66%)	3 (20%)	2 (14%)	15
2006	16 (84%)	2 (11%)	1 (5%)	19
Total	**45 (70%)**	**9 (17%)**	**7 (13%)**	**61**

Source: Chief wildlife warden's office, Dehradun.

old and mangy. Seen the other way, it is often thought that big cats become man-eaters because they are mangy or injured or very old.[23] Kipling's own Shere Khan was lame and, hence, killed easier prey like cattle. Contemporary examples of man-eaters, however, disprove such beliefs by showing that oftentimes the animal is a young and healthy felid.

Climate Change

In Uttarakhand, most of the half-dozen leopards and the three man-eater tigers I have encountered over the course of my fifteen-year research have been relatively young and healthy. Their fitness to hunt other prey was always remarked on, especially when the corpse of the man-eater was publicly displayed in its territory of operations.[24] These man-eaters' youth and lack of injury are what fuel suspicions that they have alien origins and other such theories of the more conspiratorial nature. In recent years, the health of man-eaters has been studied in correlation with another intriguing trend in the Himalaya. It is noteworthy, both anecdotally and statistically, that the majority of attacks in the Himalaya take place during the winter season. In table 1.1 below, given to me by the head of the Uttarakhand Forest Department, 70 percent of the deaths in 2004–2006 took place in the winter. According to these statistics, a total of sixty-one deaths were caused over three years by man-eating big cats. For a variety of complicated bureaucratic and knowledge-gathering reasons that I discuss in the next chapter, these official statistics present us with an extremely watered-down scenario of conflict between humans and big cats in India, but they do point out a seasonality to the attacks.

Pulling these two strands together, the district authorities came up with a very particular theory on the cause of the increase in man-eaters. According to them, in the winter leopards are pushed down by snowfall from the higher reaches of the Himalayas to spaces inhabited by humans, such as the town of Gopeshwar. Previously, there was abundant prey available for them (sheep, goats, deer, and so on). However, due to resource degradation and biodiversity depletion in Himalayan Uttarakhand, the leopards now find themselves faced with sparse options for hunting their regular prey and are, thus, constrained to turn on humans. In conversations with me, in meetings, and in official explanations to disgruntled citizens, state officials expressly made a connection between "climate change" and conflict between humans and big cats. Such causality is being established not just in Uttarakhand but also in all of South Asia. The rising number of articles in the international media on human-animal conflict is evidence of the latent potential of the discourse of climate change to make issues of human-animal conflict in hitherto marginalized areas widely accessible.

Good examples of this from a different part of India are the regular news items in the international media that relate the story of man-eating tigers in the Sundarbans.[25] Records of man-eating tigers in the Sundarbans can be found as far back as the sixteenth century, but until the recent entry of climate change as a possible explanation, the cause of the man-eating remained a mystery. When considered a tangible indicator and direct result of climate change, human-animal conflict suddenly received more public attention. For instance, in May 2019 the *New York Times* ran a story on the projected extinction of Bengal tigers due to climate change according to a study by the Intergovernmental Panel on Climate Change (IPCC).[26] The news item noted that "as the Sundarbans flood, confrontations may grow between humans and tigers as the animals stray outside their habitat in search of new land."

Depressed and/or Traumatized Cats

Much like the discourse about climate change, which has marked an entry in India in the last decade as an explanation for conflict between humans and big cats, a new psychologizing discourse is also gaining ground. Big cats are believed to possess an interiority and a psyche that can be disturbed, depressed, or—most commonly—traumatized. Thus, they suffer from trauma due to breakdowns in relationships with fellow big cats as well as with human animals; natural disasters that lead to a tiger, lion, or leopard plague; capture and relocation; excessive hunting; and a deteriorating environment. I have been hearing crooked cats described as "depressed," "psychotic," or "traumatized" for a long time, but it is only over the past few years that I have seen that this psychologizing reading of individualized and anthropomorphized big cats has been transformed into practice. There have been a few cases of medicating man-eaters with antidepressants. These medicines are the same as those prescribed to humans and are being tried particularly on the tigers as they are hard to kill or keep captured for very long. Captured male leopards are beginning to be surgically castrated before they are released back into the wild, as wildlife officials believe that this will make them less "frustrated" and "angry" and, hence, they will stop attacking humans. But man-eaters or man-killers are not merely given medication or operated on. They are additionally being "kept under observation," and any signs of depressed or strange behavior are noted down as indicators of a psychological malady. Most famously, a white tiger called Vijay was kept under observation by a team of Delhi psychologists and psychiatrists (of humans) for two weeks after he killed a man who had entered his enclosure in the Delhi zoo (see chapter 3).

If the climate change explanations are global in their framing, these psychologically derived ones are intensely individual and anthropomorphizing. In a country where most humans do not have access to mental-health-care facilities and where depression and other forms of mental illness remain taboo subjects carrying significant social stigma, there is no small irony in this contemporary turn in the management of man-eating big cats. Various studies are now establishing what my interlocutors in the Himalaya would agree with entirely: that animals are capable of complex emotions. From intelligence (Godfrey-Smith 2017) to grief (King 2014), we are only now coming to fully comprehend through studies of animal cognition and biology how nonhuman animals feel, live, love, mourn, or become crooked.

†

With both the explanations for man-eating big cats that are rooted in climate change and those that target an individual nonhuman animal's psyche or personality, the question remains: How are humans going to respond to them? As I describe in the next chapter, the human practice of governing what British colonial reports are fond of describing as "fierce, handsome tigers," "royal lions," and "sly, cunning leopards" has for long been a fraught enterprise. Crooked cats are well-nigh impossible to govern not just because they make prey of humans. Rather, their ungovernableness is due to what this opening chapter has tried to lay out through its brief exploration of the wide-ranging explanations for why big cats go crooked in the first place: there is no one comprehensive explanation that stays stable across time and space that can account for big cats' predation of humans.

In addition to the lack of consensus on why big cats become crooked, the fact that for each theory that exists we can find counterexamples to negate it adds further complications. For instance, the lions of Gir were said to have started attacking humans due to the existence of "lion shows" wherein they were lured by bait (live goats or large hunks of meat) for the purposes of human exhibition and entertainment. Jawai in Rajasthan has no record of human-leopard conflict in the past 150 years. This zero friction remains despite the sizable number of leopards that live very close to humans and make themselves public in broad daylight around a set of hills.[27] Leopards in Jawai are unafraid of humans due to the same reason as the lions in Gir: up till fifty years back they were "baited," as the process is described, for the purposes of show by the local maharajahs (kings). Even though baiting ended in the late 1960s, the leopards continue to come out to the same three hills in groups and display themselves, attesting once again to the strong possibility of intergenerational memory. Similarly, lions in Gir also congregate often in the spaces where lion shows used to take place. We have here a contemporary situation where in one case baiting leads to conflict, and in the other it produces a zone where even the talk of something like conflict is absent. Again, in some cases the lack of fear of humans is considered dangerous in big cats, as in the Himalaya. But in other cases, such as with the leopards in Mumbai and the tigers in parts of central India, the lack of fear is said to mark them as safe. The changes over time of explanations are also noteworthy. Thus, in the contemporary moment explanations rooted in climate change and/or the psychological distress of individuals are gaining traction. Not so long ago, the dominant theories were rooted in causes such as old age or "opportunism" or just the plain beastliness of an Orientalized, uncivilized land.

I can end, however, by making some assertions with some measure of confidence. Firstly, there are some explanations that are more convincing than others and that are supported by a range of evidence, from the statistical to the behavioral to the anthropological. Translocation, for one, should be seriously reevaluated as a method of dealing with crooked cats. Ample evidence has piled up that shows translocation further intensifies conflict between humans and big cats instead of controlling it. Hunting, too, doesn't seem to be the best option, not just due to the endangered status of big cats but also due to its lack of precision (in terms of identifying and killing the correct animal) and its lack of long-term efficacy in curtailing the problem. Rather, as an extraordinary Mumbai experiment that I will discuss in more detail in this book shows, new ways have to be devised for humans to learn to live with big cats, just as big cats have been adapting to humans (unbeknownst to humans!) over centuries past. Conservationists and the Indian state would be best served by experimenting with creative forms of coexistence between humans and big cats. The focus, in other words, needs to shift away from trying to separate out humans and big cats and further cosseting the latter by devising ever more punitive measures against humans. As I have argued in my previous work (N. Mathur 2016), there is a profound counterproductiveness to the intense big-cat protectionism of the form adopted in India. The strict conservationist legal regime and the bureaucratic state practices that implement it are, tragically, serving to fuel a greater human animosity against big cats, as evidenced in the rising incidences of brutal big-cat murders that periodically rock India.

Climate change is but one of the explanations that is offered, and it is offered by elites such as forest officials, nongovernmental organization (NGO) workers, wildlife writers, the IPCC, and international media. But if we read all these varying theories on big-cat crookedness together, we can see how human acts—hunting, translocation, actions undertaken in the distant past—merge with cosmologies centered on reincarnation and retribution. At the same time, the role of the state and the use of political power, which come across particularly strongly in the so-called conspiracy theories, are considered critical. History isn't separate from politics and religion, and there are complex interconnections that are constantly made by varied actors. This is the Anthropocene—that capacity of human actions to have such a huge impact that we are collectively acting as a geological force on the planet—at work, in evidence through a coming together of empire, capital, ecology, the state, notions of karma and reincarnation, and the conceit of certain types of humans.

Strikingly, these varied beastly tales of why big cats might become crooked demonstrate a significant overlap between what is termed indigenous, local, or native knowledge and the so-called scientific knowledge. Hunting, poaching, translocation, historic and political practices, and other human actions all affect relations between humans and big cats, according to new studies in biology, conservation, animal histories, behavioral sciences, and animal cognition, among other disciplines. Narratives about alien big cats, individual idiosyncrasies, and the capacity of big cats to remember, identify, and take revenge for past ills all sit comfortably with these findings. The emergent work on nonhuman animal emotions (e.g., Montgomery 2015), too, overlaps with the discussions of individual, named, known big cats that we encounter all through this work. Tiger, lion, and leopard plagues and events that can lead to breakdowns in human-animal relationships—concerns of a growing breed of multispecies ethnographer—are discussed matter-of-factly by humans who share space with big cats. Just as residents of the Himalaya have a visceral awareness of the character—especially the dangerousness or the harmlessness—of every individual feline, they also know that the big cats in return possess an inscrutable knowledge of them. It is not, then, merely indigenous knowledge and scientific knowledge that overlap and intersect in intriguing ways in the context of crooked cats. Rather, nonhuman animals with their own powerful presence, history, memory, emotions, and experience of humans enter the fray to disrupt a neat way of knowing, experiencing, and acting upon the world.

TWO

Murderous Looks

> I saw the way he was looking at me. His eyes met mine with full confidence, they didn't flinch even as I delved deep into his. That confidence convinced me he was guiltless and I refused to shoot despite the prodding of everyone around me.
>
> —Famous hunter of man-eaters (interview by author)

> You could always see it in his eyes.
>
> —Valmik Thapar, a.k.a. Tiger Man, celebrity tiger conservationist, describing the culpability of a tiger called Ustad whom he declared a "man-eater" ("Ustad," *India Today*)

> This guy [Ustad the tiger] . . . had an aura of a man-killer.
>
> —Aditya "Dicky" Singh, owner of a lodge in Ranthambore and "wildlife enthusiast" (blog post)

> On the basis of the evidence provided that the said leopard is a man-eater, I permit you, by the power vested in me, to hunt him down. You must ascertain, prior to the killing, that the hunted leopard is, indeed, the man-eater. To that effect this hunting license is valid only in a 2 km radius of the location of the last kill.
>
> —Generic requirements in most hunting licenses issued by the government of Uttarakhand

How does an individual tiger, leopard, or lion, out of the several that inhabit the same territory, come to be identified as *the* man-eater by humans? There is, I show in this chapter, no single overarching modality for arriving at such a beastly identification. It is only in the rarest of rare cases—when the attack by the crooked cat is caught on camera or there are several eyewitnesses or when the big cat is operating in a territory where there are no others of its species—that the evidence is indisputable and identification foolproof. In the vast majority of instances, the argument is built up against a specific cat on a case-by-case basis *after* it has been trapped or, worse, killed. Yet, the official government guidelines and legal strictures require that this identification be correctly made and fully verified anterior to the hunt.[1] All participating actors must, therefore, pretend that the right big cat—the man-eater—has been neutralized. In other words, the killing of a big cat enjoins a conspiracy of silence upon all involved.

Much as in the previous chapter, there are several theories that are applied in a variegated manner to identify the beast. In keeping with the highly individualized mode of culprit ascertainment that is practiced, this chapter too will proceed on a case-by-case basis. I begin with a cause célèbre, that of a tiger named Ustad who hails from the western Indian state of Rajasthan.

On May 8, 2015, a fifty-three-year-old forest guard called Rampal Saini was killed by a tiger in Rajasthan's Ranthambore National Park. The culprit, it was decided by the park authorities, was a nine-year-old tiger called T-24 or, more popularly, Ustad. Given that Ranthambore has a population of sixty-two tigers over a territory of 392 square kilometers, how was Ustad identified as the villain?

The most convincing evidence against Ustad was his "reputation." He has, as Ranthambore lodge owner and self-proclaimed "wildlife enthusiast" Aditya "Dicky" Singh noted, the "aura of a man-eater."[2] The celebrity tiger activist Valmik Thapar was convinced of Ustad's guilt too and made this judgment on the grounds of a long-standing familiarity with the tiger. Thapar is India's most famous and oft-quoted tiger specialist, who goes by the moniker of "Tiger Man." Through several books and wildlife documentaries he has established himself as the leading voice on tiger conservationism. Given his singular authority in the adjudication of whether a tiger—in this case Ustad—is or isn't dangerous, it is worth quoting him in full: "In my 40 years of experience of the tigers of Ranthambore, T-24 is the most dangerous tiger I have ever encountered."[3] Elsewhere, Thapar stated, "You could always see it in his eyes. He watched you even when your back was turned."[4]

As a cover story in *India Today* (figure 2.1), India's largest national English-language magazine, that questioned Ustad's conviction put it, "Ustad had always been a little off-kilter."[5] This tiger was reported to be not camera shy. On the contrary, he would take his kill onto the middle of the road and eat it in full sight of everyone. The field director of the national park also claimed that Ustad was different from all the others in the park, particularly in his

2.1. Cover of the *India Today* issue on Ustad the tiger.

capacity to stare down humans. Knowledge of this reputation, it appears, was not limited to elite tiger conservationists or officials. The victim's family, too, said in several interviews that Ustad was the only tiger in all of Ranthambore that Rampal was scared of. To back up this perception of Ustad's aura and bad reputation was information about the territory where the past four human killings in the park had taken place. In this territory, Ustad was known to be the dominant male, and that made him highly suspicious. The clinching evidence against Ustad came from eyewitness accounts. These eyewitnesses claimed to have seen Ustad return to the very spot of the kill and sniff the ground as if he was trying to track the corpse. Ustad was duly captured and has been sentenced to life imprisonment in a zoo near Ranthambore. This imprisonment led to a massive outrage in India. Most people believe, as the *India Today* story put it, that Ustad was "framed." There were candlelight vigils held for him across the country, petitions were lodged at all levels of the judiciary and bureaucracy, and both on social media and in the popular press there was an outcry against this unfair imprisonment of Ustad.

A vast diversity of actors believed—and continue to believe—that Ustad has been unjustly punished precisely because of the question of proof or evidence. In a landscape where there are many other tigers and it is physically difficult to distinguish one big cat from another, how do we know for certain that Ustad was the killer? All the evidence that was marshaled against him—the testimony of experts like Thapar and Singh, the territory of the kill, his reputation, and eyewitness accounts—can be and continue to be disputed as not, in and of themselves, forming convincing evidence of the culpability of this charismatic tiger.

In the case of Ustad, several legitimate questions were asked. The first was a simple one regarding just the killings in Ranthambore. There is a high density of humans in and around the park—not just of tourists but also of park staff and villagers. If Ustad really was a man-eater—a cat that is habituated to human flesh and seeks it out—then why would there be only four humans killed in five years? Further, it would appear that two of the four were accidents as the corpses had not been eaten by a tiger. Secondly, there were allegations of a conspiracy against Ustad by the tourism lobby in Ranthambore. This lobby is financed by an incredibly wealthy and powerful conglomerate of premier five-star hotels in the country. The conspiracy theory in circulation held that this industry did not want the rumors of a man-eater around to scare off tourists. The hoteliers vehemently denied this, with a couple of them claiming that, in fact, man-eaters increase tourism. Indeed, given that tourists get to enter the reserve in jeeps with security and a driver and are, additionally, well protected in their luxury hotels, with little fear of a crooked cat making prey of them there, it is quite believable that man-eaters don't dent business but might, in fact, attract a greater number of people (figure 2.2). Thirdly, human culpability in turning Ustad into a man-eater has been strenuously discussed in the media and by tiger experts like Thapar. It would appear that Ustad suffered from various ailments, including constipation, and minor injuries, such as an abscess in the paw. To treat these he was tranquilized several times. Tiger experts claim that both the processes whereby he was tranquilized and treated were badly botched, causing Ustad much "trauma" and creating an adverse relationship with humans.

More than anything, though, the culpability of Ustad has been questioned by the work of big-cat activism. A growing literature on animal

2.2. Sign placed outside the Ranthambore National Park, Rajasthan.
Credit: Photograph by author

rights activism and conservationism in India has sketched out the powerful agents that propel it and lend it much force, ranging from the former prime minister Indira Gandhi (Rangarajan 2009) to her estranged daughter-in-law Maneka Gandhi (Dave 2014) to the urban middle classes (Mawdsley 2004). Taken together, this work shows the class-based nature of conservationism even as it outlines distinct ethical considerations that underpin this heterogeneous grouping of activists lobbying for animal rights in India. The force of animal rights activism, especially as it becomes realized through state practices and policies, is immense (Shahabuddin 2010). Among the animals that are in need of protection, big cats occupy pride of place.

Big-cat conservationists strenuously question the very existence of big cats that are fundamentally crooked and decry any punitive actions against them. Are they all merely what the government of India terms "man-killers"?[6] The implication in such a framing is that the big cat has killed a human but sans intent or malice. This questioning increases exponentially in the case of tigers—the most beloved and endangered of big cats in India—and especially in the case of what I describe as "celebrity big cats." These celebrity big cats are named, identified, and known beasts who are publicly adored, and when they die or are hurt in any way, they are deeply mourned.

Ustad's incarceration causes great consternation, even more than a natural death would. Huge public protests broke out immediately after Ustad's identification as a man-eater that should be put away from the public for their safety. These protests were not limited to just Rajasthan (the state in which Ranthambore falls) but spread across the country. On social media, the hashtag "je suis Ustad" proliferated. Memes, documentaries, and placards were made, and protests and even candlelight vigils were held in defense of Ustad. A petition was filed challenging the capture of Ustad, and the Rajasthan High Court held a special sitting during vacation period—a rare occurrence—to deliberate on the matter. They, too, arrived at the conclusion that Ustad was indeed a man-eater, and he remains incarcerated in a zoo/prison to this day. The *India Today* story laments that Ustad is now a broken beast. A battle to get Ustad out rages on in several courts in India. The grounds for his release center largely on the core concern of this chapter: How can we ever be sure that this particular big cat *is* the murderer?

Gopeshwar-wallah Bagh

Let us move on from the celebrity Ustad to the humbler big cats that don't make it to the BBC or the front pages of national English-language magazines. The difficulties with beastly identification first struck me in 2006, with the crooked cat of Gopeshwar. The legal and social protection provided to endangered big cats has created a climate in which it takes great persuasion and the production of incontrovertible evidence of the dangers caused by a big cat for it to be legally killed by the state. Central to this is the production of a document called a hunting permit that allows for any action against the guilty cat to be undertaken. It was only after this permit had been "won"—as local bureaucrats described it—that the district administration could recruit a licensed hunter (*shikari*) to come up to Gopeshwar to hunt down the culprit.

By the time the hunting license was "won," the man-eater had already haunted the town for close to two months, killing at least three humans and wounding over a dozen, according to the official estimates that were released. Professional, licensed shikaris were invited to come up to Gopeshwar from the adjoining state of Himachal Pradesh. These shikaris stayed in town for a fortnight and were unsuccessful in killing the real man-eater. They were, however, successful in killing a leopard who, as it turns out, was "innocent." In this case, the innocence of the leopard was ascertained even before the official declaration of the end of the terror and before any form of public ceremony such as the parading of the corpse of the big cat through town—a common practice in the Himalaya as a demonstration of the certain death of the murderous animal. This certitude that the wrong leopard had been killed came about through an analysis of pugmarks. The leopard that had been killed was a young male adult, not even two years old, while the man-eater was an older female. The death of this innocent leopard was never entered into the official books, nor was it allowed to be published in the local newspapers. His corpse was also quickly buried before the local media or activists could get hold of photographs. I heard about it only because I was interviewing the shikaris the morning after the killing. They were semirueful about the death but also said, matter-of-factly, that every time they kill a big cat they cannot know till after the fact whether it is the man-eater. Indeed, it is commonplace for many leopards to be hunted down before the real culprit is targeted (see also Govindrajan 2015). Yet, the bureaucratic procedures and the law dictate that the correct and *only the correct* big cat can be killed. The identification of man-eaters on the ground before the hunt is undertaken through a variety of techniques. Which mode of guessing is to be adopted depends on the individual hunters, forest officials, terrain, and region of India. Yet, the bureaucratic and legal procedures that regulate the hunting of man-eaters remain uniform for all of India.

In January 2013, the National Tiger Conservation Authority based in the Ministry of Environment and Forests in New Delhi issued a "Standard Operating Procedure [SOP] for dealing with emergency arising due to straying of tigers in human dominated landscapes."[7]

The SOP suggests a series of measures to be established for the monitoring of man-eaters, after sternly warning that they can only be undertaken after the invocation of clause 11(1)(a) of the Wildlife Protection Act of 1972. These measures involve the setting up of an expert committee that would monitor the daily movements and actions of the strayed tiger or leopard. Repeatedly, the SOP enjoins that the animal must be "ID'd" before it is captured or tranquilized and definitely before it is shot dead. The SOP reads, "Obtain / establish the ID of the aberrant animal causing loss of human life, through the committee constituted for the purpose, through camera trappings or direct sightings or pug impressions if camera trappings could not be done, besides collecting pieces of hair / scats of the carnivore (if available) for DNA profiling."[8]

Camera trapping is the most preferred mode of identification of man-eaters, largely because it lends an aura of scientific authority to the entire endeavor. Camera trapping is a relatively recent development in India, emerging only over the past decade, and even now it remains limited to urban areas such as Mumbai and Shimla. Camera trapping is, furthermore, extremely difficult in mountainous regions like the upper Himalaya. Perhaps the most problematic aspect of camera trapping is that it requires the luxury of time and highly skilled experts who can, firstly, take the images, analyze them, and then make sure before the hunt that the targeted cat is the same one that they have observed and identified—over a period of time—as the man-eater. Similarly, collecting hair or fecal matter doesn't aid the process in the moment of the hunt for a man-eater. In my experience, camera trapping has been used only once in order to aid the identification of a leopard that had gone "rogue," as it was claimed. This usage took place in 2017 in an area of Mumbai called Aarey Colony, where a leopard had killed several children over a short period of four months. As there are approximately forty-one leopards living in and around this region, it was vital that the correct leopard be identified and trapped. A group of volunteers and wildlife enthusiasts who had been working in Mumbai for several years undertook an intense camera-trapping exercise in all of Aarey Colony and the adjoining Film City. Through a process of identifying the forty-one leopards and physically tracking one that had been seen in the vicinity of an attack and was "behaving badly," they decided that the guilty one was the leopard they had named Regulus. On that basis, they eventually trapped Regulus in a cage, and he now lives in captivity in Mumbai.[9] This, however, is a novel case that was largely aided by its occurrence in the megalopolis of Mumbai, with its resources, flat terrain, and limited space for leopards to move in given the vast human population surrounding them.

Tranquilization as an option is difficult in India for a number of reasons. The first is quite simply the terrain. In other parts of the world where there are clear landscapes with low numbers of humans, it is possible to spot the beast and dart it. In India, the landscape is difficult—it is mountainous, hilly, heavily forested, and, most critically, populated by large numbers of humans who often gather together in big groups in order to protect themselves from or attack the big cats. Amid the chaos of these situations, it becomes difficult to dart a feline. It is also worth pointing out that the equipment for such tranquilization is almost entirely absent, as is the expertise, in regions like the upper Himalaya. To know the correct dosage for a tranquilizer gun and to actually possess the required equipment is extremely rare in most parts of India. Many a horror story has emerged of attempted tranquilizations going badly wrong. In these cases, instead of being zapped down, the animal either dies, gets grievously affected, or turns even more aggressive for the time it takes for the sedative to take effect.

ID'ing Big Cats

What are the modes through which, in practice, big cats are "ID'd" before they are killed?

A commonplace and, it would appear, relatively effective practice is to check pugmarks at the sites of all the kills. As in the case of the Gopeshwar leopard, pugmarks can immediately indicate whether the right big cat was hunted down. However, once again, this ID'ing is only ever done retrospectively. As the hunters in Gopeshwar told me, they saw a leopard and shot at it immediately because, obviously, they couldn't check its pugmark beforehand (as the leopard would have escaped). Only when you have been directly tracking the cat can the pugmarks give the hunter a sure-shot indication that the big cat is, indeed, the one that is being hunted. With leopards, tracking normally cannot be undertaken since they are lithe and jump on trees and camouflage themselves very well. The heavier tigers and lions are more amenable to tracking in the forests.

Another common mode is that which the hunting licenses spell out (albeit after protecting themselves by saying that you had better ascertain the ID of the big cat): the territorial thesis. Hunters, when out seeking their quarry, work on the related assumptions that big cats are territorial animals and will, eventually, return to the area they have recently killed in. Thus, hunting licenses are issued only within a certain territorial circumference of the past attacks. Hunters, too, scour the landscape or set up *machaans* or stake the ground in the same general territory as the most recent killing. This type of method can, however, go terribly wrong, as it apparently did in the case of a leopard in Dehradun in 2015.

In mid-March 2015, in the early evening, seventeen-year-old Samiksha was talking on her mobile phone outside her house in the Forest Research

Institute (FRI), Dehradun. The FRI is a colonial-era institution that was founded in the late nineteenth century in the aid of "scientific forestry." Combining Greco-Roman and colonial architecture, the 450-hectare FRI campus occupies an important place not just in Dehradun but also in India more broadly. The campus hosts a training academy, museums, a university, and sprawling colonial bungalows of forest officers. Samiksha's father is a daily wage laborer who lives in a "servant quarter" in one such bungalow. That evening in March Samiksha was attacked and killed by a leopard in her own backyard. Family members found the leopard feasting on the teenager's body. In January 2015 another young boy had been killed by a leopard in the same FRI campus. This attack had happened in the late afternoon and similarly was said to be unprovoked, for the boy was merely playing cricket with his friends.

The two killings and the characteristics of the space in which they took place—in the famous and well-populated FRI campus in the heart of Dehradun, itself the capital city of Uttarakhand—were enough to win a hunting permit out against the leopard. A team of the state's most famous hunters was assembled, and within a few days they claimed to have found and killed the guilty leopard. FRI has several camera traps installed on its campus as it is a lush green area with plenty of wildlife, including—as the camera-trap images made clear—several leopards. The method the hunters adopted in ensuring they were on the prowl for the culpable leopard was staking the ground of the most recent kill. They set up a *machaan* (a high platform on trees that gives you a good vantage point) and kept watch through the night for any leopard that was found lurking in the region. When this leopard came into their view, they shot and killed her. Unfortunately, the shot was not a clean one, and the leopard bled excessively before dying. On closer examination it was found to be a heavily pregnant leopardess who was carrying three cubs and was almost to term.

The disclosure that the leopardess had been pregnant with triplets reverberated through a shocked city. This fact seemed to make everyone think—for some reason—that they had killed the wrong big cat. There is an innocence associated with pregnant or young "mother" big cats. Either there is an assumption that she is eating humans out of a compulsion to feed her children and sustain herself and, hence, this maternal instinct (almost) justifies her desperation for nourishment, or, as happened with the FRI leopardess, there is strong speculation that a pregnant leopardess just *cannot* be a killer. In the case of the FRI leopardess, what exacerbated this belief was some supposedly secretive thinking aloud between the hunters that was overheard by a journalist and published in the *Times of India*, a leading English-language national newspaper. The journalist told me that she heard the hunters wondering if, in fact, they had killed the wrong leopard. To make matters worse, the very next day another leopard was caught in a trap that had been originally set out for the man-eater right at the point where Samiksha had been killed. The capture of this leopard allowed the journalist to write a story questioning the territorial thesis that the hunters had been publicly proclaiming. The publication of the story gave ammunition to the conservationists that protest each and every kill.[10] The anger, in this case, was so livid that the hunter had to swear to "put down his gun" and never, ever hunt again. As this book argues, hunters are never certain if the correct (read: crooked) leopard or tiger has been hunted down. The fact that the FRI leopardess was heavily pregnant and was on the verge of giving birth to three cubs and, hence, four leopards had been killed was certainly a tragedy. Yet, the hunters did what they almost always do: kept vigil in the region where the young woman had been killed in the FRI and shot the first leopard that appeared there. This kill happened in the dark and very quicky on the basis of the territorial explanation. Other identifications can take more time and require deeper and—what many would claim—more scientific study.

One such scientific study was undertaken in June 2016 in the Gir jungles in the state of Gujarat. Seventeen Gir lions were rounded up on charges of killing three humans and attacking six. All seventeen were kept in captivity for twenty-five days, and on the basis of their feces and pugmarks, three were adjudged to be guilty and were sent to "prison." The male lion now lives in a zoo, and the two females have been put away in a lion rescue center. The seventeen were "arrested" through the means of trapping cages as well as some careful tranquilization over a two-month period. In addition to their pugmarks and fecal matter, their behavior was also studied. As wildlife expert Ruchi Dave told the BBC, "The officials are also studying the animals' behavior. Man eating lions usually get aggressive at the sight of a human being."[11] Indeed, the "behavior" of big cats is a key component in the identification of man-eaters and is only gaining in importance. In practice, what constitutes the "behavior" of a big cat that alerts humans to its crooked nature?

"It Is in the Eyes"

By far the most commonplace mode of identifying a man-eater just before his or her kill is by the eyes or, more specifically, whether eye contact is made. Interestingly though, the judgment is out on whether the making of eye contact makes you guilty or innocent. The big hunters and tiger experts like Thapar are convinced that the making of eye contact is a sure-shot sign that the feline *is* a man-eater. Thus, as in the case of Ustad, one of the points that added to his conviction was the fact that he did look deep into your eyes. He would stare back and snarl or growl menacingly. According to this school of thought, tigers and leopards—the normal ones—are wary of humans and do their best to avoid them. However, when you see one in the wild who is not thus inclined, then you can be sure that big cat is an aberration and most probably the man-eater.

In contrast to this account is what several shikaris told me is their sure-shot way of establishing guilt: whether the leopard or tiger "looks guilty and ashamed," for it too would know it has gone against the order of nature by killing and eating humans. Mr. Singh, one of the most famous hunters of Uttarakhand, loves to tell me this story. He was scouring the mountainside in an area that has a substantial army presence near the Sino-Indian border. A man-eater had made life very difficult in the cantonment and had killed and attacked several soldiers. To aid him on his hunt, he had a posse of several soldiers with him. Suddenly, they came upon a huge leopard sitting nonchalantly in a tree above them. The leopard looked down at them disdainfully. The moment the other soldiers saw the big cat, they gestured to Singh to kill him. However, says Singh, "something stopped me. The leopard was looking down straight into my eyes. He met my gaze but didn't flinch. There was such confidence and lack of fear in those eyes that I just knew he was innocent [*bekasoor*]." So Singh refused to shoot him. He lowered his gun and backed away. All this time the leopard had been holding his gaze. The soldiers and their senior army officers were livid with Singh for letting him get away.

The eye lock and the gaze of the nonhuman animal have been extensively discussed, with Jacques Derrida most famously wondering about his cat looking at him in his bathroom. Haraway wonderfully extended the look by noting that "Derrida failed a simple obligation of companion species; he did not become curious about what the cat might actually be doing, feeling, thinking, or perhaps making available to him in looking back at him that morning" (2008, 20). The curiosity that Derrida did not display is very much in evidence with the hunters I worked with, who read guilt or innocence in a matter of seconds on the basis of that affective moment of encounter. Had the leopard really been the man-eater, claims Singh, he would have had at least a shred of guilt or an iota of fear in those beautiful amber eyes. In that moment Singh could not, just could not, get himself to shoot an innocent leopard. For Singh that gaze was evidence of innocence, and it prevented him from making prey of the leopard. In an interesting reversal, Kohn (2013) describes how he was warned in Ecuador to sleep face up so that if a jaguar was passing by he could look back at this potential predator. The returning of the gaze would allow the jaguar to see the human as a self, instead of as prey, thus protecting him.[12]

In Singh's case, the returning of the gaze by the leopard had the effect of protecting the big cat. If Singh had not had such a formidable reputation as the ace hunter in the mountains, there might have been legal action taken against him. Singh is the direct descendant of a former princely family, and his father was, he claims, an early conservationist of big cats in India. Singh is one of those (former) aristocrats who learned hunting from their fathers and uncles at a very young age. When I went to visit him the first time in his grand old mansion in Dehradun, the first thing he showed me were his grandfather's diplomas from Oxford, where he had studied wildlife biology. The house was filled with taxidermied tigers, lions, and leopards. All these had been shot by him or his ancestors. This material culture attests to what he claims to be an innate and hereditary knowledge of big cats. "No manuals," he told me, "can teach you what I know about tigers and leopards. It runs in my blood."

Many of the formerly aristocratic hunters were often at pains to point out to me these deep connections with large felines in India. This enduring connection, they argued, provides them with an innate, inherited knowledge of the animal. It is on the basis of this that they are able to distinguish good tiger or leopard from bad tiger or leopard in the wild. The links between power and hunting are now well established, with a particularly rich literature emerging from South Asia, where one of the central tasks of a ruler—whether a king or a white colonial official—was to hunt down man-eaters in India (Hughes 2013; Pandian 2001). What is less commented on is how these associations of aristocratic and state power and duty with the hunt persist, in subtle ways, in contemporary India. One of the most overt signs that the hunt continues to be considered an aristocratic act is the open disparagement that the hunters I worked with showed toward those they considered mere "native shikaris." The native shikari is one who has learned hunting on his own (they are all men). He is someone who has taught himself or learned it from his encounters in the jungles and mountains. The knowledge of the beast is not one that "native shikaris" are believed to possess.

Whatever their lineage, all the shikaris I have worked with speak of this instinctive knowledge and connection with man-eaters. The eye lock is central to the construction of this knowledge, but the manner in which it is interpreted remains debated. Some are of the opinion that the eye lock means the big cat is confidently guiltless. Others are convinced that it is the very opposite—it establishes the fact that there is something dangerously crooked about this cat. Whichever way you read the eye lock, what does become apparent is this kicking in of an instinct and a particular intimacy with the beast in the moment.

Leopard Sacrifice

The notion of the sacrifice of leopards is a commonplace one. In Uttarakhand, where, for all the reasons I describe above, it becomes hard to correctly identify the man-eater swiftly, officials do allow for the sacrifice of a big cat in the hope that it is the correct one. But in these cases of sacrificed leopards, the issue at hand is the killing of a beast in order to stem the pressure of the locals—what bureaucrats, conservationists, and bodies such as the National Tiger Conservation Authority describe as "mobs."[13] The *Hindu*, in an article that disapprovingly notes the rampant killing of big cats on accusations of man-eating but with no conclusive proof, quotes an anonymized forest official in Chamoli District: "On one occasion, eight of his men were doused with kerosene and confined to a room by villagers who threatened to set them on fire if the man-eating leopard wasn't killed. The official had to deal with the situation with no direction from his boss who had switched off his phone. With no space for negotiations, the man said he was forced to sacrifice a leopard. He agreed it was illegal, didn't solve the problem, but at least, it appeased the villagers who set his staff free."[14]

As Govindrajan has noted, what is common to many of the anthropological analyses of sacrifice is "the principle of substitution—the use of a surrogate victim for an original other" (2018, 38). Again and again, bureaucrats would tell me of how they had to "sacrifice" a leopard in Uttarakhand in order to maintain peace and order in their region, to ward off the anger of their subjects. Here sacrifice is neither symbolic nor about establishing kinship in the manner described by Govindrajan. Rather, it is quite simply a ritual that wards off unrest for a short period of time, a ritual that is necessitated by the very nature of the task set before officials in which there is a profound uncertainty of ever knowing whether the original has been taken down. What the official in the interview is acknowledging is the difficulty of every really knowing whether the right big cat has been adjudged the man-eater and killed.

What further complicates the picture of identifying man-eaters is that many times, even after a big cat is killed, it is not always possible to unambiguously ascertain whether it was or was not a man-eater. The most common method of checking, before an autopsy, is to study the pugmarks of the dead big cat against those that were found near the killings. The pugmarks are not, in and of themselves, enough to determine whether it is the guilty leopard. In the Gopeshwar case that I discussed, it was possible to ascertain that the wrong big cat had been killed only because of the obvious difference in size and sex of the two leopards. The most "scientific" manner in which the guilt of the big cat can be proven is through the conducting of an autopsy. This was not technically possible in Gopeshwar, as we did not possess the expertise for it. Hence, in such a situation, the corpses of the big cats are sent to bigger towns, such as Srinagar or Dehradun, to be dissected. After a postmortem, too, it is not always indisputably established that the big cat was a man-eater. Often, human remains are not found, but that might just be because the big cat has not feasted on them for a while. Sometimes, the evidence that is found is suspect. For instance, Sankhala (1993) notes an autopsy after which the hunter produced silver bangles worn by a woman who had been one of the victims of a man-eater. He came to entirely distrust the hunter's claim, for the bangles were in a perfect round shape, which, he argues, was not possible given the fact that tigers don't gulp down or swallow flesh but, rather, tear away at it before having small pieces, making it impossible for them to swallow a full silver bangle without altering its shape.

When—If Ever—Can We Know?

The closest approximation of full proof of the death of the man-eater—and hence his or her correct identification—emerges if attacks on humans stop immediately. Thus, after the hunting down of the Gopeshwar-wallah bagh by Lakhpat Singh Rawat in January 2007, we were almost certain that the dead cat was the correct one because the pugmarks matched perfectly, she was found lurking in the part of town that she had been killing in, there were some eyewitnesses who claimed "this was the one" they had seen previously, and so on. Furthermore, another duo of shikaris had also previously spotted her and fired but missed killing her, but the bullet had grazed her tail and the mark remained there. The possession of the hunting permit allowed the district administration to publicly display the dead big cat, to broadcast their triumph in overturning the reign of terror of the big cat. However, as a precautionary means there was a letting up of regular security measures—such as walking in large groups with torches of fire and keeping large bushes or long grasses from growing too much—only about ten days after the cat's death, when no further attacks or sightings had been reported.

In places like Gopeshwar where there tends to be only a single man-eater that "visits" the town, this ending of attacks and sightings can be taken to be proof of the man-eater's extermination. In other parts of Chamoli District, particularly in an area called Gairsain, this proof was much more difficult to establish because there were multiple man-eaters operating simultaneously there. Furthermore, due to poor reporting and low manpower, it was very difficult to know when, where, and how some of the deaths had taken place and therefore when they stopped.

So what of those leopards and tigers that are killed legally—that is, through the means of a hunting permit—and turn out, after an autopsy, to not be man-eaters? What are the legal repercussions of killing an innocent big cat for the hunters and officials involved? In the Wildlife Protection Act there is no provision for what happens when a man-eater is killed accidentally because of mistaken identity. It is clearer on the implications of killing a big cat without a hunting permit though. An offense involving a species listed in Schedule I or Part II of Schedule II, or an offense committed within a sanctuary or natural park, attracts a mandatory prison term of three years, which may be extended to seven years. There is also a mandatory fine of at least ₹10,000. For a subsequent offense, the prison term remains the same, while the mandatory fine is at least ₹25,000.[15] So when a big cat is killed on the assumption that it is a man-eater but is subsequently found to not be one, the kill can technically fall under the legal category of an unauthorized murder of a highly endangered species and thus invite a prison term and fine. In practice, though, this is never enforced when the culprits are government officials.[16] In national newspapers there are repeated reports on the killing of a leopard that was not the man-eater where no action was taken against either the hunter or the officials. What we don't know from these reports is what eventually happened to the "real" man-eater.

Beastly Identification

My concern in this chapter has been to ask what happens when identification cannot be established till after the fact even though the legal requirements dictate otherwise. I stress the point that all shikaris make, which is the inherent impossibility of being able to incontrovertibly identify a big cat prior to killing it. Yet, given the transnational drive of preserving big cats and in the context of India's own conservationist regime, the legal clauses, bureaucratic documents, due process, and public maintenance of the facade of correct identification remain on, often as impediments to swift action and always as a necessary fiction of the reasoned government of big cats.

The implications of the argument of a radical doubting of the identifiability of a big cat are immense. The entire conservationist regime around big cats in India is premised on the belief that only the guilty individual—the so-called "man-eater"—will be captured or killed. Given the looming danger of extinction, there should be no big-cat sacrifices, and only the aberrant big cat should be imprisoned or lose its life. With conservationism, the issue that is normally brought up is the stricter application of the law. I have argued here that these difficult-to-follow rules and laws create complexities in the government of big cats. They lead to many silences, including the hidden sacrifices of big cats and the murder of innocents (be it big cats or human victims of man-eaters). They also deflect attention away from the fact that uniform laws cannot apply for all of India due to differences in terrain, forest cover, history, and state capacity. Thus, Mumbai can make camera trapping work to some extent, whereas Chamoli District in the upper Himalaya emphatically cannot. Yet, they are both governed by the very same bureaucratic-legal apparatus—an apparatus that is, I would argue, in need not of tightening but rather of radical reform in order to absorb and appreciate the difficulties in knowing nonhuman others.

Secondly and relatedly, it is not just the bureaucratic papering over or the disappearances of big cats' corpses that are rendered invisible in the process of the government of big cats. What is also eliminated is an intimate knowledge of big cats, what I discuss as beastly intimacy. Worryingly, the silencing and effacement from the public of actually existing identificatory practices, such as the look in the eye or the gut instinct or the gendering of man-eaters, due to their seeming nonscientific nature, is disallowing the development of more effective modalities to govern big cats and humans. In the Anthropocene, when wildlife extinction and exacerbated human-animal conflict are burning issues,[17] these intimate forms of knowing, identifying, and marking out crooked big cats need to be acknowledged and understood. It is these knowledge systems and modalities of operation that form the government of big cats and not, as most reports and studies assume, conservationist policies or legal apparatuses and bureaucratic guidelines. The existing scientific, technological, and legal-bureaucratic means are, I have argued, inadequate to the task. Rather, what really comes to the fore through long-term immersion and what must, therefore, be acknowledged and valued is the intimacy of living with big cats. In multispecies worlds, what we find are profoundly localized and embodied knowledges—of the animal, the terrain, humans, history—and momentary acts of recognition. What is also apparent is that these modes of knowing big cats never quite achieve a perfect certainty; they are merely honed over time and through experience. Humans live and work through these tentative and ever-questionable forms of knowledge, even as they know that they must never vocally express these uncertainties.

THREE

The Cute Killer

For some time from late 2014 onward, white tigers became the most popular soft toys in the shop of the Delhi zoo. Intriguingly, all these white-tiger soft toys were given the same name: Vijay. Not only were Vijay toys bought for children, but also they became a valued gift for one's romantic partner. Around the time of Valentine's Day in 2015, for instance, the white tigers rapidly sold out from the shop. The intense popularity of the white-tiger/Vijay soft toy was accompanied by an exponential increase in the number of visitors to the Delhi zoo and to the white-tiger enclosure (figure 3.1). Official figures released in 2015 showed an increase of two lakh (two hundred thousand) visitors to the zoo, because of the white tiger called Vijay who resides there.[1] To understand Vijay's intense popularity—as a real, living, breathing, pacing big cat and also as a cute-ified, commodified form as a soft toy—we need to dwell on an event that took place on September 23, 2014.

On this day, a young man named Maqsood Pardesi entered the white-tiger enclosure in the Delhi zoo. What happened subsequently was captured on smartphones and in a video clip uploaded onto YouTube.[2] The video shows a white tiger—Vijay—examining with (giant) kitten-like puzzlement a crouching, quaking human. Maqsood, sitting on his haunches, attempts to flap away the tiger almost as if he were a fly. In the background you can hear the horrified screams of the other zoo visitors. What is also discernible is the voice of a zookeeper who is shouting at Vijay to move away ("hat jaa Vijay, jaa jaa"). For a few agonizing minutes this continues—Vijay keeps staring at Maqsood, and the trembling Maqsood keeps making batting-away gestures with his hands as he rocks back and forth on his haunches. At some point the zoo visitors get louder, and you see stones and sticks being pelted at Vijay. Whether as a result of the noise or the minor pelting or entirely

3.1. Sign warning against entry into the white tigers' enclosure in the Delhi zoo.
Credit: Photograph by author

other reasons, Vijay picks up Maqsood from his neck and takes him further into the tiger enclosure away from the crowds. We cannot see what happens then, but we hear subsequently from the zoo authorities that Maqsood died in that act of being carried away by Vijay. The zoo was careful to state that Vijay did not attempt to eat the human; the corpse was left on the ground.

Immediately after Maqsood's death in the zoo, strident defenses of Vijay's actions were swiftly mounted. The "innocence" of the big cat was believed to be visibly available for all to behold in the freely circulating video recording of the incident. Vijay was merely "curiously inspecting" the foreign body in his home, as the zoo spokesperson put it; he was *bekasoor* (faultless). Subsequent to the killing, zoo authorities told the public that Vijay has been placed "under examination," though how and for what remained unclear. After some time, there were further announcements made by the zoo that declared Vijay fit and described him as behaving "normally." An e-petition was furiously circulated on the web with the objective of preemptively stopping any call to put the big cat down or to punish him, given that his actions were adjudged to be entirely sans intent. The defense for Vijay moved from general conversations in Delhi to the penning of blog posts that were written from the tiger's perspective—thus forming a type of autobiographical confession—on "how I became a murderer, though I did not want to be one."[3] In everyday chatter as well, the perspective that was adopted was Vijay's, and his lack of culpability in Maqsood's death was highlighted.

We learned a lot about Vijay through the death of Maqsood. Vijay's ancestry and pedigree were discussed extensively. It turns out that this big cat was born in captivity seven years before the "Delhi zoo incident," as it is now known. Vijay's parents—Laxman and Yamuna—trace their "lineage" to those tigers captured from the wild by the rulers of the princely state of Rewa in Madhya Pradesh. We read and heard about Vijay's daily schedule, what he eats and how he does so (apparently he languidly chews on his food), what he likes, and what he dislikes. Subsequently, the press announced the news that Vijay has become the "proud papa" of four little cubs. Inside and outside the Delhi zoo, there is an intimacy with the life and deeds of Vijay—an intimacy generated by all this tiger talk and the extensive reporting on every aspect of his life.

It was not just Vijay but also his unfortunate victim whom we suddenly became acquainted with. In the aftermath of the Delhi zoo incident, stirring obituaries were written up for Maqsood. These pieces, appearing in mainstream newspapers[4] and on critical blogging sites[5] alike, poetically lamented the life of the young man that had been irretrievably lost. The chain of events that led to Maqsood's ultimately fatal entrance into the tiger's enclosure will forever remain uncertain. Yet, the person we saw cowering in front of and eventually being carried away by the big cat has become identifiable, knowable, and ultimately grievable. His death has been rendered mournable, for we know him as a human being with a name, an address, and kin relations, including an unborn child and a tragically young widow. Ironically, had Maqsood died in more ordinary circumstances, his death would almost certainly have gone unremarked on, given his socioeconomic situation and the brutality of life in the metropolis of Delhi. He has been publicly mourned partly because the manner in which he died was, by all measures, extraordinary and has been made available to us all by being captured on film. Furthermore, his death occurred at the hands of the most intensely protected and loved animal in India, the tiger—and, even more specially, a rare white tiger. Any sighting of the rapidly disappearing tiger is now considered a treat, even if it is within the restricted enclosure of a zoo. But a video of a tiger playing with and killing a human in a freak incident makes for almost 2.5 million YouTube views.[6]

For the Delhi zoo, Maqsood's death has resulted in not just a massive upsurge in visitors and frenetic sales of white-tiger soft toys from the souvenir shop but also the creation of a celebrity inmate in the zoo. There are now throngs of crowds at the white-tiger enclosure, which has led to much stricter policing of this specific part of the zoo. When I went to the enclosure in the winter of 2015, more than a year after "the incident," many of the visitors were shouting out "Vijay, Vijay," to white tigers that may or may not have been Vijay, as there were two other tigers in the same enclosure. Others went to the zookeepers or guards and asked them to point out Vijay or bring him out of his cave so that they could inspect him. When Vijay was announced to be in the public view, there was hushed silence followed by the flashing of cameras and excited murmurings on having seen the white tiger of "the incident." The guard claimed to be able to distinguish Vijay from the other tigers instantaneously and would point him out to the eager onlookers.

On a trip to the zoo, I was amused to see a young boy holding a white-tiger soft toy—a Vijay—in his hands outside the white-tiger enclosure. When he spotted a tiger that he thought was Vijay, he playacted a tussle with the soft toy in which the ending was reversed—that is, the young boy succeeded in overcoming the big cat and not vice versa. The little mock play was heavily applauded by the assembled group of spectators. In my chat with the young boy's mother, she told me that he, like many of his friends, had become obsessed with Vijay. She had been forced to not just buy him the soft toy but also constantly transport her son to the Delhi zoo so that he could see the object of his obsession—Vijay the white tiger. When I asked the young boy why he was so taken by Vijay, he answered, "Woh itna cute hai" (he is so cute).

There was, indeed, a particular rendition of Vijay as "cute." The other word that is often used is *pyara*, or "lovely." I want to point out that this particular cute-ification occurred subsequent to the killing of Maqsood. The other white tigers in the Delhi zoo—the non-Vijays—were not described in the same rapturous tones. This elevation of Vijay to the status of a cute animal—both in his soft toy form and also in flesh and blood—allows us to ethnographically further explore how specific named, known animals can and are cute-ified and acquire charisma.[7]

Innocence appears to be central, as was clear from the consistent way in which Vijay was portrayed after the death of Maqsood. This innocence (he did not know his own strength; he is just a big cat who picked up the human like domesticated small cats pick up their kittens; he never tried to eat or feast on the body) is coupled with vulnerability (he was born and bred in captivity; there was an intruder in his space; he was being abused and pelted by the zoo visitors), all of which make him even more endearing.

Secondly and relatedly is the freakish nature of "the incident." It is centered on a young man who was obviously obsessed with tigers. Many press reports claimed that his family members said Maqsood suffered from poor mental health and would go to visit the tiger enclosure in the Delhi zoo daily. Rumors were afloat that a tattoo of the goddess Durga astride a tiger had been found on his body, also attesting to his unnatural obsession with big cats. The fact that this entire incident was captured on video also allowed for voyeuristic viewings and re-viewings, which accentuate the "freak nature" of the event. Freakishness allows for an intensification of the cute (Harris 2000). Subsequent to Maqsood's death, we suddenly began to read and hear more about similar deaths and injuries that had occurred within zoos and at the hands of big cats in India. However, it is noticeable that when such an incident takes place in a Guwahati or Alipore zoo, it is not covered in the national and international media with quite the same zeal as was the one that occurred in the Delhi zoo. It is almost as if the site of the death—the national capital of India and within the precincts of the historic Old Fort, in which the zoo is set—makes this an even more freakish incident.

Soft toys are, as Ngai (2012) has noted, the archetypal cute objects. However, soft toys tend to be stripped bare of their danger or brute animality, as in the case of teddy bears.[8] In the case of Vijay, it wasn't the eclipsing of a violent act and killing—albeit accidental or unintentional—that increased his popularity and made him lovely (*pyara*) and cute. Rather, it was *as a consequence* of the death of Maqsood that Vijay's cuteness was amplified and he was elevated to the status of a celebrity, attesting to the close, if ambivalent, relationship of the cute and the monstrous (Brzozowska-Brywczyńska 2007). There are, as Chua has noted for orangutan conservation, "contradictions of cuteness" (2018, 874). In Chua's case orangutan conservation hinges on the cute-ification of orangutans as animals worth preserving, which leads to the creation of publics that express a desire to, for instance, cuddle the animal. But such physical expressions of affection are considered dangerous for the continual preservation of orangutans. In Vijay's case, he killed a human being. In all the other beastly tales narrated in this book, the act of killing a human did not render the big cats "cute" or *pyara*. Vijay, however, became cute *because* he is a killer—he is a cute killer.

Becoming a cute animal is a process forged of commodity relations and encounter values (Haraway 2008). This process of cute-ification has a temporality too. Is Vijay going to remain a celebrity forever, or will his fame die out and his charisma deplete as the Delhi zoo incident gets slowly forgotten? Vijay does keep popping up in the most unexpected of places though, such as in a Hindi film, *Masaan*, that tells the tale of forbidden love and a sexual encounter between an upper-caste woman and a Dalit man in the north Indian city of Varanasi. The backdrop to a central scene—when the two meet in a seedy motel—is dominated by the news playing on the television in the background. As the two young lovers nervously examine one another, we hear—loudly—the news of a tiger called Vijay that killed a young man who had entered his enclosure that day in the Delhi zoo.

The Delhi zoo incident continues to live on in popular memory, even if the tragedy of Maqsood's untimely death appears forgotten. As for Vijay, his fame within the Delhi zoo remains strong at the moment, with the authorities actively working to keep his celebrity status burning. For instance, Vijay's tenth birthday was celebrated with great pomp in 2017. As far as I am aware, none of the other tigers—or indeed other nonhuman animals—have such flamboyant birthday bashes thrown for them. A cake was cut by schoolchildren who sang and wished Vijay a very happy tenth birthday. A large cutout of a white tiger and "Happy birthday, Vijay" posters and balloons adorned the zoo.[9] The cuteness of Vijay in his various forms—as soft toy, movie backdrop, psychologically hurt nonhuman, birthday boy entering his teens, poster, cake, young papa—has effectively displaced even the whiff of an allegation of crookedness against him.

FOUR

A Petition to Kill

> The state has today put the worth of a big cat greater than the worth of a human. Is there no value left to human lives in Indian democracy?
>
> Who is bigger? A tiger/leopard or a human?
>
> —Petition submitted by the Nagrik Manch of Chamoli District, demanding the killing of a crooked cat

An e-petition to Jacob Zuma protesting against the killing of Cecil the lion and asking for a ban on trophy hunting has gathered, at last count, one and a quarter million signatures.[1] The petitions that this chapter studies constitute the polar opposite of this monster petition for a celebrity cat. Here, I examine petitions that are asking for the killing of leopards or tigers in India; they tend to be written by either an individual or a handful of people, and none of them have ever reached the fame or circulation of the petition for Cecil. I am interested in examining those petitions that appealed for the capture or death of big cats *and* turned out to be efficacious. By efficacious, I do not mean that the demands set out in the petition were necessarily met, but rather that the appeals were given an audience, heard out, and acted on.

My interest in efficacious petitions arises from, broadly speaking, two fronts. The first and foremost is that the vast majority of these petitions are *not* efficacious. The norm is, in fact, quite the opposite—they are dismissed, burnt, lost, filed away and forgotten, or deliberately sat on. This studious ignoring of petitions arises partly due to the sheer volume and dizzying diversity of petitions that every wing of the state receives.[2] In an institutional culture where bureaucrats describe the level of petitioning as excessive, often medicalizing it as a pathology of Indians, the question arises: How do some elicit a response?

What further propels me to think about those petitions that have been efficacious in the specific context of big cats is that in contemporary India it is extremely difficult, legally and bureaucratically speaking, to take *any* punitive action against big cats.[3] From the late 1960s onward, a series of wildlife conservationist legislations and measures have been passed that serve to provide a formidable level of protection for all wildlife. And this is particularly the case for tigers, leopards, and lions, which feature in Schedule I of the Wildlife Protection Act of 1972 that serves to provide them with the strictest protection of all. Contemporary India has a powerful wildlife-protection lobby as well as a plethora of rules and guidelines that are aimed at the conservation of big cats in particular. While this conservationist infrastructure has not necessarily been successful in its objective *and* hasn't ended the poaching and trafficking of big cats, it has made it extremely difficult for the state to openly and legally capture or kill these charismatic animals (N. Mathur 2014). Central to the governance of big cats in contemporary India is the production of evidentiary proof—in the form of documents—that attests to the aberrance of a specific big cat (in the form of a man-eater, as they are officially termed) and thus allows for his or her capture or death. Petitions by affected or frightened citizens are a key part of this process. Petitions presented to local officials allow for investigations into a specific big cat to commence. They help prove that the cat in question is, in fact, dangerous and deviant and hence should be either hunted down or kept in captivity.

Within the state bureaucracy and in the English language, petitions most often get described as letters, complaints, grievances, applications, or just petitions. In northern India, the word most commonly used in Hindi and Urdu to refer to a petition is *arzee* (Travers 2019). *Arzee* is a capacious term that includes "request," "representation," "appeal," "demand," "humble desire," and "presentation of information." There is a dense assortment of meanings associated with *arzee* and its root word—*arz*—particularly if one is attentive to *arzee*'s usage in colloquial speech in northern India. An arzee is most commonly a piece of paper on which one types or handwrites an appeal, but, through the ethnographic material presented here, I will argue that this is not always the case. To make an arzee means to submit a petition, but it also encompasses a whole range of other actions around that act of submission. As the wider anthropology of claim making has shown, there is a need to be attentive to the various forms an arzee can take. Beyond the very medium of the arzee—be it on paper or, as I show below, via smartphones—there is a need to capture those moments and utterances through which an arzee is made, the forms it can take, and the types of follow-up actions that need to be or are undertaken in order to fully make an arzee. An arzee then is not just a thing—the petitionary message via a specific medium—but also a process.

Alongside this discussion of an expansion of the category of the arzee itself, I ask what happens when we bring the animal into the petitioning process. In the first place, we see a strong questioning of the wildlife conservationist regime, which comes across not just as too stringent in its rules and regulations but also as inexplicably valuing big-cat lives more than human lives (Jalais 2011; N. Mathur 2016). Secondly, the animal comes across as highly agentive, more so than the humans. Animal studies has wrestled, in different ways, with, firstly, whether animals have agency and, secondly, how to access and describe such nonhuman agency if it does indeed exist.[4] As arzees swing between the legal-rational and affective-visceral modalities, they produce strong imaginaries of the beast in question. The creature is not just described physiologically as big or small, young or old, healthy or injured, and possessing particular markings. More importantly, it also has a personality and possesses agency of a form that dwarves the most agentive human. Thus, certain adjectives are used for the animal, such as cunning (*chatur*), aberrant, vicious, scheming, powerful, dangerous, ill-mannered (*badtameez*), uncouth, all-knowing, and—even—devout. In the arzees and the speech that accompanies them, we are made aware of a presence that is eerie but also compelling. This feline presence is often anthropomorphized, but very often there is a nonhuman terminology evoked that individualizes the cat and allows for a peculiar beastly intimacy.

Uttarakhand has, as has already been argued, a very long history of conflict between humans and big cats, with the earliest available records from the late nineteenth century showing that leopards were considered "destructive" (Atkinson [1881] 2002, 16). Jim Corbett, too, makes frequent mentions of arzees written to him by villagers living under the reign of terror of man-eating tigers and leopards. For instance, a petition printed in Corbett's *Man-Eaters of Kumaon* (first published in 1944) beseeches Corbett (misspelled as "Carbitt" in the petition) to come and rescue the villagers from a tiger that was subsequently named the Mohan man-eater. It was originally written in Hindi but was translated into English either by Corbett himself or Oxford University Press, the publishers of *Man-Eaters of Kumaon*. This is a good example of what is termed "a humble petition" due to the extremely deferential language it utilizes and the faith it reposes in the benevolence of Corbett (figure 4.1). The petitions I encountered in present-day Uttarakhand break from this mold of beseeching and humbly requesting even if they don't entirely abandon some of their elements, especially the expression of faith

COPY OF PETITION
SENT TO THE AUTHOR BY THE PEOPLE OF GARHWAL

The Promise mentioned on Page 125, was made after receiving this petition

From The Public of Patty Painaun, Bungi and Bickla Badalpur District Garhwal
To Captain J. E. Carbitt, Esq., I.A.R.O., Kaladhungi Distt. Naini Tal

Respected Sir,

We all the public (of the above 3 Patties) most humbly and respectfully beg to lay the following few lines for your kind consideration and doing needful.

That in this vicinity a tiger has turned out man-eater since December last. Up to this date he has killed 5 men and wounded 2. So we the public are in a great distress. By the fear of this tiger we cannot watch our wheat crop at night so the deers have nearly ruined it. We cannot go in the forest for fodder grass nor we can enter our cattles in the forest to graze so many of our cattle are to die. Under the circumstances we are nearly to be ruined. The Forest Officials are doing every possible arrangement to kill this tiger but there is no hope of any success. 2 *shikari* gentlemen also tried to shoot it but unfortunately they could not get it. Our kind District Magistrate has notified Rs. 150 reward for killing this tiger, so every one is trying to kill it but no success. We have heard that your kind self have killed many man-eater tigers and leopards. For this you have earned a good name specially in Kumaon revenue Division. The famous man-eater leopard of Nagpur has been shoot by you. This it the voice of all the public here that this tiger also will be killed only by you. So we the public venture to request that you very kindly take trouble to come to this place and shoot this tiger (our enemy) and save the public from this calamity. For this act of kindness we the public will be highly obliged and will pray for your long life and prosperity. Hope you will surely consider on our condition and take trouble to come here for saving us from this calamity. The route to this place is as follows Ramnagar to Sultan, Sultan to Lahachaur, Lahachaur to Kanda. If your honour kindly informs us the date of your arrival at Ramnagar we will send our men and cart to Ramnagar to meet you and accompany you.

We beg to remain
Sir
Your most sincerely
Signed Govind Singh
Negi
Headman Village Jharat

Dated Jharat
The 18th February 1933

followed by 40 signatures and 4 thumb impressions of inhabitants of Painaun, Bungi and Bickla Badalpur Patties.

Address
The Govind Singh Negi
Village Jharat Patty
Painaun P. O.
Badialgaon Dist., Garhwal, U.P.

4.1. Petition written to Jim Corbett, published in *Man-Eaters of Kumaon.*

in the ultimate benevolence of the state. Below I compare and contrast the arzee to Corbett with an arzee that was submitted in December 2007 requesting the killing of a man-eater. This arzee was submitted to the district magistrate (DM) in Chamoli District.

On December 21, 2007, a group of over one hundred people took part in a procession (*jaloos*) under the banner of the Chamoli District's Residents

Forum (*nagarik manch*). Amid the beating of drums and cries of "Uttarakhand Shasan Hai Hai" (Shame on Uttarakhand administration) and "District Magistrate Murdabad" (Death to the district magistrate), the procession met the DM to give him a petition. For the past six weeks a man-eater had been haunting the town—Gopeshwar—that is also the administrative headquarters of the district. Over a dozen attacks had already taken place, and, thus far, there were three confirmed human deaths. Despite the obvious presence of a man-eater in the town, the district officials had been unable to officially declare the big cat a man-eater and, consequently, unable to obtain a hunting permit that would allow for it to be legally killed. The DM accepted the letter and made a short speech in which he claimed that he was doing all that he possibly could to regulate the leopard.

Petitions in Uttarakhand are normally written in the Hindi language and almost always demand death for the leopard or tiger. The subject line of the one given to the DM in December 2007 reads, in bold and in a large font size, "The terror of the man-eating big cat in Gopeshwar, district Chamoli."[5] It begins with reference to the spread of the terror in different districts of Garhwal that is regularly reported in local newspapers. "Yet, the central government, Uttarakhand government and district administration do not regard it gravely. The state has today put the worth of bagh greater than the worth of humans. Is there no value left to humans in Indian democracy today?" (*Sarkar ne aaj manushya ke moolya kee apeksha, bagh ka moolya adhik bada diya hai. Kya bharatiya loktantra mein manav ka koeen moolya nahin reh gaya hai?*)

The letter goes on to list a series of recent attacks by the leopard, stressing the manner in which in broad daylight (*din dahade*) the increasingly fearless leopard was barging into houses and grabbing children and attacking women. "After the experiencing of these incredible incidents, too, our sarkar remains mute." (*In unghatit ghatnaon ke ghatne pe bhi hamari sarkar maun sadhe hooeen hai.*) "The people are frightened; they are terrorized and our *sarkar* [state/government] is sleeping a peaceful sleep." (*Janata bhaybheet hai; atankit hai aur hamari sarkar sukh kee neend sau rahin hai.*)

The letter sets out four demands (*maange*) to the chief minister, including requests for amendments to the Wildlife Protection Act of 1972 and the provisioning of better compensation for victims. The demands were as follows:

1 To protect the common man there must be instant amendments made to the Wildlife Protection Act of 1972.

2 Provisions must be made for immediately killing the man-eating leopard wherever it might be. A provision must be made for compensation and the

amount for the death of a human being should be immediately raised to 10 lakhs of rupees.

3 Set up a tribunal to look into compensation for the death of domesticated livestock.

4 Whoever takes on a bagh must be awarded with a prize (for that person's bravery).

The petition was signed by over a dozen "eminent" citizens of Chamoli, including social workers (*samajik karyakarta*) and conveners of associations such as the Himalayan Peace Foundation, the Retired Soldiers Welfare Organization, the Municipal Corporation, and the Women's Forum. Interestingly, it was addressed to the chief minister and not the DM or the divisional forest officer, who are more directly responsible for the leopard in this region. Mr. Rawat, who was the chief drafter of this arzee, said that they were tired of waiting for the DM to act and knew that the only way to exert pressure on the district authorities was by going over their heads to the "big boss." They had also gotten the petition delivered by hand to the chief minister in the distant state capital, but their main line of attack had been to personally assemble a large number of people, rent the drums, and march through the town shouting slogans. They had also made sure to check that the DM was in the office today, as they wanted to personally hand over the petition to him so that later on he could not pretend that the file had never reached him. Indeed, one of the defining features of an arzee is that it is delivered by hand—you don't just post it in the mail, you make sure to hand it over yourself to the highest-possible official. Mr. Rawat and the other arzee signatories put great emphasis on the affective charge of the moment when he and his fellow petitioners confronted the DM in person in front of his office and the assembled crowd of onlookers, presented him with this letter, and related their fear and anger to him. The procession had also roped in some influential members of the local press, who stood by with their cameras. The next morning I saw pictures in almost all the local Hindi-language newspapers of the procession head handing over the petition to a somewhat beleaguered-looking DM. The petition and the press coverage around it gave the DM the space to press home his demand for a hunting permit from his superiors in the distant state capital. After he had won the permit, the DM rang up Mr. Rawat—to inform him of the "victory" and to thank him for his petition.

In arzees in Uttarakhand that one can find buried in district archives, a recurrent theme is the value of human life. Members of this particular procession kept repeating the sentence that appears prominently in the petition: Is there no value to human life in Indian democracy? Questions asked by this procession and found repeated in archived petitions include, Can it be that the Indian state values the life of a big cat more than a human's? Who is bigger, cat or human? (*Kaun bada hai?*) One said, "You are my mother-father, yet you value the big cat more than my child?" Another stated, "It would be brave [*bahadur*] to kill the man-eater; the bravery doesn't lie in protecting it. It is us humans who need protection from this wild beast. Or is it that you are a coward?" Yet another petition read, "But what idiocy is this from you, my lord, who knows so much? It is but the aunt of a cat [*billi ki mausi*] and I am a human."

What is striking in the petition sent to Corbett in 1933 in contrast to the petition sent to the chief minister of Uttarakhand in 2007 is the assessment of what the state is doing to alleviate the terror. In the case of the Mohan man-eater, the villagers wrote that the DM, the gentlemen shikari, and the forest officers are doing everything they possibly can. Unfortunately, those persons don't seem to have had much success, and given Corbett's fame in Uttarakhand, the villagers are writing in to request him to kill their enemy, the tiger. In the case of the Gopeshwar man-eater of 2007, the petitioners are furious with the state for doing nothing and for sleeping a peaceful sleep while the people are terrified. There is a constant reference to the (sorry) state of democracy (*loktantra*) in which the big cat appears to be valued more than a human. The 1933 petition is cajoling and respectful; the 2007 petition is angry and makes demands that exceed the mere hunting down of a man-eater. Though both were petitioning for the same cause—the hunting down of a crooked cat—the rhetoric employed in each of the letters is remarkably different. The wording of the arzees, particularly those that contain veiled or even open threats to wage a revolt against the state, carries import. It allows local officials to use the fear of a breakdown in "law and order" to speed up the process of getting the truant cat killed or captured. Note also the constant comparison between human life and animal life. The anthropocentric assumption would be that humans are valued above nonhuman animals, at least by fellow humans. But what the petitions buried in district archives all over Uttarakhand keep discussing is a species betrayal, one wherein big-cat life is valued much more than human life. The rhetoric of the arzees aside, the accompanying performances also make a big difference in the eventual acceptance or denial of demands. In the context of the petition that was received in December 2007, it was the theatrics around the submission of the petition that allowed the district magistrate to quickly marshal it and win a hunting permit against that particular leopard.

Chakkar Marna

In addition to careful wording and the public spectacle at the point of submission, a key tactic of petitioning the Indian state involves following up the original petition with further forms of pressure. The phrase used most commonly to describe this follow-up action is *chakkar marna,* or "to go round and round." In Hindi, one would describe the circumambulation of a temple as chakkar marna, but when used in the context of government offices it is meant to exude a sense of exasperation as well as an ensuing dizziness. Chakkar marna can and often does include follow-up arzees by the same supplicant or new ones for the same cause. There is an interesting trend of what I think of as piggyback petitions, or petitions that ride on the original appeal or grouse but also slip in an extra demand or two.

For instance, villagers or residents of a town will send out arzees requesting the death or capture of a predatory leopard or tiger. Their local political representatives—members of the two leading political parties, the Indian National Congress and the Bharatiya Janata Party—will follow up with petitions requesting the same. They do so on their letterheads with the symbols of the parties stamped on them. These arzees not only emphasize the need for the death or capture of the truant cat or a greater alertness on the part of forest and police staff but also include requests for electrification, clearance of shrubs from roads, and the construction of pukka roads. Piggyback petitions aside, follow-up action on arzees expands above and beyond a written document that might, indeed, have formed the original arzee. Chakkar marna highlights the processual nature of petitioning—it is, in other words, not just a thing, an arzee that you submit once, but also a series of steps taken in the valiant hope of getting your appeal heard.

In the case of hunting down man-eaters, when petitions such as the one described above proved to be ineffective for whatever reason—the district was unable to find a hunter or the hunting license was not issued or the hunters were unable to kill the right leopard—the agitations would gradually increase, and the situation would arise whereby one would dispel altogether with pieces of paper or those letters that veer between humble request and outright threats in order to adopt other methods to put greater pressure on the state. The most common of these methods is the staging of a dharna and sitting on the body of a victim.[6] I personally experienced this only twice in Uttarakhand. The situations went thus: a number of humans were killed by a leopard; patently these were not accidental deaths, and, in fact, there was a man-eater at work; a petition or a set of petitions would be submitted to the district magistrate and the forest department; but this would be to no avail. In such situations, a common tactic in the mountains is to not allow for the body of a victim to be cremated. The family and other villagers or townspeople will sit around the victim's rapidly decomposing body and chant slogans against the state—"death to the DM," "down with the state." Both the demonstrations took place in key spaces of the town: the first at the entrance of the bazaar and on a major road, the other right outside the forest department headquarters. On both these occasions the pressure on local officials to quickly hunt down the leopard—any leopard—and present it to the victims' families became particularly intense. It allowed these officials to ring up their superiors in the capital and beg for reinforcements, be it extra policemen or hunters or both, as the situation might pose a threat to "law and order."

The writers of administrative letters and official accounts in India appear to be perpetually in fear of unlawful and disorderly behavior. This discourse is mimicked in official letters in Uttarakhand despite the fact that such disorder has rarely, if ever, occurred in the mountains of Uttarakhand.[7] The only experience of this constantly anticipated brute behavior in the last decade, at least, took place in the district of Chamoli about two years back. There is one particular region of this district that experiences extremely high levels of conflict between humans and big cats for reasons that remain unclear. As it is a poor region, sparsely populated and far removed from the district headquarters, the presence of man-eaters is constantly ignored. This neglect stems partly from an absence of canny petition writers who can bring the situation to the attention of senior district officials. Instead you have overworked and underresourced ground staff who are only able to send across handwritten reports that list the details of deaths and request for some form of action from their superiors.

Two years ago, there were frequent attacks being reported, and nothing was being done about it. The suspicion was that there were simultaneously not one but three man-eaters in that region. One day, a procession of about fifty people—most of them men—turned up unannounced at the forest department headquarters and doused four of their staff in kerosene. The staff members were physically dragged out of their offices by the protestors, and the head of the forest department was sent a message saying that he had to give them a *likhit ashwasan*—a "written promise"—that the leopards would be immediately hunted down, or else the four men would be set ablaze. The written promise was extracted, and in the absence of a hunting permit, hunters were immediately sent out and killed a leopard the very next day. We will never know if that hunted leopard was indeed a man-eater, but its death nonetheless had the effect of calming down the residents and the release of the four forest department hostages. The official who gave the written promise and then ordered the immediate hunting of any leopard that they saw described the situation as one of "law and order" that necessitated the "sacrifice of a leopard" (see chapter 2). The dead body of the leopard was then presented to the villagers—again an unheard-of occurrence, as the corpses are always sent to the capital city for postmortems. The corpse of the dead leopard was then paraded around town. This incident is well known in official circles and in the press, largely because it remains thus far a relatively rare occurrence. None of this story appears in the government files, of course, making it quintessentially a public secret.[8] But it is not only through the threat of force that arzees to kill big cats are immediately acquiesced to. As the next example of an arzee shows, there are other mediums and moments that can unleash a visceral response and culminate in state action.

WhatsApp Arzees

In early 2016, when I was living in a large town in Uttarakhand, I woke up to find a WhatsApp message on my phone. The message, in Hindi, simply said, "Hume insaaf chahiye"—"We want justice." Accompanying the message was a photograph of a young boy—called Krishna—who had become the latest victim of a leopard in a village adjoining the town. A particularly enterprising young man in this village had come up with the idea to send the horrific image out through WhatsApp. The simple but powerful text and its accompanying photograph of a half-eaten child circulated furiously in the town and beyond. It was sent as a mass message to dozens of people, including senior wildlife and administrative officials. The next day some of the local newspapers carried it too, with headlines such as "Another innocent has been martyred to the protection of leopards" and "What was his fault?" (*Iski kya galti thi?*).

The WhatsApp message was also sent to the concerned forest official who issued a hunting permit—via SMS—to three of the state's most accomplished hunters the very same day. They were rushed into the city, and, in a few days' time, the leopard was hunted down. In normal circumstances, the killing of every leopard and tiger in a big town becomes magnified in the local press, with animal rights activists, wildlife organizations, and other assorted big-cat lovers leaping to the defense of the dead feline. In this case, though, the speed with which the big cat was hunted down and the widespread dissemination of the photograph with its simple demand for justice led to a hushing up of the event. Furthermore, there is no paper trace left of the death of this leopard in the official accounts—the "arzee" was a

WhatsApp message that wasn't filed; the hunting permit was an SMS that is equally recalcitrant to filing, unlike a document; and a lot of the discussions took place via the telephone. At the moment there is an ongoing, heated discussion in India on the extent to which new technologies such as SMS or WhatsApp messages can be used in lieu of the regular paper-based technologies. While it is too early to see where these new technologies lead and how they shape the form of government in India, it is worth making one initial observation on the basis of the WhatsApp arzee.

The *kaghazi raj* (paper state) that formed the basis of colonial rule and continued into postcolonial South Asia has, as I have argued in my previous book (N. Mathur 2016), only been strengthened by the recent push to transparency and accountability or the so-called "good governance agenda" in India. In an ecosystem in which we are witnessing the profusion of paper-based forms of functioning and evidence making in government offices, SMS and WhatsApp messages such as the one described above possess some noteworthy qualities. The first is the sheer brevity of the message. Unlike the three-page arzee that lays out the big cat's heinous actions and bullet-pointed demands, we have short and punchy messages. The demand for justice—which is what often lies at the very heart of all arzees—is presented in its sheer simplicity. There are no details, no remonstrations, not even specific demands beyond *insaaf* (justice). The power of the message is propped up with the photograph. Together, they make for an extremely potent petition. I would often observe during my time in government offices in Uttarakhand how bureaucrats, especially the senior ones who felt overwhelmed with petitions and paperwork, never *really* read the (paper) petitions seriously. They would skim one briefly or even just ask their personal assistant what the missive was about before tossing it in a file or out folder, marking it off to someone, or, in some cases, ripping it to shreds.

Going through the archives in different districts of Uttarakhand, I saw scores of petitions demanding the capture or hunting of man-eaters or pleading for compensation for attacks and kills. I was certain that many of these petitions had never even been seen by the officials they were addressed to. As I mentioned at the outset, there is a similar fatigue with the volume of petitions in the development wing of the state. In such an environment of "pathological petitioning" and dizzying volume of paper, what I think of as the "WhatsApp arzee" has the capacity to elicit not just a response but also a quick response.[9] The second aspect of the arzee sent through WhatsApp or SMS is its speed. Both the writing process and the time it takes to evoke a response are short. In the case of the Gopeshwar petition, it was after two kills and several attacks and several weeks that the petition was penned. While there was one enterprising person—a Mr. Rawat—who wrote it up under the banner of a larger organization, that petition circulated among several persons for their signatures. Once it had been signed and printed, there was plenty of organizational labor involved in the assembling of the procession (*jaloos*), the hiring of loud speakers, and the synchronization of the petition's submission with the DM's movements. Compare this involved process with the WhatsApp arzee, where one young man in the village just sent it out within an hour of the first death. Again, with the Gopeshwar petition the DM called an emergency meeting that lasted for hours, there were letters and telegrams written, phone calls were made, and a committee was set up. The hunting license was eventually won, but the entire process took a long time, despite the state being in "emergency mode," so to say. With the WhatsApp arzee the officials met the next morning and sent a hunting license through SMS before lunchtime.

The Human Petition

I want to end this chapter with a story of a long-term petitioner who carried her arzee on her very self, so to say. This story is also worth considering, for it is one in which we aren't sure what—if any—role was played by crooked cats. What is noteworthy, though, is that they loom in the background as a spectral presence reminding us of their existence and their capacity to wantonly destroy human lives.

The arzee of this woman, whom I shall call Uma, was related to the sudden disappearance of her twenty-year-old son from a town in Chamoli District. The reasons for his vanishing remain unclear to date. Some suspected he had run away from home to make a life in urban India in the plains—a somewhat common phenomenon in the impoverished Himalaya. Others wondered if he had met with some accident, such as falling down a cliff or into the river Ganges, or had been killed and eaten up by a big cat. There was a crooked cat haunting the vicinity of Uma's village at that time, but the remains of her son were never found, so everyone preferred to think this was not the fate that had befallen him. It is worth noting that when we would discuss the disappeared in the mountains, there was as much speculation on whether they had run away to the plains seeking a different life as there was on whether some tragic fate had befallen them, such as being eaten alive by a beast. In Uma's recitation of her story, she woke up one day and everything was normal in her life. Her son had breakfast, took his lunch box, and headed off to work, but then never returned. She had just one photograph of her son—a passport-sized one that had been used for his college ID card—which she attached to an arzee she had gotten a professional petition writer to pen nine years ago when her son disappeared. That arzee went into a fat file on missing persons in the district office as well as with the police.

I first met Uma in the DM's durbar-like office in Gopeshwar, where I was waiting to speak to him alongside six other people. All of the others held documents—some type of petition or form—in their hands. Uma, however, walked in empty handed, with tears in her eyes and hands folded in supplication. She stood quietly behind the seven of us. There was something so obviously distressed about her that the DM gestured to her to come ahead of us. She stepped forward near his desk but remained mute. It was then I realized the DM was already familiar with her. He asked her to speak, but when she chose to remain silent, he, not unkindly, dismissed her, saying, "We will look at your arzee again and do what we can." When I had finished my work with the DM, I went out in search of this silent, paperless petitioner. I found her in the adjoining room, where a clerical officer who, again, seemed to know her was looking through a thick file. From this he extracted a faded piece of paper, which I realized was her original arzee. He got the peon to make two photocopies of it, giving her one and marking the other to the police department with that day's date and a scribbled note that read "Please see." Uma took the copy that was given to her and walked out of the office, with me trailing beside her trying to strike up a conversation. We walked together to a Hanuman—the Hindu monkey god—temple located in the office compound. In the temple she muttered a small prayer under her breath and deposited the arzee near the main shrine.

This ritual was repeated every first Tuesday of the month for the year I spent in the district. Even when the DM was transferred and a new one came in, he was prepped about the sorry plight of Uma, who yearned to be reunited with her missing son. Uma knew that her arzee in the Hanuman temple—like the many others that were deposited there alongside hers—was swept away by the cleaner the next morning and put in the garbage bin. Yet she persisted in placing it there on the day of the week—Tuesday—that is considered the designated day for the Hindu god Hanuman. While her repeat appearances in the offices were more familiar—this is classic chakkar marna—I was curious about the additional trip to the temple. When I asked her about it one time she shrugged her shoulders and said to me, "Kya pataa? Kaun kahan sun le?" (One never knows. Who might hear you where?)

The practice of depositing bureaucratic petitions at shrines or temples, especially those located close to government offices, is not uncommon. In Uttarakhand there is a famous temple to the god of justice—Golu—that is devoted almost entirely to the submission of official petitions. As Malik (2016) has argued, there is a public intimacy that is created through the sharing of these extremely personal testimonials alongside an open expression of faith in Golu (see also Taneja 2013). In November 2015 the *New York Times* carried a story on what the journalist considered a peculiar petitioning practice.[10] The site for this practice is the ruins of a fourteenth-century fort called Firoze Shah Kotla that was built by the sultan Firoz Shah Tughlaq in Delhi. The petitions are submitted to a jinn who is believed to live in the ruined fort. Drawing on the work of an anthropologist, this piece notes—in amused and amazed tones—that the petitions are more "bureaucratic than worshipful": they include police reports, detailed contact information, and multiple copies of the very same form, "as if addressed to different departments of a modern bureaucracy."[11]

By way of an arzee-like conclusion, my submission is that an ethnographic account of arzees allows us to drop the incredulous tones of the *New York Times* article variety by expanding our imagination of what it means to make an appeal and, relatedly, what forms an arzee can take. Arzees challenge dichotomies; they do not allow for the maintenance of uncontaminated, pure spaces where, for instance, the legal is kept safely distinct from the sacred, or the bureaucratic from the poetic. They question the assumption of a separation between the sacred (such as a Hanuman temple) and the bureaucratic (such as a clerical office). They question the difference between a language that is bureaucratic and legal and a language that is worshipful; or, similarly, the difference between documents that are bureaucratic and those that are deeply affective. An arzee can have long details on which clause of which statute needs to be amended and in what manner even as it simultaneously offers musings on the meaning of life and pontificates on the inevitability of death. Just as arzees can be presented to a state official, so too can they be handed over to jinns or simply strung onto temple bells. Equally, arzees work through notions of the durbar, or a royal court; through the hope of a *darshan* of an official, a viewing that holds connotations of the sacred; and through much more of-the-moment institutions like a grievance redressal cell, or email addresses and phone numbers where you can offer suggestions, or a WhatsApp account where you can send your arzees using photographs and emoticons.

As far as documents found in bureaucracies and state archives go, arzees are uniquely genre defying. They carry elements of the humble petition and snatches of the worshipful, but just as much they can be combative, angry, and even threatening. In the same breath we go from "You are my mother-father" to "but what is this that you have done?" and "I submit to thee my humble lord; but be warned this submission is not absolute and I, too, can roar like a hungry tiger." One arzee that was furious and threatened a bloody revolt manned by Maoists shipped in from neighboring Nepal signed off, "But I shall remain forever your humble servant."[12] I want to suggest that these are not confused or contradictory petition writers, but rather that ambivalence is written into the very heart of contemporary arzees that, in their quest for justice, find themselves battling big cats and the legal and bureaucratic apparatus of the Indian state.

Humans, in these arzees, appear in a peculiarly vulnerable position, especially vis-à-vis the charismatic nonhuman animal. The big cats, on the other hand, come across as powerfully agentive in their own right, an agency that is further bolstered by the bureaucracy and the legal regime that have been set up to conserve them. In the demands to kill the big cats, power and the right to life are flipped around: it is the big cat that is valued more than humans, claim the petitioners, even though it should, by all rights, be the reverse. This flipping around of the value of lives—big-cat ones over human ones—is, on the one hand, the perverse outcome of conservationism. It appears to be quite literally true, with the state more concerned with protecting big cats than protecting humans. Besides literality, though, petitions also demonstrate a radical moving beyond the assumed anthropocentrism of state processes. In these documents, WhatsApp messages, verbal exhortations, prayers, and processions, we see that the big cat occupies central ground, with humans receding into some distant horizon. The world is not just being carefully nurtured for the tiger or leopard but also being dominated by these big cats, with an explicit subjugation of the human. Arzees do not just, then, defy a neat genre or encapsulation within a space, medium, or series of petitioning practices. They can also serve to open up debates on peaceful multispecies coexistence and challenge a conservationist discourse that assumes big cats to be peculiarly agentless and in dire need of human protection. In the arzees described here, it is the human who deserves protection from being preyed on by crooked cats. Even as they ascribe agency to the crooked cats, these petitions compel us to ask once again and further complicate the question, Who is the real beast of this tale? And how did we come to arrive upon this pass?

FIVE

The Leopard of Rudraprayag versus Shere Khan

> These jungle stories by Jim Corbett merit as much popularity and as wide a circulation as Rudyard Kipling's *Jungle Books*. Kipling's Jungle Books were fiction, based on great knowledge of jungle life; Corbett's stories are fact, and fact is often stranger than fiction.
>
> —M. G. Hallett in the 1944 introduction to Corbett's *Man-Eaters of Kumaon*

If you google "Rudraprayag," the search items list "Rudraprayag leopard" as the first item. If you go to the Wikipedia page of this town and district, there, too, the leopard features in the opening lines. Arguably, the crooked cat who is the chief protagonist of the book *The Man-Eating Leopard of Rudraprayag,* by Jim Corbett, is one of the most famous leopards in the world. Corbett not only slayed this leopard but also made him immortal by writing about him. There is a plaque located prominently along the national highway in Rudraprayag District that commemorates the hunting down of this crooked cat (figure 5.1). It reads, "On this very spot was killed the man eating leopard of Rudraprayag by Jim Corbett on 2 May 1926."

This remembrance spot falls on the side of the road as you drive further up the Garhwal mountains toward the district of Chamoli. I would often stop here, for a string of nice little *dhabas* (roadside food stalls) that serve chai and Maggi noodles and other snacks are clustered around this spot. Unsurprisingly, they are all called *Corbett dhaba,* or Corbett tea point. One of the *Corbett dhabas* became my regular, and its owner, someone I will call Sunil, soon became friendly with me. Without fail, every time I would stop over at *Corbett dhaba,* Sunil would come up to me to tell me—as if for the first time—the story of the man-eating leopard of Rudraprayag. Even if I protested by saying, "But I know this story well," he would insist on

5.1. Plaque at the spot where the man-eating leopard of Rudraprayag was shot dead by Jim Corbett. Credit: Photograph by author

repeating it, saying, "But you must hear it again *here*." The bare bones of Sunil's narrative are similar to Corbett's claims.

There was a fearsome leopard that operated over a large territory of Garhwal from 1918 to 1926. He was known to have killed at least 125 humans, though it was suspected that there were probably many more that never made it into the record books. Several shikaris tried to kill this fiend, and the government of India set many traps for him, but he managed to outwit them all. In the end, Corbett was called in—by petitioners from the affected villages as well as the government authorities—from neighboring Kumaon (figure 5.2). And, of course, Corbett managed to kill the leopard right on this very spot where we were currently sipping chai. The dhaba owner was certain that the mango tree that formed a protective canopy over his garden was the very same one on which Corbett had staked out his prey in early 1926 and then fired that "shot in the dark" that proved to be the one that—finally—killed the leopard.

Sunil was of the opinion that such a dangerous leopard had previously never existed in Uttarakhand and never would again. But why, I would ask, was the Rudraprayag bagh so special or different? After all, we were living in a world where there were so many crooked cats in our immediate vicinity that it had become difficult to create a hierarchy of evil leopards. For Sunil, there were two factors that distinguished this historical leopard from all others. Firstly, he had killed many—125 at a minimum—and over a vast territory that

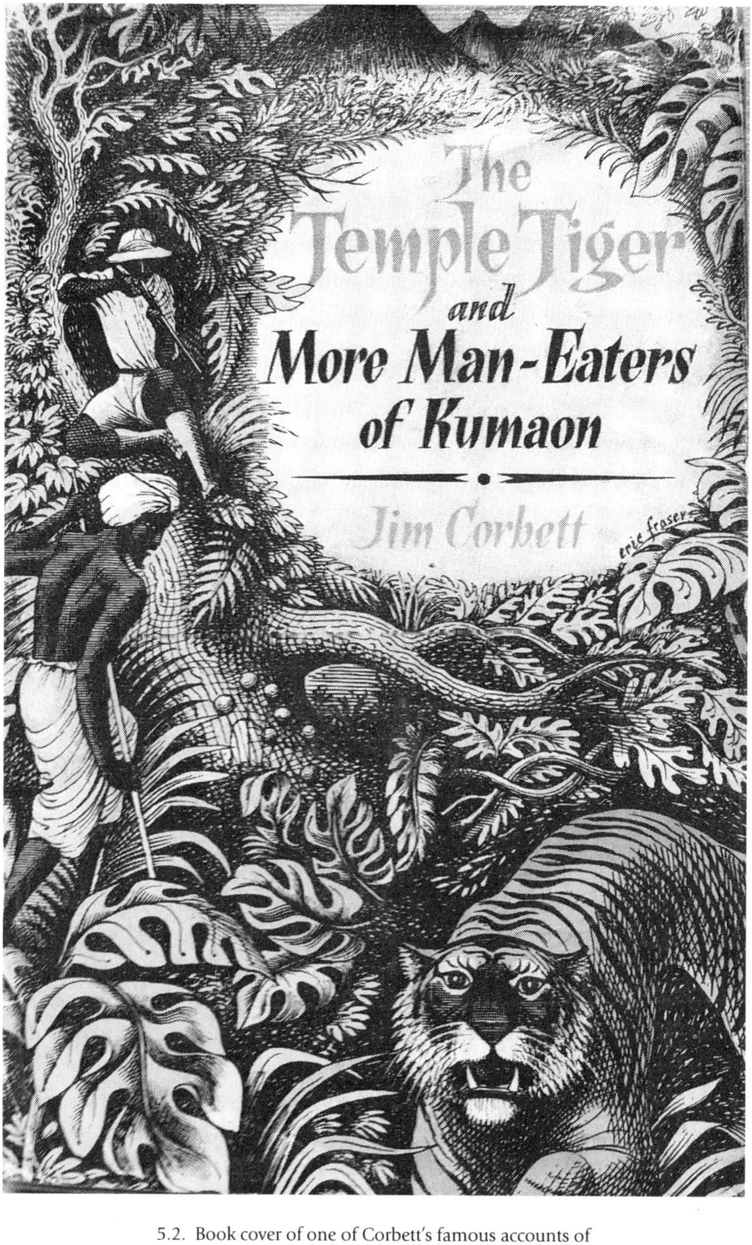

5.2. Book cover of one of Corbett's famous accounts of man-eaters in present-day Uttarakhand.

extended from Rudraprayag all the way up to the distant and inaccessible Kedarnath temple. Secondly, this leopard was more cunning than the ones we now "know." He was able to avoid the bullets shot from the guns of the most practiced hunters; no amount of cyanide poison could kill him; he had supernatural powers, like being able to make himself invisible or not make a sound at all; he could swim across the icy and raging river; he was able to unlock doors like a human or make his way past tiny slits of windows; and he was even able to calmly eat the bits of an animal that had been placed in a trap without getting trapped himself. These are, indeed, all claims about the deviousness of this specific big cat that Corbett makes in his book. *The Man-Eating Leopard of Rudraprayag* has been translated into dozens of languages, including Hindi. Sunil had, of course, read the book many times over. But he and others who reside in and around present-day Rudraprayag say that they didn't really need to read the book, for everyone knows about this adamkhor; they all grew up hearing stories of his cunning and treachery.

Indeed, everyone in Uttarakhand seems to know this particular leopard, and most tend to agree that he was more fearsome and evil than any that had previously or subsequently haunted the *pahar* (mountains). But celebrity big cats don't just achieve their fame due to some innate character, and cunning is, in fact, the defining feature of all crooked cats. As is the case with the other publicly known big cats in India that are discussed in this work—Avni, Shere Khan, Vijay, Ustad—there is something that sets them apart. In the case of the crooked leopard of Rudraprayag, the role of Corbett's putative biography of him is undeniable. The book is a global best seller, and Corbett himself commands a powerful afterlife in India.

Jim Corbett is always distinguished from other white colonial writers such as Rudyard Kipling through recourse to a stark distinction between fiction (*The Jungle Book*) and fact (*The Man-Eaters of India*; *The Man-Eating Leopard of Rudraprayag*; etc.). While critical historical scholarship has effectively challenged narratives of the white savior male who came to the rescue of terrified natives through the masculinist hunting down of man-eaters in colonial India (e.g., MacKenzie 1988; Sramek 2006; Storey 1991), this foundational distinction between fact and fiction endures. Das makes the point that Corbett, contrary to popular perception of him as a compassionate shikari and a lover of India and the paharis, was in fact a "fully-paid up imperialist" (2009, 20). Das, like Booth, who is one of Corbett's biographers, points out Corbett's hypocritical practices of advocating for the preservation of big cats and simultaneously organizing large tiger hunts for VIPs.

The intimacy between hunting and conservationism has been demonstrated by several historians of wildlife and the environment (Rangarajan

2005). Booth (1986) has listed what he charitably considers "mistakes" that Corbett made in his book, but we can perhaps more critically assess them as a form of self-mythologizing: there are, for instance, significant differences between Corbett's accounts and those maintained by the government of India on the dates when several man-eaters were killed. Corbett claims he killed the Panar leopard and the Muktewar tiger in 1907, while official records note it was 1910. In other words, it was three years later, after scores more humans had been killed, even though Corbett had ample opportunity to try to hunt the crooked cats much in advance.

It is not just differences in dates but also other seemingly small details of discrepancies between Corbett's accounts and the official records that can be endlessly listed. Perhaps these discrepancies aren't all that surprising given both the slipperiness of memory, the culture of imperialism, the white male hunter-savior syndrome, and the desire to write slick shikar stories. The point here is not to prove that Corbett isn't the hero everyone appears to think he is, for that is a different sort of historical debate that has already been undertaken to a large extent by the vast literature on hunting, imperialism, and masculinity. My interest here lies not in disproving the facticity of Corbett's accounts (though I am skeptical of many of the claims made in them). Rather, I wish to query the distance between fact and fiction via ethnography, which in turn occupies an ambiguous position between what is factual and what might be considered fictional.[1] Through the ethnographic experience of having lived in the vicinity of crooked cats and observed their killing, I want to query the assumption that what Corbett wrote was the real, was anchored in the facts of what transpired, and hence is even more thrilling than the fantasies of Kipling. In other words, can it be that Shere Khan, the menacing tiger-villain of *The Jungle Book*, is not all that much more fantastic a beast than the Rudraprayag leopard?

The book *The Man-Eating Leopard of Rudraprayag* is long—almost overly long—with digressions on the pilgrimage and fishing practices of Hindus. Like Corbett's other accounts, it builds up the tension like a suspense or crime novel. It is at pains to state that the Rudraprayag leopard was the most famous animal in all of the world at that time—his name had appeared in several international newspapers, and even a question had been asked in the British Parliament about him. Corbett notes that the manner of record keeping on deaths and attacks is faulty, and that this leopard certainly caused more than the 125 official human deaths. However, Corbett is somewhat more circumspect when it comes to the issue of difficulty in identifying the beast. The area that this leopard was meant to be covering—five hundred square miles of steep Himalayan territory that is also divided up by a fast-paced, ice-cold river—is remarkably large. In present-day Uttarakhand, at any given time there are several man-eaters operating in the same area. Corbett notes, as do present-day shikaris, that the pugmark gives a good idea of identity and also allows for forms of recognition, especially to those who are familiar with big cats. On the basis of the pugmark near the kill, he could see it was an oversize male of about eight to nine years of age. Corbett's own method of hunting the man-eater is similar to what takes place today. As soon as news of an attack on a human is heard, the shikaris run to the spot. They then track, on the basis of pugmarks or other eyewitness accounts, the movements of the leopard. They scour the nearby region or keep watch over the body of the dead human or nonhuman animal. As in the case of the Gopeshwar-wallah bagh, Corbett killed a wrong leopard first. Unlike the jubilant natives and even the colonial official Ibbotson, who had accompanied him on the hunt, Corbett somehow *just knew* this wasn't the correct leopard:

> The animal that lay dead before me was an out-sized male leopard, who the previous night had tried to tear down a partition to get at a human being, and who had been shot in an area in which dozens of human beings had been killed, all good and sufficient reasons for assuming that he was the man-eater. But I could not make myself believe that he was the same animal I had seen the night I sat over the body of the woman. True, it had been a dark night and I had only vaguely seen the outline of the leopard; even so, I was convinced that the animal that was being lashed to a pole by willing hands was not the man-eater. (1991b, 492)

So certain was Corbett that he made Ibbotson warn the people not to relax precautions against the man-eater, and he did not telegraph "the government" that the man-eater had been killed. But, of course, Corbett was right. The very next morning, they got news of the death of a woman by the man-eater in a different part of the region, on the far side of the river. What is noteworthy here is that Corbett, like many of the mini Corbetts of today, just seemed to know when he had the right one or not. When he finally killed the correct leopard, then, too, he just *knew* it, even though he had fired in the dark from atop a tree at an animal he could not see (or "ID," as present-day government guidelines specify).

Corbett, in all his writings, distinguishes himself from the natives not just by referring to his superior tracking and hunting skills but also by firmly stating that he knows the beast at work is an animal and not, as the simple mountain folk are given to believe, an evil spirit or a supernatural being.

5.3. Shere Khan with wolves, *The Jungle Book*.
Credit: Maurice de Becque. From Biblioteca Academiei Române, Wikimedia Commons

Again, in my experience in the Himalaya and in Mumbai I have not come across anyone who believes that the man-eater is anything but an animal—a crooked animal, but an animal no doubt. Popular accounts and media accounts, too, might refer to notions of destiny, bad karma, ill omens, retributive justice, and the sheer, staggering bad luck at the presence of man-eaters and/or of being victimized by them. But they do not describe these big cats as supernatural beings. Where Corbett and present-day accounts do perfectly match is when it comes to discussing the extraordinary cunning, deviousness, and treachery of man-eaters. They are crooked and evil like no others, to the point where you wonder how this individual got so very tedha when his fellow species mates are so seedha and so careful to avoid humans.

Shere Khan, the tiger in *The Jungle Book*, was born lame, with even his mother calling him Langri ("the lame one"). He was disparagingly known to kill only emaciated cattle as it was hard for him to hunt any bigger prey (figure 5.3). His weakness made him turn on "Man," but the weakness—as discussed by others—was not just a physical one (an incapacity to hunt due to a disability) but also a moral one, for he was attacking the most vulnerable. Shere Khan's revenge fantasy that was centered on Mowgli arose out of an interspecies conflict with wolves, especially Mowgli's wolf-mother Raksha (as I discussed in chapter 3). In the end, Mowgli—with some help from his other nonhuman animal friends—outwitted the tiger and had him killed by being stomped to death by a charging buffalo herd in a ravine where Shere Khan found himself trapped. Mowgli then skinned the ten-foot tiger alone and symbolically nailed his hide on the Council Rock where several disagreements with Shere Khan had previously taken place. In *The Jungle Book,* animals speak, love, feel, make friends, and conspire together. These are rich interspecies relationships that are governed by what Kipling often refers to as the "Law of the Jungle"; this is no space of brutish lawlessness, then, but rather one that has hierarchy, a semblance of order, and even specified times and places for disputation and discussion.

What makes *The Jungle Book* a piece of fiction other than its own self-description as one? Is it the dense web of interpersonal relations, the distinctive personalities of animals who have names and nuclear families, and the fact that they talk and hold heated councils to discuss the right way forward? There is, in my reading, something deeply real about Shere Khan the putative crooked cat. He hunts as he does due to an injury, he is scared of wolves and elephants, he is scheming and cunning, he has a particular temperament, and he is after one specific human as prey. All of these traits are recognizable in crooked cats in India today as well. What is refreshing in this work of fiction is the lack of a heroic white male figure. Mowgli does, in collaboration with his friends like Akela and Bagheera, outwit the tiger, but it isn't a masculinist cleverness that gets him ahead. He, in fact, says on observing the trampled-to-death tiger, "Brothers, that was a dog's death" (Kipling 2018, 107). There is a mocking of the "cattle-thief," as Shere Khan was referred to, and his incapacity to fight like a tiger, but also a touch of sadness at the type of death that he eventually got. Compare this story of interspecies love, intimacy, and collaboration that is filled with complex anthropomorphized characters with the singular arc of Corbett's shikar stories. The latter are dubious in their facts, occlude so much that must have occurred, and never, ever allow for the vulnerability of the narrator. Most crucially, the leopard that is the supposed man-eater in Corbett's book remains somewhat unlikely and unrecognizable to me, quite unlike the figure of Shere Khan, whom I can almost see walking with his limp and scarred face in a forest—or a big city—in India today. Both Kipling and Corbett clearly had the imperial project of rule over India and a sense of racial superiority ingrained in them—they both carried that "white man's burden" that the former so unforgettably wrote of. It is not the authors of these famous tales but rather the beastly portraits they sketch of their respective crooked cats that I am considering here.

Shere Khan, the man-eating tiger of *The Jungle Book*, remains one of the greatest villains in fiction; the Rudraprayag leopard is one of the greatest in fact. My proposition is that if we were to study both through the contemporary ethnography of crooked cats in India, this distinction would become blurred. Fact is not just stranger than fiction; rather, that which is considered fact might be more fantastic than that which we have thus far considered a mere figment of the imagination.

I want to end with another tale of humans recounting stories about tigers. This is a story that presses home this question of what is fact and what is fiction. How do we tell the difference, and what purpose does the boxing off of accounts into different categories with marked relationships to that which we consider real and true—or what Fassin (2014) has described as true life and real lives—really serve?

Ruskin Bond is a contemporary Indian writer who lives in Uttarakhand and has written children's stories, adult fiction, including ghost stories, and nonfiction on life in the Himalaya. Bond has a fascinating book that, somehow, perfectly illustrates this form of writing that we are pondering here: it is technically fiction but laced with so many truths that it becomes hard to consider it purely in that genre. The book is entitled *Tigers for Dinner: Tall Tales by Jim Corbett's Khansama* (2013). *Tigers for Dinner* is based on someone called Mehmoud who was the cook (*khansama*) in the Bond household. He had glowing testimonials from, supposedly, Corbett himself. Ruskin Bond is, as he notes in the introduction to the book, often asked if Mehmoud is a real person, as the book is a children's storybook and could be fiction, for all we know. Bond says that, yes, Mehmoud was a real person who served as the family cook when he was himself a small boy. The stories in the book all come across as impossible tall tales, involving comical crocodiles and the rescuing of rajas from wild boars as well as wrestles with cobras. All of the most dangerous animals that are found in northern India are included, in other words. Tigers, of course, figure prominently in the book, with Mehmoud recounting how he smacked a huge tiger on his nose with a frying pan and the tiger didn't like it and ran away into the jungle howling with pain. On the question of the veracity of the stories, Bond states, "As to the tales themselves, well—like all good storytellers, Mehmoud was given to a little exaggeration so we must allow him some poetic license" (2013, 9). Bond could almost be talking about Corbett, rather than Corbett's one-time cook, here. Corbett is a marvelous storyteller too, and the impact of the stories he has spun about man-eaters in India continues to echo through the Himalaya and well beyond. These tales have the capacity to linger on across time and generate manifold effects in the world. What better example is there of the power of storytelling? *The Man-Eating Leopard of Rudraprayag, The Jungle Book,* and *Tigers for Dinner* all remind us of the need to find new ways of narrating the beastly tales of crooked cats—preferably ways that can shine a light on the climate crisis and describe what life in the Anthropocene looks like.

SIX

Big Cats in the City

Imagine yourself in a bustling big city in India, with its noises, sights, and smells, in the midst of people, close to major urban landmarks, when a leopard enters into your sight.[1] What possible scenarios would this entrance of a big cat in the city set off? Possibly three distinct ones.

In the first scenario, panic ensues. Crowds gather. Petitions are written to the forest department requesting that they immediately hunt down this beast that dared stray into human land. Traps are set up, and the big cat is either captured or killed.

In the second scenario, there is still widespread concern. Yet, instead of asking for the capture of the big cat or even its death, the urban residents come together to discuss modalities through which they can avoid or minimize any unpleasant encounters with the animal. The leopard is allowed to stay on, and humans find ways to live beside one another. It is only if the big cat turns out to be crooked that some form of punitive action is considered.

In the third scenario, the city dwellers consider this sight rather normal and unthreatening. No action is taken. The leopard and the humans share space with equanimity.

Now what if I were to say that all three scenarios exist simultaneously in India and, in fact, tend to map onto particular cities? Each city, in other words, provokes its own response to the presence of a big cat. So, it isn't the presence of the feline per se that structures the series of human actions that will ensue as much as it is the space in which the big cat appears. There is an assumption that, in certain spaces, the entry of an animal, especially a predator, immediately means the animal is out of place; it is "escaping" or "straying" from its own animal land into human land, or from animal spaces into beastly places, as Philo and Wilbert (2000) put it.[2] Many works of academic literature—ranging from animal geography to multispecies ethnography to animal histories—have demonstrated how notions of in/out-of-place beasts have developed and have undertaken the intellectual work of dismantling these assumptions (e.g., Wolch and Emel 1998; Velten 2013). In India, there has been some significant work arguing against the popular perception that big cats live within their prescribed spaces, such as wildlife reserves. It is increasingly evident that leopards in particular thrive and are found in substantial numbers in human-dominated landscapes (Athreya et al. 2013; Odden et al. 2014; Landy 2017). This chapter discusses beastly presences in the urban, with a focus on the differentiated reactions they can provoke. I follow the arrival and movements of big cats in three cities of India—Dehradun, Shimla, and Mumbai—and study the particular responses they have evinced. As we will see, instead of a generic reaction, there is a city-specific and, sometimes, leopard-specific response. Not only are a fear of the big cat and the recourse to some form of capture or hunting not necessarily the automatic outcomes, but also these very reactions can be shifted over time through human (and, concomitantly, feline) interventions.

In the bagh diary that I maintained during my time in Gopeshwar, I noted that a question that would often be posed to me in the mornings in office was "How is your neighbor today?" There was a double meaning to the question, because on the one hand it referred to my literal neighbor, as it was widely believed that the man-eater was living in Kund Colony, the very same residential complex I was renting a room in. At the same time, it also referred to the fact that it was widely believed that the leopard was a maidani, or one who—like myself—hailed from the plains. In that morning greeting during the reign of terror of the big cat, so much was compressed: deep worry over the perambulations of the big cat and the desire to monitor her every movement; a genuine belief that I might be more aware of her movements through the city as we (as in the big cat and myself) were quite literally neighbors; a historic disgruntlement with the plains people of India for their consistent neglect and/or exploitation of the Himalaya; and a disbelief that a crooked cat such as the man-eater of Gopeshwar was a kindred pahari (mountain person). I was only dimly aware of this condensation of a variety of emotions and questions into that seemingly innocuous sentence at the time. My interest here lies in considering how that everyday question asked of me by my friends all those years back relates to an animating question of this book: How do we come to know, understand, and live with potentially predatory nonhuman animals?

The Panoptic Leopard

The leopard's movements through the town of Gopeshwar as well as his chosen points of location were considered the strongest indications of his nature: cheeky, insolent, cunning, and definitely crooked. In other words, space was central to this quest to seek out who the cat was. In the first was his "home" in Gopeshwar. This home was widely—and rightly—considered to be at the very summit of the town, just above a residential complex for the bureaucrats administering the district, called Kund Colony. Gopeshwar is laid out on a large mountain, with Kund Colony located right at the top end, much like hill stations from the British colonial period where the top (white) officials lived in bungalows on the upper ridges of mountains. At the very top of Kund Colony is a telephone tower. The tower is in a small jungle that provided a good hiding spot for the leopard. He was located not just in the poshest part of town but also at a point where he could command a panoptic view of the entire town, thus keeping a close eye on everyone's movements and lending an added layer of fear through the Benthamite proposition of surveillance.

Kund Colony was also home to all the powerful agents of the state, ranging from the police force to the local district administration. By locating himself—literally—above everyone else, the leopard was asserting his full sovereignty over the town. But he further declared his insolent disregard for state power and human hierarchies of deference through several other actions, again spatial. One night the bagh decided to wander around and spend some time in the colonial-style bungalow of the district magistrate, the highest representative of the state. This "visit" was reported on the front pages of all the local newspapers the next day and became the subject of much hilarity for the longest time. On the basis of his pugmarks, it was made clear that the bagh walked around the DM's garden, took a short nap near a rosebush, and then made off in the morning before being spotted by anyone, including the various guards stationed permanently in this compound. The local newspaper headlines the next day ran, "Bagh visits DM, but catches him napping." This incident proved to everyone in Gopeshwar that the bagh, *chatur* (cunning) as he was, was fully aware of how incapable the agents of the state are, and therefore he felt no fear of them either. In "visiting" the DM residence and trampling through his neatly laid-out rose patch, the bagh sent out a clear signal to the sleeping state (N. Mathur 2016).

One evening he turned up right outside our office in Gopeshwar at 5 p.m. precisely. This particular big cat, then, knew not only where the bureaucrats work but also when they knock off their work. Yet again, this was a show of strength and cheek by this individual. While the bagh did subvert human hierarchies of the state, he appeared careful in abiding by godly ones by, for instance, not entering the sanctum sanctorum of the town's central Gopinath Temple. Several people claimed that the bagh, too, worshiped the Hindu god Shiva, as the cat had been seen circumambulating the temple.

Burton writes of the "evil reputation" of the Sundarbans as the territory of man-eating tigers (1931, 143).[3] In Chamoli, the town of Gopeshwar and the development blocks[4] of Karnaprayag and Gairsain possess a similarly evil reputation due to the high incidences of man-eating leopards in these regions. Of the two blocks, Gairsain has experienced multiple attacks by not one but two and sometimes even three man-eating leopards that would haunt the region simultaneously. Despite the gravity of the situation there, local administrators—the subdivisional magistrate and the block development officer—told me how much more difficult they found it to obtain hunting permits for leopards in their areas of command than in the district headquarters town of Gopeshwar. According to them, this difficulty arose from the "remote," distant location of Gairsain within the district of Chamoli itself. Further, here the attacks were happening in "interior" or "remote" villages that were not very close to the road and did not possess good communication links with the block's headquarters, located in the tiny town of Gairsain.

Certain spaces—such as villages in the Himalayan "interior"—are seen as potential big-cat territories. When big cats turn on humans in rural areas or in the perceived jungle, then these episodes are made invisible not just due to lack of documentation and evidence but also due to the gradations of the value of human life. Furthermore, there is a belief that a jungle, the mountains, and even villages are spaces where wildlife belongs and, thus, such incidents are bound to occur. Their presence in such spaces—rural, in the mountains, forested, far away from roads—doesn't provoke the same response as when a big cat turns up in Himalayan towns such as Gopeshwar. This after all is the district headquarters, is larger than the villages, and is considered an important space due to the presence of the top state officials there. However, even Gopeshwar is, in the end, in the mountains and is surrounded by forests and is close to the Nanda Devi Biosphere Reserve. The bagh is cheeky and insolent in his saunterings through Gopeshwar, especially compared to his fellow felines in Uttarakhand who tend to visit smaller, more remote spaces. Yet, the sort of outrage big cats provoke here is nothing compared to what reactions are seen when they enter big cities in the plains.

A sign (figure 6.1) in the Forest Research Institute (FRI), a colonial-era institution that was at the beating heart of scientific forestry in India, captures

6.1. Warning sign at the Forest Research Institute (FRI), Dehradun.
Credit: Photograph by author

perfectly the conception of space in Dehradun. There is big-cat territory and there is human territory. And one dare not intrude on the other. The FRI was established in 1906 as the Imperial Forest Research Institute and is spread over a sprawling 450-hectare campus in Dehradun with thick forests and large green areas. It features in many Bollywood films and is described as a "magnificent building, marrying the Greco-Roman and colonial style of architecture."[5] Several hostels for students/trainees and large colonial bungalows for officers are located on the campus in and around forest clumps and gardens. The Himalayas form an incredibly picturesque backdrop to the campus. Even in this walled and policed estate, there are distinctions of space that are marked out and displayed. Stop here, for this is leopard territory. You can go elsewhere, for that is human territory.

Such a distinction almost assumes, as my nephew once said to me, that leopards can read Hindi and English and follow human orders. Yet, this is precisely what you find all over the state of Uttarakhand—this strict demarcation between human territory and big-cat territory—with the FRI or the discourse of the cheeky, *badtameez* leopard in Gopeshwar serving as microcosms of this widely prevalent attitude. The fact that Uttarakhand has a high density of big cats as well as incredibly high levels of conflict probably contributes to such a demarcation of space.[6]

Looked at from another perspective, though, it is somewhat curious that a region with such a large number of big cats that are regularly sighted in putatively human territory would insist so adamantly on such a beastly/human spatial partitioning. In Dehradun, Gopeshwar, and other urban areas of Uttarakhand, more so than in most other places in the world, such distinctions are rendered untenable by daily life. In Gopeshwar, I spied a leopard sitting out in a sunny spot of the mountain near the busy bazaar area and in full sight. In Dehradun, from my residence near the FRI, I saw camera-trap images of leopards walking on the main road and interviewed dozens of people who would regularly encounter them in places such as the temple on the road or the tea plantations next door. Here, big cats are everywhere and, quite literally in some cases, very in your face. It is noteworthy though that leopards started attacking humans only in the recent past. Many long-term residents of Dehradun told me that these cats began becoming crooked only in the 2010s. Even though a number of leopards have lived in and around the town, they started consistently entering these spaces and acting peculiarly over the last few years. This temporality is important to keep in mind, and I return to it later on, but let us first ask, Why is there this strong insistence on marking out separate territories?

My proposition is that this distinction flows from two reasons, both harking back to the colonial period, the very time when Dehradun was first set up as a garrison town. The first is the presence of certain institutes such as the FRI, the Survey of India, and, more recently, the Wildlife Institute of India. The work of all such institutes was, and still is, to scientifically map, survey, and categorize their subject matter—be it forests, people, mountains, or animals. Emplacing or finding the "correct" space for their subject matter flowed naturally from such projects of classification, categorization, and scientific scrutiny (T. Mathur 2018). Alongside the upmarket boarding schools that too are engaged in similar disciplinary projects, albeit of young, elite boys and girls (see Srivastava 1998), these institutes predominate the character of Dehradun. This was a particular kind of city, one that was orderly and picturesque and derived much of its allure from colonial discipline.[7]

In addition to the very architecture and planning of the city, the personality of one individual looms large in Dehradun and Uttarakhand, specifically when it comes to big cats and their regulation: Jim Corbett. Corbett, as mentioned previously, is a heroic figure whose charismatic legacy underpins and centrally forms any discussion of big cats in Uttarakhand. He gained fame as a remarkable hunter of man-eaters in this region and, globally, as an incredibly popular chronicler of these hunts. The shikar story is a very particular genre that has been mastered by Corbett like almost nobody else. His name is internationally recognizable and has become synonymous with man-eaters. Indeed, the very term "man-eater" is one that has been popularized by him with his best-selling books entitled, for instance, *Man-Eaters of Kumaon*, *Man-Eaters of India*, and *The Man-Eating Leopard of Rudraprayag*.

It is difficult to describe the larger-than-life presence of Corbett in Uttarakhand. He has centrally shaped the manner in which Uttarakhand responds to big cats, especially man-eaters, or what I prefer to term "crooked cats." Corbett was a complex personality who ended life as a staunch conservationist. The first tiger reserve in India, in Uttarakhand in fact, was named after him. His writings follow the standard narrative of a shikar account. They begin with an account of the menace that is the tiger or leopard and how many people the big cat has killed and consumed. The narrative then spends a considerable amount of time discussing the difficulties that Corbett faces, often with "his men," who are natives completely effaced from the heroic account. When they are given a name, it is only to show how frightened they are of the beast and how much faith they repose in Corbett's capacities. The hunt nearly always has a twist or moment(s) when Corbett is almost outdone by the cunning beast. Yet, he always emerges triumphant. At the moment that he kills the truant big cat, there is a mixture of jubilation and sorrow in the man. His "love" for tigers and leopards is unmistakable, particularly in the strong, if flawed, defenses he mounts of them. The point remains that these hunts are now legendary in Uttarakhand. Not only have his writings been translated into dozens of languages, including Hindi, but also his legend in the mountains remains strong. One of the ways in which he lives on, so to say, is through the young men who wish to emulate him. I have lost count of the number of hunters and forest officials in Uttarakhand who have told me that they model themselves on Corbett. Hunters, in particular, actively wish to emulate the methods and style of Corbett, often quoting him extensively in interviews. Lakhpat Singh Rawat, for instance, who killed the Gopeshwar bagh, is known as "Chamoli's Corbett" (Chamoli is the district in which he lives). Joy Hukil—another famous hunter in Uttarakhand—refers to himself as "a latter-day Corbett." And Shafath Ali Khan, who is a hunter from Hyderabad, similarly liberally invokes Corbett's prose and writings.[8]

When you model yourself on Corbett—and this applies to not just hunters but also senior forest officials—and feel deep pride in his belonging to this region as well as his professed love for what he wrote about as "my India," then it is but natural that you will take similar actions to his, including hunting big cats even as you praise their beauty. When I first went to Mumbai I was astonished by how the manner of dealing with problematic big cats was so different and the fact that killing them was the absolute last resort. Similarly, in the neighboring state of Himachal Pradesh, in the city of Shimla, leopards are rarely—if ever—hunted down. The norm is that they are captured in traps and then rehabilitated or translocated. In Uttarakhand, leopards and tigers are killed with a far higher frequency and significantly lower levels of remorse. This culture of hunting might, in fact and as argued in chapter 1, explain why the crookedness of big cats is rampant in this region of India.

Corbett lives on not just through the men who desire to be native Corbetts but also in material and spatial terms. There are hundreds of cafés and restaurants named after him in the state, and his home in Kumaon is a major tourist destination. Of course, the Corbett National Park is one of the oldest tiger and leopard reserves in the country and, indeed, the world. Corbett's books have inspired native spin-offs, such as *Kumaon Ke Khaufnak Adamkhor* (Terrifying man-eaters of Kumaon), published in 2010, by Thakur Dutt Joshi, who is known as "Mini Corbett." Bookshops, newsstands, and sellers of pirated books on footpaths carry the original Corbett's books. There are T-shirts, mugs, notepads, and even a tea towel with Corbett and his big cats printed on them.

To understand how leopards and tigers live in certain spaces—whether in a specific region or in urban areas generally—then, is to also understand these very particular legacies. On the one hand is the afterlife of the white colonial hunter/conservationist Corbett, who continues to enthrall long after his departure from India and his death with his sensational stories of man-eaters. Much has been written on the fundamentally imperial nature of Corbett's actions (e.g., Das 2009). More generally, Shresth (2015) has shown how the colonial hunt was central to a paternalistic, imperial ideology that produced the figure of the hunter-administrator or sahib.[9] What is less commented on is how a sahib-shikari like Corbett *continues to inspire* men in postcolonial India to act like him when it comes to both the conservation of big cats and the protection of native lives from the reigns of terror of man-eaters. This peculiar simultaneity of professing a "love" for big cats but feeling compelled to kill the crooked ones in order to discharge a masculinist, paternalist, protective due, which Corbett epitomized, is very much there within the new Corbetts, mini Corbetts, native Corbetts, and Corbett wannabes. In sum, what endures is not just the ghost of the sahib from the British Raj but also the disciplining of space and the imposition of the supposedly scientific and rationalized practices of counting, categorizing, classifying, and governing people, nature, and the animal kingdom.

Living with Leopards in Mumbai

Mumbai has the densest population of leopards and humans living in proximity to each other in the world (figure 6.2). The Sanjay Gandhi National Park (SGNP) that lies within the megalopolis is said to have had a population of forty-seven adult leopards in 2018, according to a study released in March 2019.[10] The levels of conflict, or the crookedness of big cats in Mumbai, have fluctuated over time. So much research has been done on Mumbai leopards and they have been featured so often in the media that the story is one that narrates itself.[11] I first heard it from a journalist who is a wildlife enthusiast and photographer over chai at a dhaba in Aarey Colony. Aarey Colony, also known as Aarey Milk Colony, is a neighborhood in a suburb of Mumbai called Goregaon (East). It adjoins SGNP and has been the site of many human-leopard encounters, including several deaths in the recent past. The journalist and his two close friends started laying out the entire story of leopards in and around Aarey. Slowly, a crowd gathered around us, with people chipping in to the narrative here and there. I tried to keep up with the pace of the tale by jotting quick notes in my diary. When the storytelling ended after more than three hours, one elderly man from the largish group that we had by now spontaneously become said to me, "It is all politics, just politics."

As I read more secondary literature from Maharashtra and interviewed other prominent actors on the "leopard scene in Mumbai," as a student put it, it became evident that a particular narrative has stabilized around human-animal relations here. The leopard scene in Mumbai has been

6.2. A fiberglass tiger spotted in a Mumbai suburb.
Credit: Mumbai Paused

interpreted quite comprehensively by now, not just in popular media and through documentaries but also by academics. Landy (2017), for instance, considers the leopards to be heuristic animals that unsettle nature/culture dichotomies as well as spatial categories of urban/rural even as they help us rethink both the types of actors in Mumbai and the space of the metropolitan city of the twenty-first century. Ghosal and Kjosavik (2015) study the Mumbai leopards for the light they shed on moral and social relations in the region and the modernity of conservation that shapes leopard-human relations; both sets of relations coexist in negotiated tension with each other within fields of power. I briefly regurgitate the account that was narrated to me by the spontaneous collective that first day in Aarey not to endorse or critique it but to note that this is becoming a stabilized account of the Mumbai story. I re-present it here as another one of the beastly tales that we are telling ourselves on relations between humans and big cats and the sharing of space. This tale is becoming part of the historical narrative of how Mumbaikars came to, as it is now commonly said, "live with leopards."[12]

Central to the Mumbai leopards story is the narrative that the adivasis who have inhabited the region in and around Aarey for a long time are the ones who are most able to live with leopards peacefully. They practice what Greenough describes as a form of "interspecies accommodation" (2012, 337). They know, for instance, that the leopards prey on dogs and other pets, are attracted by litter, and are nocturnal. They also worship a god called *waghoba/vaghoba* who is in the form of a leopard or tiger (Athreya et al. 2018) (figure 6.3). The word *bagh* or *vagh* is Sanskrit for "big cat" and is used for tigers, leopards, and lions indiscriminately. This narrative of the indigenous inhabitants living peacefully with big cats is dominant in much of the literature, be it South Asian or African. In recent times, this narrative of

6.3. A waghoba idol.
Credit: ProjectWaghoba.in

peaceful coexistence is being disturbed, with diverse authors locating several reasons for this perturbation, including transformations in regional rural economies (Margulies and Karanth 2018) and climate change (N. Mathur 2015). More generally, the imaginary of indigenous communities living in peaceful eco-harmony with nonhuman animals has also been questioned for its romanticism and lack of consideration of historical change.

To return to the Aarey story, a disruption to this living-beside is said to have been posed by the arrival of immigrants who are new to the landscape and ignorant of the mores of the natives, human and nonhuman alike. In Mumbai, this disruption is linked to the immigrants from neighboring states who were "illegally" settled in and around Aarey by the right-wing political party the Shiv Sena in order to gain vote banks. It is electoral politics, with the need to get more votes, that has, in this one telling, changed the local human dynamics with leopards. The newcomers to Aarey are not aware of how one lives with leopards and are, in particular, careless with their waste (the trope of "dirt" was consistently invoked by the old-timers in my interviews). The littering and the absence of a deep-seated knowledge of other animals in the region lead to unfortunate encounters with the beast.

The poor immigrants are problematic, but perhaps they are not as bad as the middle classes and the corporate groups, with their greed for green land and their hatred of the wild in their own backyards. There is a campaign to "save Aarey Colony," which was originally conceived of as a green space and a dairy colony at the outskirts of Mumbai. As the city expanded exponentially, this outskirt became incorporated into the megalopolis, with important landmarks like Film City and the Indian Institute of Technology Bombay coming up near it. Big corporate actors, like the Ambanis of Reliance Industries and the Adani group, are vying for this green land to develop industries. The upwardly mobile middle and upper classes also have made residential buildings, and the super rich are constructing weekend bungalows in the vicinity of the green belt. All of these actors want an animal space and a human space to be very clearly demarcated within this area. SGNP can and in fact should house leopards that can then be observed during safaris as the beautiful, charismatic animals that they are. However, they should not be allowed to escape or stray out of this space into the human habitations, which should be expunged of all signs of the "wild." The middle and upper classes want the wild and "nature" to be separated out of their own urban residential lives. When a leopard is sighted or, more egregiously, when it kills/eats a pet dog, then there are outcries and complaints to the builders. In the conservationist discourse it is the middle classes, the immigrants who are unsocialized to big cats, and the industrialists' greed for land—which will inadvertently displace the animals and lead to interspecies conflict—that are causing problems in and around SGNP.

What perturbs this neat categorization is the presence of big-cat lovers within these groups that would appear, at first sight, to be hostile to the animals. In the other two cities discussed here, Dehradun and Shimla, conservationism is undertaken largely through the work of organizations such as animal rights groups or through a few well-known individuals who tend to have a background either with NGOs or the government and now spend time conserving big cats. One of the most fascinating aspects of big cats in Mumbai is the presence of a large number of citizen conservationists. These include journalists, foresters, NGO workers, tiger and big-cat lovers, students from the different universities in Mumbai and adjoining areas, and even just regular people who live in the neighborhood of big cats. The organization Mumbaikars for SGNP (MfSGNP) has been very effective in bringing these diverse actors together and in working with the forest department to find workable methods of living with leopards.

In addition to the citizen conservationists are prominent big-cat lovers who dot the cityscape.

The national park is named after Indira Gandhi's first son, Sanjay, who is widely considered the brains behind the Emergency and whose excesses against humans are well documented. During the Emergency, he initiated the compulsory sterilization plans and the forceful resettlement of the poor. Yet, he—like his mother—is a known animal lover, proving paharis right in their claim that certain people can love big cats and simultaneously have the utmost disdain for humans.[13] Similarly, Uddhav Thackeray, the leader of the right-wing Hindu nationalist party Shiv Sena, is another prominent photographer and wildlife enthusiast. Thackeray is currently chief minister of Maharashtra, is a renowned big-cat lover, and has undertaken several measures to conserve wildlife in the state. Finally, the charismatic personality of a particular Indian Forest Service (IFS) officer who was posted as field director of SGNP for a while is marked out as having made a difference in conservation. This officer believed, much like the other conservationists in Mumbai, that human-leopard conflict is caused by human actions and has nothing to do with the leopards. Therefore, if humans adapt to living with leopards, then conflict will be avoided, if not entirely eliminated. A series of training programs was set up to sensitize local residents and the media in how to coexist with and report on leopards, respectively. Everyone in Aarey noted the care that this IFS officer put into the lives of leopards in the region under his control. He was said to know the names of those in captivity and checked in on them regularly. He would remember if one needed extra attention or if one wasn't eating properly and would make sure to look them up in the rehabilitation center.

One of the many ways in which the narrative around leopards has been shifted in Mumbai is by the words and actions of these prominent individuals and the labors of the citizen conservationists. Mumbai is also the home of the Hindi film industry, and several Bollywood stars have lent their weight behind big-cat preservation programs. In 2011, a leopard from SGNP decided to visit the bungalow of one of India's biggest actors from the 1970s, Hema Malini. Her house is located close to SGNP, and one morning a domestic worker entered it at 5 a.m. to find a leopard lolling in the lobby. He immediately locked the door and called the forest department and the police. As this leopard had the temerity to stray into the house of the heroine who was popularly known as "Dreamgirl" for her beauty and acting chops, this became a big news item. The leopard was apparently trapped inside the house for over six hours, till it managed to escape back into, one assumes, the national park. The most interesting aspect of this incident of a big cat straying into the city was not how this news item went viral—again, attesting to the hierarchies of space and persons with regard to when a leopard or tiger is considered as going beyond the pale or the moment the big cat becomes *badtameez*. The most intriguing aspect of this was the interview that Malini gave to a news channel. In it she went counter to the TV anchor's concern about her well-being to state bluntly that she and her family are fine but she is more worried about the leopard. She noted that SGNP had been set up by the government to protect (*suraksha ke liye*) leopards, but the government is utterly failing in this objective. The poor leopard has nowhere to go as more and more land from SGNP is being sold off to humans. Malini also claimed, in a particularly astounding sentence, that she wished she had been home to look after the leopard (*tendua ki dekh bhal karti*). She criticized the government for not taking adequate measures to protect leopards who were now so hungry and lost. Malini is herself a politician and belongs to a political party, the Bharatiya Janata Party, that is different from the then-ruling party in Maharashtra, the Shiv Sena. So part of her blaming of the government for being unable to look after and protect big cats might emerge from this position. As the gentleman in Aarey had told me on my very first day there, "it's all politics, just politics."

I have to end this section on Mumbai though by recounting one of my favorite leopard stories that was told to me by several people, including one woman who heads a respected tiger and leopard conservation organization. This is the tale of the scratching bagh. Apparently, for many years there was a very friendly leopard that lived in Aarey (figure 6.4). When early morning walkers or joggers would be out and about, this leopard would leap out from

6.4. Leopard strolling the alleys of Aarey Colony in Mumbai, captured by a camera trap. Credit: Nayan Khanolkar

behind the bushes and playfully scratch their legs and then dash back again into hiding. It was a big leopard but acted like a little kitten. The scratches were never anything serious, just her way (everyone assumed it was a she) of reaching out to humans to show her interest and/or affection. This story has been recited to me by so many people in Mumbai that it really ought to be somewhat true. I find it hard to imagine a leopard playing scratching games with morning walkers and joggers and the latter being unperturbed by these beastly games. Yet, this story—much like Hema Malini's lament at being absent from home when her feline guest visited, or anecdotes of the loving care with which the former director of SGNP looked after every individual leopard in his custody—suffuses the landscape of Mumbai. The relatively recent rise of digital photography—amateur and professional—and the use of camera traps are only deepening this sense that in this megalopolis, one can in fact learn to live with leopards and not just love them in the distant wild or a safe zoo.

The Old and the New in Shimla

Finally, we move to a city in which encounters between big cats and humans are widely considered unremarkable. Shimla is currently the capital city of the Himalayan state of Himachal Pradesh. It used to function as the summer capital of the British Raj and, therefore, possesses good infrastructure, such as roads and rail connections and lavish constructions in Tudor and neo-Gothic styles (Kanwar 2004; Pubby 1988). These colonial-era constructions continue to dominate the city, making it India's most popular tourist destination in the Himalaya. In the last two decades, the city of Shimla has witnessed a large urban expansion outward, with middle- and upper-class Indians buying cottages and high-rise apartments and constructing bungalows that function as either retirement homes or summer getaways.

I went to Shimla with a team of wildlife biologists, conservationists, and photographers who were—in collaboration with the forest department in Shimla—undertaking a leopard census of the city. Big cats in India are now being counted through the use of drones and, most commonly, camera trapping. A camera trap is a remotely activated camera that is equipped with a motion sensor or an infrared sensor or uses a light beam as a trigger. Set up in strategic locations, camera traps are able to—through their photographic evidence—provide excellent data on movements, numbers, habits, density, and so on of big cats. The study indicates that there are approximately nine individual leopards in the city of Shimla at the moment. The human population is approximately 180,000.[14] As the total area of Shimla is about twenty-five square kilometers, this makes for a fairly dense leopard population, and, hence, sightings of the animal are fairly frequent.

Most of the residents of the city—or, more specifically, those who have lived there for long and those hailing from villages in the mountains—are not particularly perturbed by the sight of a big cat strolling around. The same cannot be said for the new entrants to Shimla, especially the retirees and the summer homeowners (most of them coming from the metros) who are not all equally sanguine. In the first place, they are unused to seeing wildlife in their own backyards. This shock that urban dwellers express at seeing big cats out of the supposed wild and this belief that the big cats are "straying" out of their own territory have been noted for the metropolis of Mumbai as well. In Shimla, it is not just that the recently arrived, well-heeled urban dwellers are disturbed by the presence of big cats in proximity to them, it is also that they are *seeing* the cats in a different way. A large number of them have installed security cameras in their bungalows or in the housing societies that they live in. The regular appearance of leopards in the CCTV imagery has, according to the forest department, led to an exponential increase in complaints against the leopards over the last seven to eight years. It is worth pointing out that there have been no deaths by leopards in Shimla in recent times and there has been only one case of an actual attack. The young man who had been mildly hurt by a leopard—a few nasty scratches—said that he had been listening to music on his MP3 player as he walked through a forested shortcut at night and was not paying attention to his environment when he "tripped over" a sleeping leopard. He considered this skirmish his own fault and was, in fact, somewhat apologetic for having scared the leopard and for having caused a bit of a kerfuffle.

Despite the complete absence of conflict—defined as unprovoked attacks on or injuries or deaths of humans—for a thin sliver of Shimla residents the very sighting of a leopard in their midst is a cause for worry. For them, this is an animal out of place. It has, as they say, "escaped" or "strayed away" from its prescribed beastly place that is a jungle or even a village and mistakenly or cheekily entered their historic city space.

The most common reaction to a leopard sighting is to pick up the phone to lodge a complaint with the forest department. Shimla City has a twenty-four-hour emergency help line that you can ring in order to report either the uprooting of trees or the sightings of leopards—admittedly two common problems, even though they appear somewhat different. The bunching together of these two complaints also attests to the relative banality of a leopard sighting: it is much like a tree being uprooted on your street. The complaints register notes the name of the complainant and the time and place of the leopard sighting, and has a separate column for the specific grouse.

The forest department responds to a chosen few complaints by installing cages with some sort of live bait—such as a dog or goat—in them to trap the big cats. Most of the time such trapping doesn't work, much to the relief of the forest department officials. In fact, they oftentimes position the traps poorly in the hope that they do not capture the leopard. If they do, unfortunately, capture the leopard, then it is sent to a zoo or a rescue center. According to guidelines issued by the Ministry of Environment and Forests (2011), a leopard cannot be kept in captivity for over thirty days unless it is proven to be dangerous to human life. As none of these leopards have been thus convicted, they are released back into the jungles adjoining Shimla within thirty days. In other words, within a month of capture these cats come right back to their homes, which we are learning—thanks to new visual technologies and human storytelling—tend to be as much on the fringes of urban areas as in the perceived wild of India. The officials have been reluctant to capture the leopards partly because they have been made nervous by the Wildlife Protection Act and assorted guidelines, but also because they have found the whole exercise a bit pointless as, in the end, the leopards, being territorial animals, will return straight back to Shimla, only now they will be—as one of the officials put it—more grouchy and grumpy (*khadoos*).

As I ran through the complaint register of the past five years, it became obvious to me that the forest department ignores most of the sightings other than, broadly, two sorts. The first is when the complainant is a person who possesses powerful contacts with politicians and bureaucrats, especially when they have some form of evidence of the leopard's regular movements in their immediate vicinity. The death of a domesticated pet dog appears to particularly provoke a response—that is, the placement of a cage near the dog's owner's home. Normally, however, the forest department responds only when there is a huge spike in telephonic grievances. There was one day when there were ninety-six complaints registered within four hours. The incident that set this off was that a leopard was sighted near the meeting place of the legislative assembly. Not only is this building located in the historic heart of the city—on the Mall Road around which the colonial city was constructed—but also the leopard's appearance was seen as particularly audacious. In an interview I was told this incident was widely described as that of "a big cat knocking at the door of the temple of democracy." Even those who were otherwise unperturbed by leopard sightings in the city seemed to object to this appearance of the big cat, for this was going a bit too far. The forest department appeared to agree, and not one but four cages were put up around the legislative assembly building to trap the leopard. Duly trapped, the leopard was sent to a zoo and now resides there, having gained fame as the *Vidhan Sabha-bagh*, or the "legislative assembly leopard."

Another person we spoke to said that he had been walking home one day at dusk when he encountered a leopard at a corner and, remembering what his grandmother had said to him about what to do when meeting a leopard or tiger in the wild, played dead. He shut his eyes and lay down like a corpse. After many agonizing minutes had passed, he opened his eyes in the hope that the cat would have gone. Instead he was looking straight into the inquisitively innocent eyes of a leopard! He screamed in shock, which scared the poor leopard, and it bounded away.

In the series of interviews I did alongside the research team in Shimla, I was struck by how a question on leopards would immediately be answered by a deflection to monkeys and dogs. There is a huge "monkey menace" in Shimla; the problem is of aggressive rhesus macaques and langurs that snatch food and intimidate and even bite humans. This monkey menace, it is now widely acknowledged, comes from the issue of their translocation as well as their feeding by tourists (see also Govindrajan 2018). It is genuinely a big problem, especially in certain parts of the city, such as around the Mall Road, which is also chockablock full of tourists. Leopards also pose a threat to humans, not so much because they attack humans as because they tend to pick up domesticated dogs. Many people mentioned the loss of either their own pets or the pets of someone they know to leopards and how it broke their heart. In Shimla, much more starkly than in Dehradun or Mumbai, the relationship between leopards and dogs and the separate issue of the monkey menace are much more at the forefront than a more straightforward conflict between humans and big cats. It is an interspecies relationship that the mention of a leopard brings out, not the animal itself or a relationship to humans that is unmediated by another species.

Space figures strongly in Shimla when it comes to questions of what sort of a leopard one is and whether it should be captured or not. This involves not just ideas of urban space but also ideas of the private and the public as well as sacred spaces. The clips of leopards walking around one's well-manicured garden are deeply troubling for many upper-class residents. When the same beast is spotted in other public spaces, it becomes semi-comical. Thus, there are some grainy images of a leopard sitting at a bus stop as if it were waiting for a bus, and one near a bank as if it were waiting to withdraw cash from the nearby ATM. These images, which circulate furiously in WhatsApp messages and as newspaper items, acquire humor; they become objects of public comedy rather than of the fear or anger seen when the private space is transgressed. However, the entry of a leopard into certain public spaces too can become—as the case of the legislative assembly leopard demonstrates—a transgression. There are some public spaces, such as the sites where democracy in India is enacted, that must remain sacrosanct.

†

Mumbai is intriguing, to my mind, not for the huge population of leopards that live cheek-by-jowl with humans but for the way in which this sharing of space has changed character over time. It has moved from sudden spurts in attacks on humans to an equanimous coexistence that is now increasingly coming to characterize Mumbai. This story opens up the possibility and hope of living-beside between humans and predators in almost unimaginable terms. It shows that we can learn to live with predators in our backyards, and organizations such as MfSGNP can lead the way in this. As the climate breakdown becomes more evident in a variety of ways—from droughts to famines to floods to big cats in the city—in India, it becomes increasingly important to be conscious of the difference that collective human actions can make. Beastly tales are not static but can and do shape-shift depending on how humans—and big cats—think, feel, respond, and act.

Similarly, it is important to consider the case of Shimla as one in which there is an absence of anything that can be described as conflict, and where the real predatory behavior comes from the rhesus macaques, which would be widely considered less dangerous. In Shimla—much like in Mumbai—the classed nature of the response to leopards is also instructive; it is the elite and the middle classes from urban areas who are uncomfortable with sighting leopards and are most enraged when big cats attack or carry away their pet dogs. The local state has responded to their grumbles in an evenhanded manner thus far, taking care to not kill or even capture unless strictly necessary. The human-animal relationships that emerged in Shimla are those between humans, leopards, pet dogs, and monkeys. Leopards in Shimla cannot be grasped outside of their predations of dogs and the distinct story of monkeys that have gone rogue due to tourist behaviors and the monkeys' translocation to the Himalaya. In this multispecies world, it is also worth holding onto the many accounts of people encountering a leopard in their everyday work and life and simply walking carefully away, or the stories of the curious friendliness with which some leopards might regard humans. The banality of these interspecies encounters, ones that are described with a nonchalant shrug of the shoulder as just an everyday encounter in this picturesque hill station, is what I wish to remember. Shimla posits an alternative to Mumbai as it has—thus far—entirely avoided the entrance of the word "conflict" and the turning of a leopard into a dangerous alien in the city.

Finally, Dehradun is instructive for its strict adherence to demarcating human territory and nonhuman territory. It is also a lesson in how quickly urban environments can change, as it is only in the last few years that we have seen attacks by leopards taking place. In interviews with residents of the FRI, there was much talk of this sudden spurt of attacks and of the many years during which they would espy leopards walking around the institute grounds while taking care to avoid humans. In this beastly tale, we see the climate crisis and its attendant effects mark an ethnographic entry. We are now coming to finally see climate change through extreme events like flooding, cyclones, and hurricanes. Contributing to the list of the signs of a new geological epoch on a damaged Earth is the literature that points to interspecies tussles over increasingly limited resources and to the change in behavior of nonhuman animals. The entry of feline predators and other nonhuman animals into spaces that they would normally avoid—such as large Indian cities—is beginning to be recognized as a mark of the climate breakdown. The increase and spread of zoonotic diseases, especially after the COVID-19 pandemic of 2020, too are finally being understood as emerging from large-scale ecological damage. In the imagery of climate politics, no animal has become more symbolically charged than the polar bear. If the polar bear drowning due to melting ice is a powerful visual depiction of climate change, so too is the more recent photograph of an emaciated and obviously starving-to-death polar bear. Without access to these animal visuals or the scientific expertise and expert narratives around the climate breakdown, my interlocutors in Uttarakhand have been saying for a long time that leopards and tigers turn on humans—and are doing so with increasing frequency—because there is no other food available to them, because their natural habitats have been wantonly destroyed by humans, and because big cats are angry with humans for killing them in vast numbers.

I have argued that in human attempts to fathom elusive leopards, space comes to serve as a form of evidence. The particular history—lived, architectural, remembered—of a city and the region it lies in and the ever-fluid contemporary politics of apprehending nonhuman others are central to the responses that big cats provoke. Against this wider canvas of the city space are the more micro processes through which big cats come to be adjudged. It is through where and when the big cat is sighted that a knowledge of its nature comes to be gleaned. As this comparison of three cities shows, it is not the cat's actions per se but rather its entrance into classed, historically constituted locations that allows humans to draw conclusions about what this animal is really like. Finally, the role of individuals—humans and big cats alike—is also critical. Individual humans and their colonial legacies or conservationist drive or discursive framings figure prominently in the processes through which big cats come to be apprehended as particular kinds of beings. Simultaneously, the personalities of individual big cats—the panoptic leopard, the scratching leopard, and the legislative assembly leopard—with their idiosyncratic appearances and highly individualized character traits help congeal imaginaries of our nonhuman urban co-residents.

SEVEN

Entrapment

This chapter forges connections between the visceral emotions that emerge from new ways of seeing nonhuman animals and the remaking of ethico-legal formations. It all began with a field trip in 2015 to a big city. I had accompanied a group of people who were involved in a new camera-trapping project to the sites where the equipment had been set up. These were extremely high-tech infrared cameras as they were owned by a wealthy Western organization with the resources to purchase them. At one point, a member of our group requested that I sit on a specific ledge so that he could take my photograph. He was, somewhat uncharacteristically, very particular about the location and angle and even the tilt of my head. I nevertheless went ahead and posed as he bade me do. He took the picture on his phone's camera and then, grinning, pulled out his tablet from his satchel. Opening a file, he juxtaposed the device next to the photograph he had taken of me minutes ago on his phone and showed them both to me. I let out a huge gasp of shock, and everyone in our group burst into laughter. What I was seeing was an image of a huge leopard sitting on the very same ledge I was currently perched atop. The date and time at the bottom of the tablet image showed it to be from two evenings back. Somewhat uncannily, the leopard had been captured in a manner that appeared, to my shocked mind, very akin to my own slightly self-conscious pose. I still remember the chill that ran down my spine when I saw those two images side by side. Once the shock subsided, I too joined the rest of the group in laughing. This chapter is about such gasps of shock and horror, chills down the spine, laughter, and even tears that are direct products of new technologies like camera traps, CCTVs, and smartphones that are aimed at capturing images of big cats.

In this chapter, I ask what happens when we see a big cat through the medium of something like a camera-trap photograph or CCTV footage, means of observing and visually encountering big cats that are relatively nascent. Seen by many as the future of conservation, these new technologies for visually capturing animals are proliferating. In the process, they are unleashing a range of emotions—from love and awe to revulsion and fury—that are often overlooked in the technocratic desire to know more about our nonhuman counterparts. What also remains unremarked on is how new forms of secretive and elite knowledges are being created and how this raises troubling ethical questions of who comes to know what about our feline neighbors and who doesn't. These questions are quickly becoming tied to new legal pronouncements, the repercussions of which are potentially far reaching. The technological means of seeing and, thus, feeling and knowing big cats are, I argue, deeply implicated in the production of emergent ethico-legal regimes that might come to conclusively change our relations with nonhuman animals. Many of the ethical conundrums and legal potentialities of the use of new visual technologies for entrapping nonhumans are just on the cusp of emerging. There is no saying where and in what directions they will eventually lead; here I merely open up some of the ethical and legal questions that these new ways of seeing nonhuman animals are posing. The Anthropocene and the era of extinction that we are living in bring with them new possibilities for the remaking of animal ethics and law. This remaking relies closely, I contend, on varying emotive responses to visual encounters of the nonhuman world (e.g., N. Mathur 2020).

Seeing a big cat is perhaps the most direct way of knowing one. Donna Haraway (1990) early on analyzed images of primates in *National Geographic* magazine to argue that they were produced by race, gender-coded roles, capital, and empire. She reads the images through an analysis of the working of the magazine and the desire of the National Geographic Society to popularize science through depictions of travel and "naked-eye science" that convert readers into voyeurs (1990, 157–60). Bill Adams (2020) has recently examined what he terms "digital animals" through the forms of data that tagging and other surveillance technologies open up about nonhumans. Importantly, he notes that the digitalization of animals "may involve the creation of new digital lives, which have no analogue in nature." Adams is concerned with how nonhuman nature is sensed no longer directly but rather via the medium of technology (of surveillance or visualization), leading to a potential breakdown in the distinction between that which is animal and that which is machine. In this chapter my interest is also in the increasing sensing—seeing—of big cats via new digital technologies. However, this does not lead me to argue for the increasing domination of digital animals (as opposed to flesh-and-blood animals in the real world), *pace* Adams. On the contrary, I argue that these digital technologies produce a whole gamut of intense emotions that are silently but effectively shaping the near futures of the nonhuman.

A striking theme in the visualization of animals is the foregrounding of their pain and suffering. Peter Singer's pathbreaking *Animal Liberation*, for instance, makes its argument against speciesism and for the ethical treatment of animals through text that conjures disturbing images of the tyranny of humans over nonhumans.[1] Animal suffering is now being widely studied, with Barbara King, for instance, looking at animal emotions and animal grief through a study of various modalities, including "videotaped evidence," to argue, along with scientists, that "more animal species think and feel more deeply than we'd ever suspected" (2014, 3). Naisargi Dave in her work with animal rights activists in India has picked up on the recurring motif that activists identify of seeing and hearing the suffering of animals. She is interested in thinking about "the idea of witnessing as distinct from merely seeing" animal suffering. To witness "means to see in a manner that is present, to root themselves when they might rather run or turn away" (Dave 2014, 440). Miriam Ticktin et al. (Multiple Mobilities Research Cluster 2017) notes that the visualization of animal suffering in, on, or against border walls does manifest the deadliness of such walls for nonhuman animals. Yet, the compassion that nonhuman animals are able to evoke in photographs through a complex mix of innocence, cuteness, and individual suffering is *not* transferable to human subjects.

There is, in short, a rich and growing literature on the visualization of animals, especially of animals grieving or suffering in some way. But what about those moments when we see nonhuman animals—especially extremely elusive ones like big cats—in unexpected yet banal ways? In other words, what does it mean to see big cats not in pain or as victims of human depredations but as other types of beings? Camera traps, smartphones, and security cameras are allowing for this new form of seeing that I describe here as a form of entrapment.

A camera trap is an automated digital device that takes a flash photo whenever movement of some form triggers its infrared sensor. They came into prominence in the late 1980s, once the technology had adequately developed.[2] In India, camera traps are increasingly replacing pugmark monitoring, especially when it comes to taking censuses of tigers, leopards, and lions.[3] The camera trap, as an article lauding its achievements has noted, "has revolutionized wildlife research and conservation, enabling scientists to collect photographic evidence of rarely seen and often globally endangered species, with little expense, relative ease, and minimal disturbance to wildlife."[4] Indeed, "digital conservation" (Arts, Van der Wal, and W. Adams 2015) is now all the rage, and camera trapping is particularly singled out as the future of conservation. Unlike radio collars or other forms of physical tagging devices, camera trapping is nonintrusive and provides all sorts of data ranging from animal habits and movements to population counts to, in some remarkable cases, the identification of new species or the rediscovery of a species thought to be extinct. For elusive animals or those considered "shy," camera trapping has proven to be a particular boon (e.g., Karanth 1995). It has allowed for the proliferation of an argument for seeing animals as they *really are;* these clandestine cameras are allowing us a peek into the animal kingdom in a manner that wildlife photography and documentary filmmaking—with their photoshopping and editing as well as deliberate chasing and stalking of the subjects—have not been able to achieve.

The benefits of camera trapping are genuinely tremendous. In conservationist literature, there is a utilitarianism that underlies the seeing of endangered animals, especially the seeing of their secret lives. This seeing becomes a means of better protecting them, not just from poaching and hunting but also by devising new ways to make a space in the world where they can flourish—ranging from captive breeding to marking out bigger protected territories. Yet, the conservationist enthusiasm for new technologies misses out on the ethnographic side effects of these new practices of entrapment. These effects include gasps of shock or awe and excited or nervous laughter at the beholding of certain visuals. But they also include an elite secrecy enjoined by the newfound knowledge of the hitherto hidden lives of big cats (figure 7.1). New questions are being opened up—ethical and political questions about whether we should share novel bits of information revealed by camera-trapping exercises, and with whom. Simultaneously, legal questions related to the copyrights and ownership of these images and knowledges are emerging as we ponder the question of the legal personhood of the nonhuman in the Anthropocene.

The literature on digital conservation also elides what other forms of visualizing and seeing nonhuman animals are doing to human-animal relationships. Smartphones, with their in-built cameras and capacity to upload files instantaneously to social media, and security cameras, with their often accidental capturing of nonhuman animals, are distinct from the project of camera trapping. The former are amateur forms of photography or videography and do not, in general, have the intentionality of science or conservation behind them. The latter is much more purposeful about using scientific knowledge to better human-animal relationships, prevent extinction, and protect endangered species. Yet, both the professional practice of camera trapping and the expansion in use of CCTVs and smartphones share something critical: they are allowing us to see nonhuman animals and capture their images in a way that is distinct from what has hitherto existed in the form of stylized

7.1. Camera trap image of a leopard wandering onto the porch of a house.
Credit: Himachal Pradesh Forest Department/Wildlife Conservation Society

hunting photo shoots or professional wildlife photography. Furthermore, the ethical issues that they are unleashing share much more in common than is immediately apparent. These are, fundamentally, new forms of entrapping nonhuman animals that I, therefore, study in tandem here.

That Beastly Gaze

Tyger Tyger, burning bright,
In the forests of the night;
What immortal hand or eye,
Could frame thy fearful symmetry?
In what distant deeps or skies.
Burnt the fire of thine eyes?

—William Blake, "The Tyger"

It is impossible to write about seeing big cats without first writing about their eyes that burn bright and the way in which the beastly gaze features in human interactions with them.[5] The Netflix series *Sacred Games* (Kashyap, Ghaywan, and Motwane 2018), based on the novel of the same name by Vikram Chandra (2006), confers a pivotal role to the exchange of meaningful looks between humans and a leopard. The series is centered largely on the life of a Mumbai underworld strongman called Ganesh Gaitonde. In a recounting of his life and the transition from being a regular immigrant from a small village to being a strongman in the metropolis of Mumbai, Gaitonde underscores the role played by a leopard and the messages that were imparted by this beast. In the TV adaptation, the leopard features twice, once in reality and the other in a seeming delirium (though that is never made quite clear). The first time Gaitonde sees a leopard is when he is about to murder an accomplice in the jungle, near a river. Just as he is about to strike the fatal blow, both he and the intended victim hear a rustle in the bushes. Both of them turn to find a gorgeous big cat, what Gaitonde describes as a cheetah in this first appearance, staring down at them. Cheetahs are, of course, extinct in India, and the animal in question is a leopard, but the words *cheetah, jaguar, tendua, bagh,* and *guldar* are often used interchangeably for a leopard and even a tiger. The cheetah looks straight into the eyes of Gaitonde. Gaitonde claims that it was at precisely this moment that he knew he was going to, one day, rule Bombay. It is a moment of epiphany induced by a beastly gaze. This is the very same eye lock that tells hunters whether a big cat is guilty of murder. In this fictionalized account, this gaze becomes a window into what the future holds for a human. In the second appearance of the big cat, Gaitonde is laid up in a hospital with a mysterious illness, with hints given that it is a sexually transmitted disease. He is weak, feeble, and delirious. Again, the leopard—this time correctly described as a *tendua* in Hindi—appears. The cat walks through the hospital with an insouciance and then peers into Gaitonde's room. This time, though, Gaitonde can't hold the feline's gaze; he is too enfeebled by various tragedies in his life and the disease. This incapacity to return the gaze is perceived by him as a sign that all his powers are depleted and he is finished. The leopard, in both appearances, has no intention of hurting the human; rather, the cat is merely communicating a message through its eyes and the capacity (or lack thereof) of Gaitonde to meet the gaze and, hence, know his fate.

A common trope in the narrations of those who encounter leopards and tigers is that the big cat displays a distinct lack of crookedness intermixed with a cool disinterest in humans that is still nonetheless laden with an intimacy that comes through in the eye lock. The human freezes. The big cat regards the human with an unblinking intensity. Then the cat turns its head and walks away. That beastly stare and the amber eyes that burn bright remain etched in human memory and, often, serve as an otherworldly message or a moment of epiphany. The big cat is telling the human something; what the message is varies from person to person. In Berger's reading, there is an element of noncomprehension between "man" and animal when they look at each other that arises from the absence of language, which is able to bridge the abyss between man and man but not man and animal: "No animal confirms man, either positively or negatively. . . . But always its lack of common language, its silence, guarantees its distance, its distinctiveness, its exclusion from and of man" (2009, 14). In Gaitonde's case, there was a confirmation—positively in the first instance and negatively in the second—by the look of a big cat. The absence of language—which philosophers, from Aristotle to Berger, see as the all-critical distinguishing trait between human and nonhuman animals—doesn't preclude vivid communication or the intense intimacy that follows from such encounters.

The intensity of this communication and intimacy increases tenfold when the big cat is encountered in the wild, so to speak. A number of men, women, and children have told me about such accidental encounters from which they came away entirely unharmed, though that moment changed them forever in some way or another. What new technologies are now doing is showing us what that moment might look like. For instance, the cover image I desired for this book—but was unable to obtain for reasons that somewhat ironically mirror the concerns of this chapter—displayed what we know is a commonplace occurrence in those parts of India where humans and big cats closely co-reside. It was from a series of images captured by a camera trap set up by an international animal-features magazine, with a particularly famous wildlife photographer sent in to shoot it. As I don't have these images, let me use words to conjure them up as best as I can: A human is sleeping under a mosquito net. A leopard comes up to his bed. The big cat regards the human with concentration for what appears to be an agonizingly long time, though the photographic marking that notes time shows it to be a matter of mere moments. The cat then turns its head away and walks off.

When this set of four images—man sleeping; leopard regarding him studiously; leopard turns head away; man sleeping on peacefully—was first shown to me by the group of people who had been putting up the camera traps, it was narrated as a moment when the leopard is considering the human as food. The main narrator, who was scrolling through the images with me, read that critical instant, when the leopard averts its head, as a decision that this meal is not of interest. To me, having heard so many stories of similar encounters—or, rather, of even more dangerous ones, as in those where the human was awake and conscious—these photographs tell a different story. This is, I immediately thought, a seedha bagh, not a tedha bagh. It isn't a crooked cat but rather one that is straightforward.

No doubt, other interpretations can be drawn from those photographs. My interest here, though, lies in the fact that these and similar camera-trap-enabled photographs are giving us further evidence, in a visual and highly aestheticized medium, of a fact that we already know—namely, that humans and big cats can and do live in close proximity. One might argue that this close sharing of space is not always known thus, especially when one is asleep. However, humans who live in tiger, leopard, or lion territory use other means to gauge such proximity, especially pugmarks, which are instantly recognizable as those of a specific big cat and can even detail the size and sex of the feline. One of my earliest memories is that of my Nani, my maternal grandmother, reciting this tiger story (*sher ki kahani*). She and my grandfather were living in Ranikhet in present-day Uttarakhand in 1953 in an old colonial bungalow. My mother was two years old and was sleeping in her cot in a room that opened out onto the backyard. My grandmother stepped out for some time, but when she returned she felt something eerie in the room, though her daughter was still sleeping peacefully. She then noticed the trail of a tiger's pugmarks leading in and out of the room. Stepping outside, she and others in the household traced the tiger's movements through the "old" method of tracking pugmarks. Evidently, the tiger came out from a nearby forest, walked into the room where the baby was fast asleep, did absolutely nothing to either her or the room, and then walked out again just as quietly as it had entered. When I would ask my Nani how she knew the tiger had visited my mother, she would say that when she re-entered the room she felt something had shifted in the room; the environment had shifted (*vatavaran badal gaya tha*) in some indescribable way. It was only her affective awareness of this change, her sense that the energy of the room had shifted somehow, that led her to seek and spot the tiger's imprints outside.

Such tiger or leopard tales are legendary in areas where big cats cohabit with humans. Due to dwindling tiger populations, the ones about tigers are no longer as prominent, but they do emerge in often surprising ways. Leopard tales of a familiar sort were told to me with high frequency in Uttarakhand. When the Gopeshwar-wallah bagh had (finally) been hunted down and the seedha leopards were our nonhuman neighbors, I would often spot pugmarks outside my little room; people in the neighborhood would nonchalantly mention the leopard they saw this morning or that afternoon just walking placidly through the bushes. The visual images that camera traps, smartphones, and surveillance cameras are now bringing out do provide one form of stark evidence, but there have always been other forms of intuiting beastly presences. As I noted earlier, one of the ways to know that you truly are an inhabitant of a region, such as the mountains (*pahar*), is when you are able to sense the gaze of a big cat on your back—when that "hard" knowledge produced by camera traps and animal censuses serves as evidence as much as an intuitive feel for space or an affordance that comes from living with the nonhuman over time does. Images from camera trapping and other such methods provide one form of evidence of beastly presences, one that is evocative and available to strangers who don't inhabit the same space. What *is* novel about these images and in need of elaboration is who has access to this knowledge and how they wish to disseminate it or, as the case often is, don't wish to disseminate it.

In the case of the man photographed sleeping under a mosquito net with a leopard watching him, he has never been told about this image or even shown it. Similarly, the adivasis who live in the mud house where the image of the leopard on the ledge was taken, which I opened this chapter with, have never been informed of the big cat's presence there. The sleeping man is, then, not alone in not knowing how close he was that night, and probably on many subsequent nights, if not throughout his lifetime, to a leopard that regarded him with such intense concentration. In another city I worked in, there was another story that revealed the same ethical issues regarding who owns this newfound, camera-trapped knowledge and when/whether one should inform the individuals who have been photographed cheek by jowl with the big cat.

The Man Who Walks with Leopards

When a team of camera trappers was looking for spots to place their cameras in one city, they came across a path that leads to a small lake. The rough path in the woods looked like ideal leopard territory to the team, but as is the norm they went around asking locals if they had ever spotted a big cat. One elderly gentleman who was walking down the path said to the team that he has lived in this area for the past twenty years. Every day at the same time in the evening he takes a walk down this path. In the past twenty years, he has never once spotted a leopard here, even though he has heard plenty of rumors of their existence. He told the team it would be futile to place a camera here. The team members were disheartened somewhat but nevertheless considered it worth experimenting with a camera trap for at least a few days just to see what it might throw up. What they went on to find was stunning. The images from the camera trap showed the same gentleman who had dissuaded them from placing the camera trap walking down at his regular hour every evening. Fifteen to twenty minutes later, they would see a leopard taking the very same path down toward the water. About half an hour later, yet another leopard would appear on the same path. In short, not one but *two separate leopards* were in that area, walked behind the man, and evidently were aware of his presence and that of each other in this territory.

Once again, this person wasn't informed of his ghostly walking companions. The reason given was that it would be too much of a shock and he would get panicked. Also, the leopards weren't hurting the man, so there was no reason to alert him to their presence.

I often think of the two nameless men in these sets of photographs: the man who unknowingly walks with leopards each evening, and the man who quietly slept on as a leopard regarded him studiously for some time. Both images have remained etched in my mind. I dwell on these men not because they are living in breathtaking proximity to leopards without realizing it. Rather, I am made uncomfortable by the fact that I know something they don't about their own lives—an aspect that can, for some, be utterly terrifying.

The reasons for this nondisclosure are complex and vary depending on whom you speak to. The citizen conservationists constantly talked about the importance of not causing panic and stress among the residents of this region. What they don't know will not hurt them, quite literally in this case. A senior forest official I spoke to named a more bureaucratic and preservationist reason for not revealing the images or details of where and when leopards are being habitually spotted: to prevent potential poaching or random killing of the preserved animal. For this forester, it was critical to guard the life of every leopard, and any knowledge that the "locals" might have of the movements, habits, and residences of these protected animals could pose a potential threat to them. Yet another reason was given by some of the photographers and camera trappers helping with the image-taking process—that these images are "owned" by a particular organization, given that the photos were taken by their equipment. So a question of copyright, loosely understood, precluded a wider sharing of the information. This is the case even though the location and placement of camera traps depend profoundly on native knowledge, as I discuss below. These silences on the images as well as the stonewalling I personally encountered when trying to obtain some of them to illustrate this book have imposed a similar censorship on me—I have anonymized the cities and not named the photographers, organizations, and magazines that were involved in these exercises due to the ethical concerns I personally have with such disclosures. The reasons for nondisclosure of visuals are thus very complex. There have been some other cases where the sightings of leopards on camera traps or CCTVs have not been made known, but for somewhat different reasons.

The Leopard with the Penchant for High-End Cars

In one of the cities I worked in, a leopard regularly visits the parking lot of a top five-star hotel, every inch of which is under CCTV surveillance. In numerous clips obtained from these cameras, one sees a rather large leopard who appears to have a penchant for lolling and napping atop high-end Jaguar and BMW cars. The time stamps and dates also show that this is a regular occurrence. The very same leopard arrives at night or around dusk, wanders around the car park, as if interested in the different car makes, and then splays himself out atop an eye-wateringly expensive SUV or luxury car. He doesn't cause any damage at all; he just enjoys the car as a perch to rest atop for a while before he wanders off someplace else. These clips, alongside petitions, were sent to the forest department as evidence of the need to capture this particularly impertinent leopard. While the manager of the hotel was very agitated by this leopard, it caused us—including the forest department officials—much hilarity, especially as the leopard has never hurt anyone or even been sighted by the guests.

There is one instance from when I myself was part of the research team that placed camera traps and never told a specific resident about what we were finding. While there are definite ethical problems with this active nondisclosure, perhaps the details of the case will nuance it somewhat. When I accompanied a team of wildlife researchers on their study of human-leopard relations in another city, we—all women—had a somewhat unforgettable encounter. A resident in one of the posh colonies of the city where we had been getting local reports of leopard sightings and dog disappearances caught sight of us as we were attempting to locate a good spot to place the camera trap. He came up to us to invite us into his house garden. We gladly accepted, as we were always keen to speak to the residents about leopard activities in their localities. When we told him of our mission and the suspicion that there is at least one leopard—if not more—residing in the vicinity, he pooh-poohed our suggestion. Firstly, he pontificated, there are no leopards in India, only jaguars. When the head of the research team, who just happens to be an extremely prominent wildlife biologist, tried to gently tell him that there are leopards in India and that "jaguar" is a term that is often used for them, she was shut down. After he had informed us of the ignorance of seeking leopards when only jaguars exist, he proceeded to tell us that we are mistaking cheetahs for leopards because they look similar. At this stage, I intervened to say that cheetahs are extinct in India due to overhunting in the colonial period. I, too, was quickly informed of how wrong I was, for he had seen, with his very own eyes, several "big kitties" in the city. These "big kitties," said the person we now refer to as "Jaguar Man," are friendly and don't hurt humans, and they also don't eat dogs. By this point, the two young women who were permanently stationed in the city to undertake this research were close to dissolving into a fit of giggles, so neither I nor the head of the research team felt we had the capacity to argue further. We made our exit as soon as possible, but only after innocently inquiring about the area he had seen the "big kitty" in. His account of the big kitty corresponded well with accounts from our other interviewees in the neighborhood, and we eventually found a safe spot to locate the camera trap in.

I then returned to Uttarakhand but was kept entertained for the next two months by emails from the research team in this city; they would keep sending us images that the camera had captured of the big kitty. It turns out that not only did this big kitty eat dogs, but also she had two little kitties with her who would often prance alongside their mother on her evening perambulations and hunts. With each email, we would wonder what Jaguar Man would make of this image or that image and whether these photographs would ever convince him that, in fact, he is living with not one but three leopards in his direct neighborhood.

I did ask the research team if we could release images from the camera traps, but there was much confusion on this as our study had been commissioned by the forest department and, technically speaking, they owned the images. Also, given the total absence of unpleasant encounters between humans and big cats in this area, we were all hesitant to put out visuals that might alter the dynamic of seemingly equanimous cohabitation. So, as with the other cases from other cities, we did nothing other than quietly hold onto the images. We felt a discomfort at possessing this type of knowledge on big cats in the city, knowledge that even its long-term residents could reasonably guess at and intuit but not prove through the very same visual means.

Every case of camera trapping discussed here poses simultaneous questions of legality and ethics. Who owns the images, and when should they feel it is incumbent upon them to release the visuals? The question of who owns the image is one that has provoked considerable debate after a chimpanzee took a "selfie" via a camera trap (figure 7.2). The now-celebrated monkey-selfie case revolved around a photograph that a crested black ma-

7.2. Naruto's selfie.
Credit: Open-access image

caque in Indonesia had taken of himself using the equipment owned by British nature photographer David Slater. The image was used by Wikimedia on the grounds that Slater couldn't hold the copyright to a monkey selfie, and subsequently a bitter legal battle was waged by PETA (People for the Ethical Treatment of Animals), who wanted the macaque to own the copyright to the image. Using the "next friend" principle, which allows people to sue in the name of another person who is unable to do so, the lawsuit entitled *Naruto et al. v. David Slater* became globally famous for the fact that a monkey—named Naruto by PETA—was suing for copyright. PETA claimed that the selfie "resulted from a series of purposeful and voluntary actions by Naruto, unaided by Mr. Slater, resulting in original works of authorship not by Mr. Slater, but by Naruto."[6] In January 2016, PETA and Slater reached an out-of-court settlement, with a joint statement between the two stating, "PETA and David Slater agree that this case raises important, cutting-edge issues about expanding legal rights for nonhuman animals, a goal that they both support, and they will continue their respective work to achieve this goal."[7]

The conferral of legal personhood to animals is already on the horizon, with, for instance, two states in the United States of America considering the well-being of animals during divorce proceedings and considering their interests in custody arrangements. The European Union had already begun to recognize animals as "sentient beings" in 2009 in an article of the Treaty of Lisbon.[8] In 2018 the Uttarakhand High Court passed an order saying that "the entire animal kingdom including avian and aquatic are declared as legal entities having a distinct persona with corresponding rights, duties and liabilities of a living person."[9] These questions regarding the ownership and morality of animal knowledges are beginning to be opened up. This question of what happens when the rights of animals are taken into account and when they appear in courts—literally, as in the case of medieval European courts where they were also executed on scaffolds (Salisbury 2011), or through their human guardians, as happened in the case of Naruto—is one that we will surely be considering in the near future. For the moment, though, let us think about the older anthropological question of knowledge making and who gets to know or, more specifically in this case, who gets to *see* what and who doesn't.

Native Knowledges and Exclusions

The ethical conundrums around who owns images that have been taken by a camera trap are perhaps even more complicated than the case of *Naruto v. Slater*. Naruto had picked up the camera and taken his own "selfie." The camera belonged to Slater and, as he claimed in an interview to the *Guardian*, "It wasn't serendipitous monkey behavior. . . . It required a lot of knowledge on my behalf, a lot of perseverance, sweat and anguish, and all that stuff."[10] Camera trapping, too, requires a lot of work. Here I draw out a brief note on what all—knowledge, perseverance, sweat, anguish, and all that stuff, as Slater put it—goes into getting a good image from a camera trap. I draw on my experience of camera-trapping exercises in Uttarakhand, Shimla, and Mumbai, where I accompanied very diverse actors as they set up, guarded, and checked on camera traps and—eventually—attained images of big cats.

I had assumed camera trapping would be a relatively straightforward exercise, for I believed it involved just setting up the camera at some point and then periodically checking in on it. After accompanying different sorts of field researchers—ranging from professional photographers to wildlife biologists to students interested in conservation—in several distinct sites, with their unique geological and demographic makeups, I began to appreciate the complexities of camera trapping. In some cases, the very spot in which you locate the camera trap is inaccessible and deep in the forest. While physically difficult to get to, the site is easier in other respects. For one, you locate the camera trap in certain obvious spots such as near a known den of a tiger or a water body where big cats come to drink or a trail that you know the animal will certainly be treading on at some point. As it is deep in the jungle, the dangers of the equipment being stolen are minimal. It is when you are locating the camera trap in landscapes where there is a significant human population that the situation becomes more complicated. Given that much of my research is in precisely such areas—where humans and big cats jostle for space and resources—the camera-trapping exercises I took part in were vastly more complex.

In most cases, we would begin the process of locating camera traps by looking up forest department records and media reports on spaces where sightings have regularly occurred over the recent past. Utilizing this data, we would narrow down on certain regions where repeat sightings were being noted. We would then undertake a reconnaissance of these locations to sniff out, for ourselves, whether they appeared akin to "big-cat territory" by, for instance, noting any sort of a forest cover or escape tracts to green areas. This assessment of whether a site appears like the habitat of a leopard or even a tiger cannot be narrowed down into a checklist of natural resources or geological features. Much like awareness of the gaze of the big cat on your back, it is something that develops over time. Once we—the camera trappers—were satisfied by the official records and our own intuition of the space, we would begin interviewing the local residents. This aspect of interviewing the natives, so to say, is absolutely vital. Much like in the discipline of anthropology, the role of the "native informant" in constructing knowledge of the big cat is central. It is local residents themselves who are best able to locate spots or paths and identify times and appearances of big cats.

They pinpoint very specific locations as ideal for setting up a camera trap. It is also to them that we must entrust the care of the camera trap, for there is a high risk of theft or vandalism of these fairly expensive pieces of equipment. While in some cases there is the option of locking the camera traps securely in place, in many cases this isn't possible, and besides, oftentimes the lock wouldn't prevent theft. This leads the research team to sometimes place the camera at night in the chosen location and then return the next morning to take it away, making the endeavor rather labor intensive. There have also been cases of researchers locking a camera trap and attaching a lemon, vermilion, and chili to it—objects that are used to ward off the evil eye as well as in rituals of black magic—in order to dissuade theft or vandalism.[11] Often, of course, the vandalism is done by the nonhuman animals themselves, especially big ones like elephants. There are also cases of tigers and leopards vandalizing camera traps.[12] Perhaps the most interesting aspect of all of this, one that points to an uncanny animal agency and knowledge, is that we now have several cases of leopards and tigers artfully avoiding camera traps. Nikit Surve, for instance, who has extensive camera-trapping experience in Aarey and SGNP in Mumbai, told me of certain leopards who appear to know where a camera is positioned and carefully avoid it (though they might be captured by another camera trap that they haven't quite spotted, or tracked through other means, such as foot imprints). Similarly, in the FRI in Dehradun, the residents told me of leopards that would actively go around a camera trap or, curiously, stare into it, resulting in some rather cute leopard selfies.

If the camera is located at a great height or is at an angle or in a location that is totally unnoticeable, the reliance on locals to protect and look after the camera trap is minimized, yet still important. In many cases, we actually placed the camera trap up in the gardens or on the walls of the locals, and in those cases in particular, we relied entirely on them to look after the equipment. In many cases, especially when the equipment is expensive and is being provided by an NGO or a Western wildlife outfit, the locals are paid for their services. In other cases, students are taken on as volunteers to keep checking in on the cameras to see that they are secure and whether they have captured any pictures. Most of these students are interested in conservation and/or photography, and this experience is made to count as an internship of sorts. What is vital though, more so than the exchange of money or goods of other forms or threats of criminal action, is the development of personal bonds of trust between the trappers and the locals.

I saw how these bonds developed over time. We would forge—or try to forge—a relationship with the locals at the point of the first round of interviews during the reconnaissance. Then, once it was decided where we would locate the camera trap and for how long, we would hold consultative meetings or group discussions with all who were living in the vicinity, but especially those individuals whose land we were utilizing for this exercise. We would try to explain to them the value of camera trapping and for what purposes we need these images. Always, the direct gain to the neighborhood would be stressed: this is a way to protect you and to reduce any possibility of interspecies violence; we will compensate you with our gratitude and resources (monetary or otherwise). The relationship would really develop, though, with the repeat visits one made to check on the cameras and see what images were being captured. If the images were good, then there was much jubilation, but when we didn't get anything, then it became even more important to return to talking to our "native informants" to see if we were missing some vital clue that was not letting us get those highly valued images.

The ritual of periodically checking on the cameras and the joy when one does capture—visually trap—a bit of a big cat are incredible. This emotion of excited happiness at the success of getting an image is vital to the entire enterprise of camera trapping and, in critical ways, underpins the profound belief that conservationists have in this technology. In Dehradun, I was involved with some college students who were placing camera traps in a region known for leopards and the occasional tiger. We spent hours walking around the area, which lies just outside the boundary of the Rajaji National Park, scouting out spots and speaking to forest guards and local villagers. For the time I was there, we didn't manage to capture much other than, once, a little bit of a leopard's tail, even though we knew—from the traditional method of examining pugmarks and from eyewitness accounts as well as some wildlife photography—that there were several leopards in this area. Evidently, we were doing something wrong, but what that was eluded us. In Shimla, I noticed how the head of the research team I was accompanying had almost a sixth sense about knowing how and where to locate the cameras. After her visit, the traps that she had only lightly modified the location/angle of started giving us superb images of big cats. I can only put her knack of knowing where and how to locate the cameras down to her long experience and knowledge of the habits of urban leopards as well as her capacity to deftly extract information from the town residents. To come back to our failed efforts outside Dehradun, half a year after my return to the United Kingdom, I spotted a news item in the local newspapers of Uttarakhand that showed an adult tigress wandering around the area. She had been captured in the very same region where we had put up our cameras, but by another set of camera trappers. The tigress's presence was subsequently confirmed by the forest department on the basis of other eyewitness sightings and pugmark impressions. News of the tigress was exciting, but all that we could think of was how we had failed in capturing her with our cameras. The sense of discovery that camera trapping induces is enormous; the joy when you capture an image is immense, as is the melancholy when you miss out on that perfect revelatory shot. Compare this entire process and range of emotions to what happens through the older, more literal method of trapping big cats—in cages.

Alfred Gell made the observation that animal traps are devices that "embody ideas, convey meanings, because a trap, by its very nature, is a transformed representation of its maker, the hunter, and the prey animal, its victim, and of their mutual relationship, which, among hunting people, is a complex, quintessentially social one" (1996, 29). As Corsin Jimenez and Nahum-Claudel have recently noted, the problem with this anthropological legacy is "that they aim to explain how traps work rather than describe the kind of work they do" (2019, 391). But there need not, I suggest, be a distinction between an animal trap as a model of how traps work and the kinds of social relationships and complex entanglements with nonhuman animals that it brings alive. I describe below the materiality and design of cages, the processes and events through which they are pressed into service to trap crooked cats, and simultaneously consider the social-political work they do.

Cages, unlike expensive and sensitive cameras, are normally rather heavy and require multiple people to lug them up often difficult terrains. In the Himalaya, there is always a mad hunt on for cages as they are in short supply. Once one is located—often from a neighboring district or region—then it is transported, with some effort, to what is deemed an appropriate spot. The placement of a cage is not as intricate a matter as that of a camera trap, for it depends on where you can prop the cage up and camouflage it appropriately. Equally important is finding live bait for the trap that would attract the big cat. The bait is normally a kid or a dog that bleats or woofs plaintively through the night. Baiting a trap with a dog is generally contentious in urban areas, as several complaints have been lodged at this usage of nonhuman animals that are considered "cute" and loveable.

Despite the presence of live bait, it is more difficult to trap a leopard or tiger through a cage than it is to capture a photograph with a camera trap. There are several reasons for this, including the fact that the cages are often quite badly designed and rust quite rapidly, leading to the levers not working effectively. I have heard of several cases of a leopard or tiger managing to grab the bait and yet, through some devious means, avoid being trapped in the cage.[13] But even once one has managed to trap the big cat, the next steps involved are complicated—and often dangerous. The operational guidelines for caged leopards indicate that one should tranquilize the leopard and then move it to another vehicle that would transport the cat to a zoo, veterinary hospital, or rehabilitation and rescue center. The tranquilization of leopards or tigers is very complicated. It requires a knowledge of the exact dosage that must be administered depending on the size, sex, and age of the big cat. Incorrect dosage can have serious consequences ranging from being lethal to making the big cat very sick to—as often happens—not knocking the cat out for long enough such that the cat wakes up, furious and woozy, in the middle of the move. I have heard several stories of humans being attacked, bitten, mauled, and grievously scratched because the big cat recovered too quickly from the tranquilization or wasn't affected by it in any way other than by becoming grouchy. Indeed, in my field notes I have put down these stories narrated to me by men—vets or forest officials—who valiantly fought off or survived a tiger or leopard that wasn't properly tranquilized under the heading of "modern-day shikar stories." Much like the shikar stories of yore, these tranquilization and/or capture stories have heroic men at the center fighting off fierce and profoundly unmanageable beasts. The endings of these stories, though, are more complicated; in the hunt it was the man who normally triumphed, whereas here the finale can be somewhat different, with, for instance, a vet left badly injured and the tiger bounding off.

To properly tranquilize a big cat, trained specialists, vets, vehicles, and equipment are required that are not always available. Another factor that often makes trapping a big cat in a cage complicated is the presence of large crowds of humans—what foresters and conservationists refer to as "mobs"—that create added stress on both the big cat and the officials. The officials have to catch or tranquilize the animal amid these vast numbers of people who can generate a lot of noise and who can panic and do things like throw stones at the big cat or assemble too close to the space where the events are unfolding. All of these human actions can make the venture of physical trapping very troublesome. Tranquilization and caging are, even when successfully carried out, not ideal for the stress they cause the big cat. As is now well established, if the big cat is rereleased into the wild or shifted to a new territory, it tends to try to return to its home territory. The saddest fate awaits those big cats that are kept locked up forever in rehabilitation or rescue centers. Overcrowding of leopards is a major problem, as is the issue of not having adequate space and proper food. As someone said to me in Mumbai about a leopard that was captured on suspicions (almost entirely unfounded) of being crooked, "Her life is finished. A creature that could travel thousands of kilometres in her lifetime is now stuck in a ten by ten cage for the rest of her life." Seeing a leopard or tiger trapped in a cage transforms the big cat from the beauteous nonhuman that the aestheticized camera images produce into a raging, maddened beast that snarls and shrieks.[14] This is her angry, shocked, raging, and trapped; this is her before that marginalization that zoos so violently inflict on nonhuman animals; this is her before the zoo brings on that blank, unseeing look and alters her responses and habits (Berger 2009).

Pothead and Wet Leopards

At moments there can be deeply empathetic accounts of interactions between humans and big cats too. One of the most common ways in which leopards, in particular, are reported in the Indian media is when humans come to their rescue when they fall into a well or get stuck in some way or another. The genre of "leopard rescued from well" in India has spawned hundreds of YouTube videos as well as newspaper articles and images of rather bedraggled "wet leopards" and tigers. The rescue stories tend to have a similar arc. A leopard is spotted stuck in a well, normally by humans but in some cases by other nonhuman animals like dogs or, more recently, monkeys.[15] When it is a dog or monkeys to the rescue, they attract human attention by barking or chattering loudly near the well or even by physically fetching a human over by dragging them to see the stuck big cat.

The forest department is informed and/or a group of people come together to find a way to rescue the big cat, as it will be impossible for it to climb out unaided. In some cases, the leopard is tranquilized and a human then goes down via a ladder and either carries the leopard up or has it pulled up through a rope or swing.[16] In many cases, especially when the forest department officials are not around with tranquilization guns, humans lower ladders down or even make them from scratch in order to let the leopard out.[17] Other times, they lower a cage down, and once the leopard has entered it, they are able to haul it back up and rerelease the animal.[18] In a particularly epic leopard rescue, widely reported for its ingenuity, the villagers lowered a bed down a well. With some gentle coaxing, the leopard eventually perched atop the bed, which was then pulled up by villagers. As soon as the bed had reached the rim of the well, the leopard leapt off it and ran away without, as anticipated, causing any harm whatsoever.[19] These stories feature as heartwarming tales against a wider background where humans are constantly being demonized for their cruelty to this endangered species, and offer a perspective on what also could be—a situation of peaceful coexistence in which evidence of interspecies friendship, empathy, and care proliferates. It is important to note that the big-cat rescuers belong to the very same communities of humans—villagers, adivasis, farmers, the poor, those who live on the outskirts of wildlife reserves and forests—who are otherwise vilified in popular accounts for their supposed cruelty to big cats and who are even deemed poachers and hunters.

In the autumn of 2015, a leopard in the Rajsamand District, in the state of Rajasthan, got his head stuck in a pot.[20] Apparently he had wandered into a village seeking water, which he found stored in this pot. He somehow managed to get his head stuck in the pot, and try as he might he could not get it off. A video of the leopard walking around blindly with a pot stuck on his head circulated widely on news networks around the world. Luckily, the forest department managed to tranquilize him after about six hours of having the pot stuck on his head, and then successfully sawed the vessel off. According to official reports, the leopard was none the worse from this pot ordeal and promptly scampered back into the bush. Videos uploaded online show several men who have collected near the leopard and are taking photographs on their smartphones. All the while they make sure to keep a safe distance away from him just in case he manages to free himself and goes back to being a dangerous animal, as opposed to this tragicomic creature that is currently in need of human rescuing. So novel was this image that Buzzfeed put out a quiz on this potheaded leopard that posed "a conundrum about life and death and our roles in both," and asked how would one respond.[21] Fascinatingly, 35,800 people answered, "This leopard did not ask to be a pothead. I shall free the creature of this misery, even if I have to risk my own life. Goodbye, world." This response constituted a whopping 79 percent of the results, with the remaining 21 percent, or 9,762 voters, saying, "Try to save the leopard and serve as its three-course meal? No way, bro. I'm sitting this out." To the extent that one can take Buzzfeed quizzes seriously, especially one about a "pothead leopard," it does demonstrate a familiar trend with online comments when it comes to big cats. Quite clearly, those on the internet are overwhelmingly in favor of protecting the nonhuman animal even if it means sacrificing human life, including—as this quiz asks of you from the security of your vast distance from the pothead leopard—your own.

Seeing That Which You Would Rather Not

And then there are some cases of seeing big cats that you wish you had rather not experienced and would dearly desire to unsee. The image of the half-eaten child that circulated on WhatsApp, which I discussed in chapter 4, is one such example. In that case, however, the child's parents were actively acquiescent in the distribution of the image, and the image helped in the revenge killing that, apparently, was one objective of allowing it to be sent out. Normally, however, images of pet dogs are what is captured. This is a new trend that is emerging out of the increased use of CCTVs and other forms of surveillance cameras.

During the reign of terror of the Gopeshwar-wallah bagh, all the street dogs were closely watched by the neighborhood. As dusk fell, we would make sure that none of "our" dogs were loitering about. I always made sure Sheroo, my beloved Bhotia canine companion, was in my room, even if it meant literally pushing him in like one would push a giant, unrelenting boulder through the door. In the mountains, one knows that dogs are primary fodder for leopards, and, hence, they need to be guarded closely. The distinction between "stray" and "pet" dogs dissolved during that period. While very few people had domesticated dogs—largely those who did were the officials posted in from other parts of the state—the stray street dogs were well looked after in a casually communal manner. One or the other of us would feed them with various leftovers like rotis and, from those who could afford it, milk. The main distinction was that the strays slept on the street and the pet dogs slept inside homes; the latter had collars and leashes and were overall better fed and groomed.

When dogs would vanish, we knew that a leopard had struck. Often we would hear howls in the night or see signs of a scuffle that would tell us a leopard had "picked up" (*utha liya*) livestock or another animal such as a dog. While it was heartrending to hear animal screams in the middle of the night or to hunt in vain for a friendly puppy that had suddenly disappeared, we didn't quite see the act. The arrival of CCTVs is upending this phase of nonseeing by providing some grisly footage. In one city, when I had gone to interview a retired high court judge who had complained vociferously about leopards in the city, we were made to sit down and watch a particular clip that his security camera had recorded. It showed his dog, a fluffy, white, well-fed Pomeranian named Paradise, sitting placidly on a veranda. Suddenly, a leopard enters the frame. Paradise starts and makes as if to run, but the big cat is far too quick for him. The cat grabs Paradise by the neck and drags him, all four legs flailing and a look of sheer terror on his doggy face, out of frame. The former judge, who was in his eighties and evidently very fond of Paradise, made us sit still in his large living room and watch and rewatch that distressing clip on loop. By the fifth time that we saw the clip, I noticed a tear rolling down the cheek of the judge. Wiping away the tear, he began to rage against big cats in general, but especially this evil one that dared to steal his beloved Paradise away from him, and right under his unsuspecting nose in the early evening too. The effect of this unexpected capture by the CCTV was that this gentleman, who has strong personal connections in the state bureaucracy, got a large cage placed near his house in order to trap the offending big cat. The cage was set up by the forest department and stood there for months on end. Much to the chagrin of the judge who still grieves for his beloved Paradise, but luckily for the leopard, the cage remained a useless undertaking and had to be, ultimately, removed.

The unintended effects of the use of security cameras include not just the ability to be able to watch things like a leopard snatching your darling four-legged companion away but also a resultantly increasing demand by privileged citizens to install cages to trap the videotaped culprits. Previously, had the dog vanished—as they so often do in the Himalaya—then a leopard or tiger might have been the prime suspect, but there would have been no evidence that could have been produced for the forest department. So the dog could have gotten lost, been stolen (dognapping of expensive pedigreed dogs is commonplace), been run over, or met with some other regrettable fate such as falling off a cliff. But with the proliferation of security cameras, now there is evidence of a crime and the criminal can be spotted in flagrante. The possession of both a security camera apparatus and a dog as a pet implies that you belong to a thin sliver of the Indian elite. These elite persons' status allows them to make phone calls or use other techniques of petitioning to capture the big cat that has the temerity to enter their private property and mess with their family members.

In Mumbai, the prevalence of CCTVs is creating significant tension in the middle-class and upper-class residential colonies that are located (some would say encroaching) close to SGNP. Given the dense population of leopards next door, it is but natural that big cats will "stray" into these colonies. Most of the time, the cats are not spotted, and when they are, it is in the more communal areas or atop boundary walls. Unsurprisingly, Mumbai has its own fair share of Paradise-the-dog type incidences. For instance, a video clip that has been uploaded to YouTube shows, in breathtaking detail, a leopard slithering into a flat.[22] You see the cat make its way stealthily in till it briefly disappears from view. When the cat reappears just moments later, it is seen dragging out a large writhing dog! The leopard then carries the dog away till they both disappear from view. I often show this clip in my talks on crooked cats, and it never fails to draw a loud collective gasp from the assembled audience, a gasp of the type that I wish to center in this chapter.

The camera in this Mumbai episode was actually a nanny cam that had been put up in order to monitor and make sure that the children of the house were safe. After this clip went viral, there were large-scale protests by residents of the upper-class apartment complex where this event had occurred. The response to the video clip included demands to increase security, raise the walls, and install cages that would capture and relocate the big cat. The demand for capturing big cats in cages and then relocating them far away from the town precincts to an imagined wild is spreading across India. While the very sighting of a big cat by eyewitnesses is enough to bring on the petitions demanding its capture, when there is further evidence of the leopard or tiger actually entering flats, houses, schools, or other types of human settlements, it becomes difficult for the forest department to ignore them. For this reason, the caged capture and relocation of big cats in India is increasing apace. As mentioned previously, there is significant evidence mounting that shows the negative effects of translocation. Instead of the smooth removal of the trouble animal that is perceived to be straying out of its prescribed beastly place, what we are seeing is an increase in crooked behavior by a stressed or injured big cat that has been displaced and seeks to return to its home. In other words, contrary to the celebratory narrative of digital conservation, the proliferation of new technologies can, in certain instances, undermine the wider project of conservation and the inculcation of an ethos of peaceful interspecies coexistence. None of this is an argument against the use of digital methods or the other forms of technology that can provide us with more knowledge and equip us with the means to foster animal conservation. Rather, this is to make an ethnographic case for considering how the unintended consequences of digital technologies that are producing emotions such as shock and anger against big cats can negatively impact the preservation of big cats. These emotions—the gasp of shock, the heartache of seeing that which one could otherwise only guess at—need to be brought front and center in the discussions on conservation, new technologies, and surveillance as much as in the legal battles over animal rights and personhood.

These new ways of seeing big cats produce a range of emotions that go well beyond the project of conservationism, even as they aid our understanding of how big cats live and, particularly, how closely to us they do so. What is intimacy if not the presence of two leopards that walk safely behind a human with a regularized frequency? What is intimacy if not that big cat that so carefully considers the human as he sleeps under his mosquito net, or that leopard that lounges comfortably on the ledge of another person's hut? Similarly, the anguish you feel watching your beloved pet being dragged off by a murderous leopard or the sympathy that is generated for a leopard trapped in a well is what allows us to know this predator with an intensity, albeit through opposing emotions of hate and love.

The question of what happens to these images produced by camera traps or to video clips that are, often inadvertently, captured by CCTV remains open. Uncertainty about the near future is, after all, a key feature of the Anthropocene. One doesn't know what will be, quite literally, tomorrow, but one is constantly guessing at it. So what are the questions opened up by these new forms of entrapment of big cats in India? They include questions about potential legal developments, such as the conferring of rights and legal personhood to animals; questions of science and conservation as they intersect in the race to maintain species diversity and prevent extinction; and ethical and moral conundrums around ideas of "native panic" and sense of safety in a landscape. All three of these aspects require a radical reimagining of what it means to share space with big cats in the age of the Anthropocene. The changing modalities of visualizing the beasts and the range of emotions and visceral responses they unleash in the process are not mere unintended side effects of the new leaps in digital conservation. On the contrary, conservationism and human relations with the nonhuman world will be—and, indeed, already are, as the legal challenges and emergent questions are showing—profoundly reshaped by the seemingly peripheral tears that roll down an elderly man's face as he watches his beloved pet dog being preyed on by the big cat that lives down the road from him.

EIGHT

Three Beastly Tales to Conclude

How does one write a conclusion for a story of which the ending remains uncertain? With the sixth mass extinction underway and the severity of the climate crisis increasingly undeniable, humans find themselves grasping for a language to name and describe the global present and near future (MacFarlane 2019).[1] *Crooked Cats* has presented beastly tales as a modality through which the climate crisis can be comprehended and life in the Anthropocene articulated. It is, therefore, only appropriate to conclude with three more such offerings. We begin with the life story of a crooked cat, a tigress called Avni.

While it might be impossible to rival the fame of the leopard of Rudraprayag, immortalized by Corbett, in 2018 a tigress suddenly and briefly became an international celebrity. Going by the name of Avni (fire), she earned global fame, partly because she was dubbed a "man-eater." In a country where crooked leopards, lions, and tigers aren't uncommon—with several killed or captured annually—this wasn't what set her apart. The reasons for Avni's somewhat unexpected fame lay elsewhere: in the novel method used to bait her. Avni proved remarkably difficult to trap, and, out of desperation, all sorts of tricks were tried to lure her. This included the sprinkling of a Calvin Klein perfume in the belief that she would be attracted to it. Something about this utilization of a high-end designer scent caught the public imagination, and global news outlets such as the *Guardian*, the BBC, and the *New York Times* reported extensively on this case.[2]

I followed the unfolding of the Avni story from afar with fascination. Erica Fudge has remarked that stories about animals form a basis that makes it possible to seek another way of thinking (2002, 16). If the story of the Gopeshwar leopard opened up and set the narrative for *Crooked Cats*, Avni's life and death almost uncannily walk us through each chapter. I thereby provide a brief sketch—a final feline biography—below to remind us of the elements that composed this work and are, once again, reflected in the life of an individual tiger.

The question of whether Avni was *really* a man-eater or not seemed to occupy everyone. So too did the question of whether something like a man-eater existed at all anymore. Avni—also known as T1, in an effort to make her a more scientific and distant subject—was said to have killed thirteen humans in the central Indian state of Maharashtra over the last few months of 2018. Even before she was hunted down, there were strong questions about whether these killings were by the same tigress; the problem of beastly identification was upmost in the minds of many. At the same time as the local state was trying to ID the big cat, there was much public debate over whether these were just accidental deaths rather than deliberate murders by her. In bureaucratic conservationist terminology, were these "chance encounters," or was the big cat "habituated" to making prey of humans?

If the questions of whether Avni was really a man-eater and whether it really was *her* (and not, for instance, some other tiger, or indeed several tigers) were voiced during the hunt, the clamor following her killing was exponentially louder. A former vet who examined her corpse publicly claimed that Avni was not a "man-eater" but a mere "man-killer." This individual said it was obvious that the tigress had not eaten for five to six days before she was hunted down and had she been a real man-eater, she would have found a human prey rather than starve thus. His second objection was a more bureaucratic one, which was that this labeling was done through a flouting of the guidelines issued by the National Tiger Conservation Authority.[3] Here we see, yet again, how the governmental regime, with its legal and bureaucratic bodies that protect big cats, merges with the so-called scientific one, with its examinations that reveal a state of early starvation in the corpse. In turn, they further intersect with a long-standing, historically constituted suspicion of "natives," who would wrongly call an innocent tiger a "man-eater."

Avni was identified through the careful tracking of her pugmarks in the ground. Camera traps were also placed in strategic locations, but good images were hard to come by. The local foresters managed to win a hunting license from the Maharashtra government, which allowed known hunters from the official government-certified board to be called on to try to capture her. If they couldn't trap her in a cage—a notoriously difficult achievement—then and only then was she to be rendered legally killable by the state. As the hunt went on, it became evident to the foresters and others on the ground that it would be hard to catch this tigress, for she was, as most crooked cats are thought to be, exceedingly cunning. In an effort to trap her, the urine of a tiger was sprinkled in areas she had been recently spotted in, all sorts of camouflaged cages were set up, and the now-famous perfume was utilized. All to no avail. Avni was eventually brought down under rather murky circumstances when the son of the official hunter—rather than the certified hunter himself—shot her down. This man, coming from a long tradition of aristocratic hunters from the former princely state of Hyderabad in central India, claimed that he had killed Avni purely out of self-defense and had in fact never intended to join the hunt himself.[4]

We see and remember Avni not through stylized wildlife photography or the more serious-minded camera-trap images but through tragic pictures of her corpse—in the veterinary center being examined, and being carried off jubilantly by the hunters and government officials. These images went viral through news outlets, on social media, and via WhatsApp. These new ways of seeing Avni sparked a nationwide outrage at the killing. Petitions had been written and submitted even before her death—including pleas to the president of India to intervene and give her a presidential pardon that would prevent her from being hunted down. None of them proved to be efficacious, as the numbers of dead humans were piling up. Media exposure only added to a very tense situation in the villages where locals were getting increasingly agitated over the tigress. These petitions became even more strident after her death. Politicians entered the fray to loudly deride the events leading up to the killing of what they considered a beautiful young tigress. They all tweeted their outrage, with some attaching official letters condemning the act. Maneka Gandhi from the Bharatiya Janata Party, who is a Union minister in Delhi and also a famous animal rights activist, described it as a "ghastly murder" and demanded an inquiry into why Avni was not just captured, *if* Avni was indeed a man-eater.[5] Aaditya Thackeray of the Shiv Sena party, who is currently serving as minister of tourism and environment for the state of Maharashtra, tweeted that the central Ministry of Forests (which manages wildlife in India and is based in Delhi) should be renamed the Ministry of Poaching as it is such a sham.[6]

What could have made Avni crooked?

As argued throughout *Crooked Cats*, we will never know for certain but can only guess at the cause. One argument is that Avni is an example of how India has become a victim of her own successes in tiger conservation. This idea arises from a statistic: tiger numbers have increased substantially, from 1,411 in 2006 to an estimated 2,967 in 2018—more than half of the world's population of tigers. This success in numerical terms has led to greater pressure over the sharing of resources between humans and tigers and subsequently an increase in what is described as "human-animal conflict." However, there are several shortcomings to this simple equation of more tigers equals more human deaths by tigers. In the first place, we should take all tiger and leopard census numbers with a grain of salt as there are significant methodological issues with enumerating big cats, and the political pressure to produce higher official numbers is intense in India (Gopalaswamy et al. 2019). More importantly, even if we were to take these numbers as valid, the rise in population shouldn't in and of itself lead to more attacks on humans. Something else has to be at play that would cause Avni—or any other tiger—to go crooked.

Avni was, it is widely agreed, *not* born in a tiger reserve. In other words, she was born in what is called a non-tiger zone, or human space, as opposed to the prescribed beastly place that is reserved for big cats by state edicts. Avni was, in turn, described as venturing onto human land—farms, village outskirts, even the villages themselves—and preying on humans and their livestock. This distinction between land that belongs to humans and land that should be occupied by big cats and other beastly animals is, as this book has argued, an artificial one, especially in a densely populated country like India. It is a bureaucratic construction that has little bearing on how humans and nonhumans actually inhabit a rapidly changing planet. The very birth and life of Avni, as well as of several other tigers and leopards in India, attest to the increasing artificiality of these spatial categorizations and separating out.

There are some landscapes that are, no doubt, human dominated and some that are more amenable to the habitation of big cats. Leopards are temperamentally comfortable in scrub forests and in and around human populations. Tigers are thought to prefer dense forests, but several recent cases—such as Avni's—are counteracting this widespread belief. We are now finding increasing evidence of tigers and leopards in human-dominated landscapes all over India. The responses to sightings of big cats in our cities vary considerably across India, for reasons outlined before. Whatever the response, it is now quite clear that big cats in our urban backyards are not mere aberrations but are here to stay. As urban areas continue to expand out, deforestation continues apace, and minor successes with tiger and leopard conservation are achieved, we should, in fact, be prepared to more openly share space with these charismatic megafauna.

Perhaps Avni was attracted to the Maharashtrian villages she hunted in for the potential prey—humans—within that have become more and more attractive in the wake of rapid biodiversity depletion and habitat degradation. In addition to humans, there were also plentiful cattle available to her, aging cattle that can no longer be slaughtered due to the controversial beef ban that was enacted in the state of Maharashtra in 2015 (Punwani 2015). Cow protectionism is central to the Hindu nationalist agenda, and the Bharatiya Janata Party government in Maharashtra was successful in pushing through this law, which forbids the killing of cows, bulls, and bullocks and even the possession of beef. As several distinct news sources noted, the real prey of the tigress might have been the cattle that the villagers were herding in forests and fields. Humans appeared to be coming between the tigress and the cow—an effect of the beef ban, whereby humans become the prey of a predator in lieu of the bovines. The images of herdsmen wearing "shields" to protect themselves from Avni as they took their cattle toward the forests to graze depict this inversion of the prey-predator relationship. It is also worth noting that Avni had two cubs to feed, which was—it is believed—placing extra pressure on her to hunt.

Leopards and tigers with itineraries that cut through large urban centers are showing the artificiality of the distinction between human land and big-cat land. It is becoming increasingly difficult for us to deny or look away from the effects of climate change. No longer are we seeing climate change only through seemingly distant reports, graphs, activist slogans, or conferences. We can also see it in the smog over north India, read it in the astronomical numbers reported by air quality indicators on our phones, and quite literally taste the acid that is the air on our tongues. Animals, too, are powerfully pointing us to the facticity of the climate crisis. The polar bears that recently "invaded" a north Russian town looking for nourishment are a case in point, as are the bears that are awakening early from their hibernation due to mild winters and, in doing so, increasing the possibility of greater conflict with humans.[7]

Similarly, when we see leopards walking almost to the gates of New Delhi—appearing in the satellite township of Greater Noida[8] or lounging on the golf course in Gurgaon[9]—we aren't seeing an animal that is merely lost or straying. When a tigress such as Avni keeps hanging around humans and, for one reason or another, develops a taste for human flesh, she isn't just one aberrant big cat. Rather, she and other big cats like her are symptomatic of what climate change is doing to our present; they represent a moment when so many of those categories and distinctions that we took for granted—such as tiger land versus human land—no longer apply, if they ever really did. The climate is changing, bringing with it not just dry riverbeds or extreme events but also big cats that are behaving and will behave more crookedly than before. Avni's tragic tale should push us to acknowledge the fact that both the fixity of the world we inhabit and the categories through which we think are no longer tenable.

†

This book, at one level, is about predation in quite a literal sense: the predatory behavior of big cats like Avni who make prey of humans. At the same time, *Crooked Cats* is an invitation to think more deeply about predation in the dual senses of the word—the preying of a living being on another, and the act of looting—and how it might help us understand what it means to live and die in the age of the Anthropocene.

There has been a steady increase in attacks by bears on humans in the Indian Himalaya, similar to the increase in crooked cats. Once again, officials have theorized that this upswing in attacks by wild bears on humans is a consequence of climate change (N. Mathur 2015). The rationale, basically, is that due to global warming, it has now become so hot even in the upper Himalaya that the bears have been "driven mad" (*pagal ho gaye hai*) by the heat. These heat-crazed bears go on to indulge in random and inexplicable acts of violence, such as the mauling of humans and the destruction of human property.

Nonhuman animals attacking, mauling, and eating humans in ever-rising numbers are but one manifestation of life in the Anthropocene. But what of *anthropos itself* as a predator?

In one powerful and polemical reading, climate change is a direct result of the (de)predations of capitalism (Klein 2014). Taking an approach that is somewhat distinct from the universalism of capitalism that figures in Klein's manifesto, *Crooked Cats* has attempted to foreground the localized accounts of colonial, postcolonial, and corporate plunder of the Himalaya that proliferate in Uttarakhand. Here, certain specified and frequently named human constituencies—those hailing from the distant plains of India (*maidani*), the agents of the state, and corporate bodies—are considered to be preying on the rich resources of the upper Himalaya. It is the historically long-standing practices of animal poaching and trafficking, hunting, deforestation, resource extraction, mining, damming of rivers, incessant construction, and the commercialization of all domains of life that have depleted the Himalaya. Historically entrenched human-made political structures—democracy, the state, relations with neighbors like China and Nepal, governance at different scales from the village to New Delhi—actively feed this slow but certain killing of the Himalaya.

Is it not, then, darkly apposite that the predators (human beings) are being predated by nonhuman animals (big cats and bears) in this age of the Anthropocene in the Himalaya?

Mutual predation is not, however, restricted to animals and humans in this epoch. Rivers, mountains, soil, and even the gods are furious at humans for their wanton destruction of the Himalaya. The fury is expressed in diverse ways, with a prominent mode being recurrent disasters (*apada*) such as floods, famines, avalanches, forest fires, and earthquakes. In June 2013 in Uttarakhand, there was one *apada* that was especially devastating, with officially 5,500 people declared dead, even though unofficial accounts put the toll at closer to 10,000. Following several days of unremitting monsoon rain and cloudbursts, flash floods inundated several regions of Uttarakhand. In addition to the uncharacteristically fierce monsoon behavior, a contributing factor to the floods was the moraine left behind by the retreating Chorabari Glacier. The monsoon rain filled the rock debris reservoir of the moraine, and soon it overflowed to join the rising river. It was the combined force of the two that led to the raging floodwaters.

In a region where one *apada* or another now forms the norm on a seasonal, if not daily, basis, this 2013 event is marked out as exceptional. Even in the otherwise prosaic and self-consciously secularizing bureaucratic language of the Indian state, it has been termed a *daiviya apada,* or a "divine disaster." The 2013 disaster was considered "divine" partly because of the scale of the destruction, which can only be wreaked by gods and demons. As eyewitnesses, victims, and residents of Uttarakhand describe and remember it, the floods and rains that were certainly *prakriti ka prakop* (retribution by nature) felt like the furious *tandava* dance of the Hindu god Shiva.

The highest number of casualties and greatest amount of damage took place in the holy town of Kedarnath, centered on an ancient Shiva temple (c. the eighth century AD). As Shiva danced his dance of death and destruction, he made sure to protect his own temple. Witnesses describe hearing a huge snapping noise followed by a gigantic wall of water descending on the Kedarnath temple and its surroundings. Miraculously, a huge boulder got lodged behind the temple, protecting it from significant damage. The location of the temple and its strong construction also protected it. This protection was not at hand for the surrounding buildings that were swept away in the flood. Along with the buildings, thousands of humans—largely pilgrims—were swallowed up by the raging river, while others were buried alive under landslides.

The image that has become iconic of the divine disaster, however, was taken much farther downstream from Kedarnath in the town of Rishikesh (figure 8.1). In it, we see the flooding Ganges River partially submerging a popular Shiva idol. With his closed eyes and beatific smile, it is as if Shiva the Destroyer is resting at the end of his dance of rage. The divine disaster is discussed as a chilling foreshadowing of the Anthropocene yet unseen: an

8.1. A statue of the Hindu god Shiva submerged by the flooding Ganges River in Uttarakhand. Credit: Associated Press

age in which prey will become indistinguishable from predator; a world in which big cats, bears, rivers, glaciers, mountains, clouds, humans, and gods will all act with a hitherto unknown extremity, ferocity, and unpredictability.

†

A final fragment of memory. One that emerges from human relationships with seemingly inscrutable nonhuman animals and is embedded in interspecies love, friendship, and care.

I am back in Gopeshwar in my room in Kund. The crooked cat's reign of terror is at its peak. I have to go to Dehradun for a meeting and for a small break from the intense tension of life with a predatory nonhuman neighbor. I am booked into a taxi—what is called a "share Sumo," as it is a Tata Sumo car that seats several people who split the cost between themselves—that is to depart from outside the bazaar at the crack of dawn. I leave from my room wearing my canary-yellow backpack when it is still dark, just after 5 a.m. The only way to get to the bazaar is by walking down, as no other transportation options exist, especially at this unearthly hour. This is one of those rare moments of the past few weeks when I am venturing out in the semidarkness. But I am not alone, as Sheroo, my loyal Bhotia dog, is accompanying me unbidden.

Sheroo now sleeps in my room at night and has, somehow, become mine. Over the months this relationship developed organically. Sheroo lives on the street and is technically a stray. However, he has never felt like one, as he would always be found with the pet dogs owned by the police officer from whom I was renting my accommodation. Sheroo would hunt and forage and generally get fed by random people. I now feed him daily and even buy extra milk every morning from the milkman that is secretly meant for him. I am closemouthed about Sheroo's milk and also feel guilty, as I know most other human residents of the town cannot afford to drink milk daily, if ever. I don't know how old Sheroo is and I am certain he has never really had milk before, but he absolutely loves it and gulps it down in a trice.

Sheroo adopted me as his mistress through an action that began a few weeks after I started feeding him and playing with him: he would on a near daily basis make his way to "my office" in the district office just before 5 p.m. to pick me up. He would saunter past the big DM's office, up the narrow stairs above the garage, to the small room in which I sat, and stretch out comfortably in the front to patiently wait while I wrapped up for the day. Everyone in the office and the town would laugh when they saw him—they would say, "Your friend is here [*aapka dost aa gaya*]." Sheroo, my dearest friend, and I would then happily walk home, side by side.

Sheroo does sometimes drop me off at the office in the morning too but almost always picks me up in the evening. He doesn't, however, go farther afield and certainly never to the bazaar, which is about a twenty-five-minute brisk walk downhill from my accommodation and almost a forty-minute walk when climbing back up. This morning is different. He walks ahead of me on the road. I tell him, again and again, to go home as the bagh is around, but he resolutely ignores me. At one point I run ahead of him and try to stop him and physically push him in the opposite direction, but he refuses to heed. I give up, knowing his stubbornness well.

It is still dark, but I can see some golden beams are beginning to emerge from behind the mountains. The Nanda Devi mountain shimmers silvery against the deep purple sky. I started out walking on the main pukka road that curves around the town but realize I am running a bit late. I decide to take the shortcut that goes through some rough steps cutting diagonally down straight to the bazaar. Sheroo is walking ahead of me and turns sharply when I call out to him and gesture toward the alternate path. Sometimes we take this when going to the office, and he knows I stumble at the more steep bits. He brushes past me to bound ahead. At the one step where I often clumsily slide, he turns back to regard me seriously—as if alerting me to it. I carefully step down from it and, for once, do not trip.

Sheroo then starts to walk behind me. I jump nimbly over the next bit of stairs, and we come to the main road again. He comes abreast with me here when, suddenly, he stops dead in his tracks. I, too, stop. He looks behind, and I turn, with a racing pulse, to do the same. I see nothing. But Sheroo is staring fixedly at something or someone. For a few seconds we both stare back in the darkness. I feel panic rising in me and turn back on the path and begin walking much faster. Sheroo joins me. He is now behind me, and when we come to another shortcut, he bounds ahead as if to encourage me to take this and move away from the main road. I follow him quickly and find myself sweating, though it is a freezing December morning. He keeps moving in front of and behind me, and I start to concentrate on walking—almost running—down the hill. I know he is thinking-feeling what I am: that the bagh is watching us; she is close by someplace.

After what feels like an age, we arrive at the bazaar, which has quite a few people out and about. The Sumo taxi is there too, rapidly filling up with travelers. Dawn has arrived, washing over everything in gold and blue. I turn to look up the mountain, as does Sheroo. We both then look at one another for a long moment. It is an exchange of knowing—and relieved—glances. I can see the concern in his deep brown eyes; I feel his affection strongly. In all the wonderings over the big cat and amid the unanswerable questions—Where is she? What is she doing? Who is her next victim? Is she really a "man-eater"? What makes her thus?—that was a moment when I was certain of two things. First, the big cat was close by, and she had been watching us. Second, Sheroo was aware of this too. He had known it would be dangerous for me to venture out alone that morning and had accompanied me simply to protect me.

Amid the unpredictability and uncertainty that are characteristic of life in the Anthropocene, with its steady dissolution of the world as we knew it, there exist such fleeting moments of pure clarity. What will it take to hold onto these moments that lay bare multispecies entanglements and deep, uncanny relationships with the nonhuman? Can we come to believe in, unembarrassedly acknowledge, and *act* according to affective knowledges of the form they demonstrate? Doing so could diminish much of the beastliness of our times and allow for the crafting of a simpler planetary tale.

†

And so I'll end the story here.
What is to come is still unclear.
Whether the fates will smile or frown,
And Bingle Vale survive or drown,
I do not know and cannot say;
Indeed, perhaps, I never may.
I hope, of course, the beasts we've met
Will save their hidden valley, yet
The resolution of their plight
Is for the world, not me, to write.

—Vikram Seth, *Beastly Tales*, 130

ACKNOWLEDGMENTS

This book began many years back now—with the arrival of the leopard of Gopeshwar in the winter of 2006—and it has changed form more times than I care to remember: from a multispecies account of human-animal relationships to an argument on the climate crisis, the role of anthropology as a discipline in speaking to the Anthropocene, and writing on India, a space that has for long been represented through recourse to images and discourses depicting the jungle/wild as populated with fearsome man-eating tigers. My most heartfelt gratitude to my many interlocutors in Uttarakhand, Himachal Pradesh, and Mumbai who have put up with my long and intermittent presence and incessant questioning.

Vidya Athreya's work with leopards in India has been critical to how we understand "conflict" and the pernicious effects of translocation. Thank you for the many conversations and links to articles and books, as well as for taking me along on an important research trip to Himachal Pradesh. Thanks also to Nikit Surve, Jairoop Riar, Nayan Khanolkar, and Persis Farooqy. In Mumbai, many thanks to Ranjeet Jadhav for the introduction to Aarey Colony and for the many chats over the years. I am grateful to the many members of the forest departments in Uttarakhand and Himachal Pradesh, most of whom would prefer to not be named, for interviews and for opening the archives to me.

I wrote vast sections of this book while I was on a British Academy Postdoctoral Fellowship at Cambridge and was continuing to be a part of the "Conspiracy and Democracy" project funded by the Leverhulme Trust. The interdisciplinary conversations that I had at the Centre for Research in the Arts, Social Sciences and Humanities (CRASSH) over those years were central to the rethinking of method with this work: my thanks to Richard Evans, David Runciman, John Naughton, Hugo Drochon, Alfred Moore, Andrew

McKenzie-McHarg, Tanya Filer, Rolf Fredheim, Rachel Hoffman, Christos Lynteris, Catherine Hurley, Simon Goldhill, and several visiting scholars, especially "the Jos." Thanks to fellow anthropologists at Cambridge: Franck Bille, Branwyn Polykett, Jessica Johnson, Alice Wilson, Chris Kaplonski, Yael Navaro, Chloe Nahum-Claudel, Matei Candea, Sian Lazar, David Sneath, Barbara Bodenhorn, Fiona Wright, and Hildegard Diemberger. I am very grateful to the space that the Department of Anthropology at the University of Sussex gave me for a year to work on this book and would like to acknowledge here the support of Andrea Cornwall, Geert de Neve, Magnus Marsden, and Filipo Osella.

Thanks are due to many colleagues for conversations, support, feedback, and invitations to panels and workshops: Eirini Avramopoulou, Amita Baviskar, Heath Cabot, Naisargi Dave, Radhika Govindrajan, Annu Jalais, Subhashim Goswami, Julie Billaud, Miia Halme-Tuomisaari, Andrea Ballestero, Manan Ahmed, Daniela Berti, Rohit De, Tarangini Sriraman, Jane Cowan, Tara Suri, Amna Qayum, Sarah Green, Ravi Sundaram, and Mahesh Rangarajan. I am particularly grateful to Jason Cons for organizing a draft manuscript workshop in Austin and Yasmine Moataz for giving me the chance to present some of this work in Cairo. Both those trips—and especially the engaged feedback received from anthropology students at the University of Texas at Austin and the American University in Cairo—have proven to be very important.

At the University of Oxford, my home for the past three years, I am privileged to be part of a flourishing South Asian studies and anthropology community. My colleagues from the Oxford School of Global and Area Studies (OSGA) have patiently borne with me as half my mind has been constantly distracted with this book: Stephen Minay, Kate Sullivan de Estrada, Tim Power, Rachel Murphy, Erin Gordon, and Miles Larmer. Beyond OSGA, I work and teach with Imre Bangha, Dilar Dirik, Fiona McConnell, Mallica Kumbera Landrus, Nandini Gooptu, Sneha Krishnan, Zaad Mahmood, Bhawani Buswala, Justin Jones, and, most of all, Polly O'Hanlon. Anthropologists at Oxford have warmly welcomed me: Sophie Haines, Thomas Cousins, Gemma Angel, Ana Gutierrez Garza, the late Marcus Banks, David Gellner, Elizabeth Ewart, Ina Zharkevich, and Dace Dzenovska. I am grateful to Wolfies Nikita Sud, and Ruben Andersson for the genuine fellowship and many meals—of admittedly varying quality—that we have had together.

Very many thanks to the series editors of Animal Lives: Jane Desmond, Barbara King, and Kim Marra. Jane has been steadfast in her support and encouragement all through this long process, from when an initial idea was pitched to what has now become *Crooked Cats*. The late Douglas Mitchell was the original acquiring editor of this book; I continue to cherish his enthusiastic emails, particularly the one in which he declared me "a big cat connoisseur." Priya Nelson picked up the project subsequently and handled it with care, patience, and some terrific editorial suggestions. Kyle Wagner has seen it through to the very end. Dylan J. Montanari and Tristan Bates have made the process of working with the University of Chicago Press so very easy and friendly. This book wouldn't feel like it really exists till it is published and widely available in South Asia. I am very grateful to my editor Siddhesh Inamdar for acquiring this work, and for his enthusiasm for this story.

Sections of this book have been previously published in somewhat different forms in *Economic and Political Weekly*, *American Ethnologist*, and *Modern Asian Studies*.

Over the years, I have been part of several collaborative projects, and while only some of them may be found directly reflected in these pages, I consider those conversations and ideas critical to my thinking. Amanda Power and I ran the Oxford Anthropocene reading group for a year, which has now morphed into our exciting "climate crisis thinking in the humanities and social sciences" research network. I have learned so much from our conversations on the Anthropocene—medieval as well as contemporary. Lisa Schipper, Eiko Honda, Tom White, Joseph Browning, and Fredi Otto are critical collaborators on this network. Thanks also to Liana Chua for our "cute animals" panel at the American Anthropological Association, our coedited book on who we anthropologists think we are, and the many conversations on orangutans and big cats; Ravinder Kaur for our "peoples' state" workshop and forthcoming book on the politics of New India; Alfred Moore for the political theory and anthropology paper on climate change that we have been working on for years; Jason Cons for discussions on the Anthropocene as method and climate imaginations in South Asia; Rohan Deb Roy, Jonathan Saha, and Sujit Sivasundaram for the "political animals in South Asia" project idea and discussions; Sarnath Banerjee for our plans for a graphic textbook on *adamkhor bagh*; and Surabhi Ranganathan for our varied conversations on techno-utopianism, interdisciplinarity, oceans, big cats, law, and Oxbridge.

I am hugely grateful to several friends who have listened to me drone on about this book for many years and contributed to it with their questions, enthusiasm, and ideas: Hulda Proppe, Sara Abbas, Sirisha Indukuri, Shumita Deveshwar, Laura Bear, Shinjini Das, Esther Major, Evelyn Ofori-Koree, Subhasri Narayanan, Perveen Ali, and Mi Zhou. Christopher Beckman read every word of this book thoroughly, and his comments have gone a long way in knocking it into some sort of shape. I cannot thank him enough for the generosity of spirit with which he treated the draft manuscript and keenly await the publication of *The Happy Anchovy*.

Shiv Kumar's delicious cooking and constant search for compliments are intrinsic to my sense of being home. Krishna and Jeetendra Rawat take such good care of us in Dehradun. My brother Gaurav Ahluwalia, brother-in-law Saurabh Endley, and elder sister Manika remain as supportive as ever. Binod Kumar refused to leave my side during an exceptionally difficult moment, and for that he has my eternal gratitude. My nephew, Saharsh, made me narrate my *bagh ki kahaniyan* to him after each field trip. In those endless oral retellings to a wide-eyed young boy, these beastly tales have assumed a particular narrative shape. This book is premised on interspecies love and friendship, enabling me to note that I desperately miss our feisty Cinnamon Bun and adore our new family member Kulfi Lodi.

I sometimes think this book actually began long before the Gopeshwar-wallah bagh with the *sher ki kahaniyan* that my Nani used to tell me, only one of which has found its way into this book. Tragically, Nani didn't live to see *Crooked Cats* in print but my very last conversation with her was about this book, and she had given me her *shabashi* then.

My first publication was a short story I had written as a child about my little sister, Tapsi. The story, if I remember correctly, was somewhat unimaginatively entitled "My Sister" and was a description of her peculiar habits. Tapsi was too young to read properly at the time, but when I showed the story to her, she spotted her name—which she had just learned to write—and promptly burst into tears. She had rightly guessed this was a less-than-flattering account of her. To stem the sobbing, my mother made me, much to my annoyance, cut out Tapsi's name and replace it with her best friend's instead. My mother then, unbeknownst to me, sent the story off to the children's section of a national newspaper. A few weeks later, my perennially proud Papa came bursting out of the bathroom excitedly waving a newspaper in my face—he had spotted it published in the weekend edition. Then, as now, my parents and Tapsi were far more thrilled for me than I myself was. Much else too remains the same: my mother still does much of the invisible labor that has laid the ground for my life, and my father continues to support me in *hazaar* ways that elude language. The one thing that has changed is that Tapsi is now the first reader of every single thing I write, which she edits with a *qainchi*-like sharpness. To her I dedicate this book, with the hope that, this time, she will let me keep her name in.

GLOSSARY

adamkhor—man-eater
atank—terror
bagh—leopard/tiger/lion
bechara—poor thing
bekasoor—guiltless/innocent
chinghaad—scream/roar
maidani—plains person
pahari—mountain person
sarkar—state/government
sher—tiger/lion
shikar—the hunt
shikari—hunter
tendua—leopard

NOTES

PREFACE

1. Sara Reggiani, "Stay Home, They Told Us...: Diary of an Italian Editor," Literary Hub, March 16, 2020, https://lithub.com/stay-home-they-told-us-diary-of-an-italian-editor/.
2. For a brilliant account of the debate on the origins of Covid-19, see Christos Lynteris, 2020. "The Imperative Origins of Covid-19", *L'Homme*, 234-235 (21-32). http://journals.openedition.org/lhomme/37062
3. See, for instance, Avivah Wittenberg-Cox (2020) on women leaders being the most successful in handling the pandemic, Krishnan (2020) on the callousness of the Indian government in its handling of the coronavirus pandemic, and Yong (2020) on how the United States failed miserably in the face of the pandemic. Also see Bhan et al. (2020) on how the pandemic should push us to not just think in terms of totality and the planetary but also pay attention to what they call the "collective life" rooted in southern urban lives.
4. Sonia Shah, "Think Exotic Animals Are to Blame for the Coronavirus? Think Again," *Nation*, February 18, 2020, https://www.thenation.com/article/environment/coronavirus-habitat-loss/.
5. Richard Adams, "Oxford to Receive Biggest Single Donation 'since the Renaissance,'" *Guardian*, June 18, 2019, https://www.theguardian.com/education/2019/jun/19/oxford-receive-biggest-single-donation-stephen-schwarzman.
6. See this open letter written by Common Ground that protests against the donation and lays out details of the role played by Blackstone (chaired and cofounded by Stephen Schwarzman) in the housing crisis of 2008 and in the deforestation of the Amazon. Oxford Humanities Centre Open Letter, "Open Letter: No to the 'Stephen A. Schwarzman Centre for the Humanities,'" Medium.com, September 17, 2019, https://medium.com/@oxfordhumanitiescentreletter/open-letter-no-to-the-stephen-a-schwarzman-centre-for-the-humanities-f9ba87077b97.
7. The resurgence of the student-led Rhodes Must Fall movement in Oxford is one striking example of this. See my brief essay on this: Nayanika Mathur, "What I Learnt at the 'Rhodes Must Fall' Protest in Oxford," Wire (India), June 11, 2020, https://thewire.in/world/cecil-rhodes-oxford-protest-george-floyd.

PROLOGUE

1. Sara Reggiani, "Stay Home, They Told Us . . . : Diary of an Italian Editor," Literary Hub, March 16, 2020, https://lithub.com/stay-home-they-told-us-diary-of-an-italian-editor/.

2. See, for instance, Avivah Wittenberg-Cox (2020) on women leaders being the most successful in handling the pandemic, Krishnan (2020) on the callousness of the Indian government in its handling of the coronavirus pandemic, and Yong (2020) on how the United States failed miserably in the face of the pandemic. Also see Bhan et al. (2020) on how the pandemic should push us to not just think in terms of totality and the planetary but also pay attention to what they call the "collective life" rooted in southern urban lives.
3. Sonia Shah, "Think Exotic Animals Are to Blame for the Coronavirus? Think Again," *Nation*, February 18, 2020, https://www.thenation.com/article/environment/coronavirus-habitat-loss/.
4. Richard Adams, "Oxford to Receive Biggest Single Donation 'since the Renaissance,'" *Guardian*, June 18, 2019, https://www.theguardian.com/education/2019/jun/19/oxford-receive-biggest-single-donation-stephen-schwarzman.
5. See this open letter written by Common Ground that protests against the donation and lays out details of the role played by Blackstone (chaired and cofounded by Stephen Schwarzman) in the housing crisis of 2008 and in the deforestation of the Amazon. Oxford Humanities Centre Open Letter, "Open Letter: No to the 'Stephen A. Schwarzman Centre for the Humanities,'" Medium.com, September 17, 2019, https://medium.com/@oxfordhumanitiescentreletter/open-letter-no-to-the-stephen-a-schwarzman-centre-for-the-humanities-f9ba87077b97.
6. The resurgence of the student-led Rhodes Must Fall movement in Oxford is one striking example of this. See my brief essay on this: Nayanika Mathur, "What I Learnt at the 'Rhodes Must Fall' Protest in Oxford," Wire (India), June 11, 2020, https://thewire.in/world/cecil-rhodes-oxford-protest-george-floyd.

INTRODUCTION

1. Unless otherwise noted, all translations in this book are my own.
2. Luciano (2015) makes the important point that the question of the periodicity of the Anthropocene (when do we say it began?) is vital for it "reflects the explanatory promise of the Anthropocene concept: it is a debate over what kind of story can and should be told about human impact on the planet." In other words, the debates on when the Anthropocene began—which I do not myself directly engage in here—have consequences for how the Anthropocene is conceptualized. For instance, did it begin with the commencement of the industrial revolution or the era of decolonization? An answer to this would have strong implications for where and with whom the burden of the devastation of the Anthropocene lies.
3. According to the United Nations Framework Convention on Climate Change (UNFCCC), "climate change refers to a change of climate that is attributed directly or indirectly to human activity that alters the composition of the global atmosphere and that is in addition to natural climate variability observed over comparable time periods" (2011, 2).
4. Similarly, see Chua and Fair (2019) on how anthropologists have treated climate change, extinction, and so forth as factors that make manifest the Anthropocene.
5. While I am referring to the same set of phenomena with both "climate change" and "the climate crisis," I deploy the latter to press home the urgency of the planet in crisis, what is also termed "the climate emergency" or "the climate breakdown."
6. I am very grateful to Jason Cons for sharing his syllabus on "Anthropologies of Climate Change: Anthropocene as Method" and for our many conversations on the Anthropocene and his comments on a draft of this manuscript that have pushed me to refine this point.

7. Anthropologists have noted that the Anthropocene enjoins nothing short of a transformation of the discipline. Latour (2014) notes this is part of the gift that the Anthropocene presents the discipline with. Haraway describes it as a "response-ability," or "a praxis of care and response . . . in ongoing multispecies worldings on a wounded terra" (2012, 302). Tsing, Mathews, and Bubandt put it most powerfully when they ask if anthropology is content to continue being regarded as a minor science and whether it is able to step up to the task of thinking differently: "In the face of the challenges of the Anthropocene, anthropology must dare to be more than the voice of parochial alterity; dare to allow anthropological stories of the 'otherwise' into concrete transdisciplinary conversations about planetary structures that 'change everything'" (2019, 187). Similarly, historians are also calling for a recrafting of their discipline in light of the challenges opened up by the Anthropocene (Chakrabarty 2009; Power 2019; Thomas 2014).
8. There is a growing body of fascinating writing on changing human-animal entanglements in different disciplines that is presented against the backdrop of extinction, environmental decline, history, and capital. For instance, see Parreñas's (2018) ethnographic account of orangutan rehabilitation centers in Borneo and her arguments on the need to decolonize extinction, by which she means that one should not attempt to stop extinction but "consider how else might it unfold for those who will perish and for those who will survive" (9). Also see Barua's (2014) work on human-elephant cohabitation in India, where he draws on postcolonial environmental history, animal ecology, and more-than-human geography to make an argument for a dwelt political ecology. A particularly rich collection of book-length accounts of nonhumans in the oceans—and the threats to their continual survival that they face—is developing. Telesca (2020) closely traces the process through which international law and its commissions that are ostensibly established for the goal of conservation have purposefully managed the extinction of the giant bluefin tuna. Probyn (2016) explores the deeply complex food politics of human-fish entanglements as she locates the ocean and fisheries as sites of entanglements of technology, politics, culture, and capital. Giggs (2020) describes the rich inner worlds of the whale as she traces the historical and institutional processes through which whales have been hunted and made into an extractive resource for humans. What looms over this book is the fact that climate change could subject whales to sudden extinction, as mass and often inexplicable deaths of them—such as in Patagonia in 2015—increase.
9. Also see Rangarajan (2013), Ghosal (2014), Rangarajan and Sivaramakrishnan (2011), Greenough (2012), Govindrajan (2015, 2018), Margulies (2019), Doubleday (2018), Shahabuddin (2014), and Divyabhanusinh (2008).
10. In contrast to human relationships with big cats in India, the polar bear—as well as its changing behavior—has been strongly linked to the climate crisis, so much so that this charismatic nonhuman animal has come to stand in for climate change, largely due to the efforts of environmental and climate-change organizations and crusaders. Polar bears' near extinction, starvation, drowning, attacks on humans, and recent invasion of a town in search of food have been analyzed through the lens of the ecological collapse (see Hutchins 2019). Fictional accounts of human-animal relations are also powerfully showing how human actions lead to changes in nonhuman animal behavior. See, for instance, Tania James's *The Tusk That Did the Damage* (2016).
11. Thanks to Akeel Bilgrami for pushing me to make clearer the connection between the intense speculation on the possibility of a big cat turning crooked and the dense proliferation of narratives around big cats. In central ways, it is this uncertainty over

whether a bagh is seedha or tedha and why it might be tedha—and the type of talk this leads to—that occasioned the writing of this book.

12. "Summary for Policymakers of the Global Assessment Report on Biodiversity and Ecosystem Services of the Intergovernmental Science-Policy Platform on Biodiversity and Ecosystem Services," advance unedited version, May 6, 2019, https://www.ipbes.net/sites/default/files/downloads/spm_unedited_advance_for_posting_htn.pdf.
13. Pooley et al. note, "In a world of shrinking and fragmenting habitats and increasing competition for natural resources, potentially dangerous predators bring the challenges of coexisting with wildlife sharply into focus" (2017, 514). They, too, argue that in discussions of human-wildlife conflict, the conservationists' concentration has been on the biology of predators and prey, with the social sciences brought in merely to improve the cost-benefit ratios of cohabitation for humans. This comprehensive interdisciplinary review of approaches to human-predator relations lays out much of the literature and makes a convincing argument for greater interdisciplinarity. This paper, in line with many of the recent writings, also cautions against the use of the word "conflict" and suggests that it may be more productive to think in terms of human-predator relations.
14. In the natural sciences literature, species interactions, especially those related to decreasing food availability and the resulting conflict, are often centered as a prime driver of species extinction (Cahill et al. 2012). The decrease in food availability due to habitat loss and biodiversity depletion is driving changes in species' ranges as animals travel farther and farther in search of nourishment. Reasons for increased human-animal conflict are regularly centered on contests over land and resources that have ensued between humans and nonhuman animals.
15. It is important to point out that I had similarly not centered the fact of climate change as much as its political actions in my own early writings on human-animal relations in the Himalaya. In an early essay, I had traced the process whereby "climate change" marked an entry in the Himalaya in the context of human-animal conflict and species extinction through very localized processes of deduction and naming by the state (N. Mathur 2015). My concern in that work lay in tracing how the very category of climate change—based in the English language and derived from the rationalism of a universalized "science," complex climate models and tables, and descriptions in reports published by the Intergovernmental Panel on Climate Change (IPCC)—traveled out from its elite spaces and assumed an explanatory power in a remote borderland of India. I also showed the political effects of the very category of climate change, how it allowed the local state to avoid responsibility for certain events, and the fact that in the hands of state bureaucrats the concept of climate change can work as a tool for depoliticization. As such, that work was interested in exploring how a category becomes real, how "climate change" marks an entry in space, and the politics of naming and expertise. Also see Paprocki (2019) for a comparable argument on the depoliticizing potential of climate change in Bangladesh.
16. This question of how the social sciences and humanities can speak to the natural sciences in the context of the Anthropocene and the climate crisis is becoming increasingly important. See the historian Julia Adeney Thomas (2014) for important thinking on history and biology. Thomas points out that endangerment is not "a simple scientific fact. . . . Only the humanities and social sciences, transformed though they will be through their engagement with science, can fully articulate what we may lose" (2014, 1588).
17. Tsing describes science as a translation machine: "It is machinic because a phalanx of teachers, technicians, and peer reviewers stands ready to chop off excess parts and

to hammer those that remain into their proper places. It is translational because its insights are drawn from diverse ways of life." In her own work she studies this translation as a messy process filled with "jarring juxtaposition and miscommunication" (2015, 217).

18. In this book I sometimes refer to conflict between humans and big cats or to their coexistence even though I am very aware of the shortcomings of such terms. A central objective of this work is, in fact, to go beyond the conflict/coexistence framing that continues to dominate conservationist and academic accounts of human-animal relations, through a reliance on beastly tales and the concept of the Anthropocene. However, I deploy these terms as a shorthand to refer to the manner in which this phenomenon is written about by other authors or has been sometimes articulated by a few of my interlocutors—primarily bureaucrats, hunters, and conservationists. For a working definition, I follow Hill in considering human-wildlife conflict as denoting "negative interactions between people and wildlife, i.e. where wildlife damage property including crops, or threaten the safety of livestock or even people" (2017, 1). As she goes on to note, "it is increasingly apparent that human-wildlife conflict is normally better understood as conflicts between different human groups" (1). Also see Pooley et al. (2017) and Redpath, Bhatia, and Young (2015) on the many drawbacks of utilizing the "human-animal conflict" phrasing.
19. An argument made about the Anthropocene is that it opens up a thinking at the level of a planetary "us" arising from a shared sense of catastrophe (Chakrabarty 2009). D'Souza (2015) has considered the claim that nations are becoming "without borders" as the inescapable urgency of working to sustain ecological worlds at a planetary level becomes more obvious. While I agree that a shift of scale from, for example, the Indian Himalayan borderland to the level of the global and then back again—is critical to our understanding of life in the Anthropocene, I also caution against the glib use of an "us" or an ahistorical, depoliticized understanding of a "we" (N. Mathur 2015). To uncritically deploy a "we" of the Anthropocene can potentially blind us or limit our attention to a cruelly obvious point—viz., not only have my interlocutors in the Indian Himalaya, with their almost nonexistent carbon footprint, contributed the least to anthropic climate change, but they will still be the ones to most intensely suffer the consequences sans the privileges that might allow for coping with its effects. Hecht (2018a) correctly notes that far too often the "we" of the Anthropocene is white and Western. As she succinctly puts it, "If the Anthropocene is to have real value as a category of thought and a call to action, it must federate people and places, not just disciplines. It requires thinking from, and with, Africa. 'They' are 'us', and there is no planetary 'we' without them."
20. In her critique of how the conversation around the Anthropocene is being dominated by the geophysical and social sciences, DeLoughrey has pointed out that "scholarship that does turn to the role of the Anthropocene cultural imaginary is focused almost exclusively on the viewpoints of the global north" (2019, 2). As such, it is important for more scholarship from the global south to take on the scholarship on the Anthropocene.
21. As Hecht has cogently argued, we need to put the Anthropocene "in place." Through a proposition of focusing on an African Anthropocene she seeks to find "a means of holding *the planet* and *a place on the planet* on the same analytic plane" (2018b, 112).
22. Amrith in his retelling of the history of South Asia through its waters notes that meteorological data collected in the 1960s and the fictional voices present in Neel Mukherjee's novel *The Lives of Others* appeared, at that point of time, disconnected: "Human lives and voices could not be fed into climate models, where readings of

pressure and wind and moisture could. But they told different facets of the same story" (2018, 230). He goes on to make the connections that were not evident at the time between the story of monsoon science in the 1960s and the story of the political and economic history of the mid-1960s droughts. It is such a type of putting together of stories that are, too often, kept apart that *Crooked Cats* attempts and that is implied in the idea of the task of the climate translator (N. Mathur 2017).

23. See West (2005) for an important argument on the political nature of all translations—whether by anthropologists or conservationists—and the caution that should be exercised in order to not ignore knowledges that don't somehow fit with "scientific" knowledge systems. Environmental translations in their drive to be seen as rational and useful for conservationist purposes can "often miss the fact that human relations with the natural world are aesthetic, poetic, social, and moral" (West 2005, 633).
24. The unthinkability of the climate crisis also emerges from the fact that, as Quentin Skinner has observed, "we are ill-equipped by our inherited traditions of thinking about the natural world to deal adequately with our current predicament" (2018, 222).
25. Forrester and Smith (2018, 1) similarly note that "climate change is the great challenge of modern politics" largely due to its "novelty: nothing quite like it has ever happened before."
26. In a comprehensive review of the Anthropocene, Chua and Fair (2019) outline four main anthropological approaches to it: (1) those that take it as a context for or backdrop to ethnographic inquiry; (2) those that interrogate the Anthropocene as a socially and politically constructed idea; (3) those that treat the Anthropocene as an opportunity for creativity and hopeful speculation; and (4) those that view the Anthropocene as the outcome of long-standing global, political, and socioeconomic inequalities. See Lorimer (2017) too, who also lays out a guide to how the Anthropocene has been taken up in the social sciences.
27. For instance, Jason Moore has argued that "the Anthropocene makes for an easy story. Easy because it does not challenge the naturalised inequalities, alienation, and violence inscribed in modernity's strategic relations of power and production" (2015, 170). Malm and Hornborg (2014) have demonstrated how the concept of the Anthropocene is ultimately dominated by the natural sciences, and the dangers it holds of underplaying the deep divisions between members of the human species in time and space and of making issues of culture and power secondary. Alternatives to the Anthropocene have been articulated, such as the Capitalocene that has been proposed by Andreas Malm (Moore 2016, xi) and Donna Haraway (2015). "Capitalocene" does not center the *anthropos* as an undifferentiated whole but claims that "capitalism is the pivot of today's biospheric crisis" (Moore 2016, xi). The argument for centering capitalism is sharply outlined in Naomi Klein's (2014) important polemic *This Changes Everything: Capitalism vs. the Climate*. The debate on whether "Anthropocene" is most apt or "Capitalocene" is preferable is also explored in a collection (Moore 2016) that brings out what is at stake in this naming debate. Also see Haraway on her critiques of both the Anthropocene and the Capitalocene and on her preference for thinking through staying with the trouble in what she terms the Chthulucene, which "can be a fierce reply to the dictates of both Anthropos and Capital" (2016, 2).
28. Similarly Hetherington notes that though he and his collaborators too tried to abandon the concept of the Anthropocene, they found themselves continuously returning to it as "it served as a placeholder for a certain mode of questioning the contemporary" (2019, 3).

29. This point—on how divisions between "nature" and "culture" and between "humans" and "nonhumans" are being collapsed by the Anthropocene—has now been identified as central to its power. Simultaneously, the Anthropocene can similarly break down the disciplinary barriers that have been constructed around these concepts, such as the one between social anthropology and biological anthropology, as outlined by Latour (2014) in his American Anthropological Association inaugural address.
30. Barnes and Dove make a case for an anthropological account of climate change by making the point that "climate change is not just about hotter temperatures and melting ice. It is also about stories and images, myth and reality, knowledge and ignorance, humour and tragedy—questions that are, at root, cultural in nature. While this collision and confusion of forces flummox climate scientists and policy makers alike, in some ways they make it all the more attractive to the anthropological project" (2015, 3). In the emergent literature on climate change, anthropologists have focused on the social and cultural mediation of climate change science, shown local practices of adaptation, and studied the processes of construction of expert knowledge on climate change, and are beginning to seriously wrestle with the question of climate justice even as they document the plight of climate refugees (see Cons 2018; Zeiderman 2016; Khan 2015). Also see Bodenhorn and Ulturgasheva (2017) for how collaboratively thinking through examples from the Arctic opens up the space for social anthropologists to suggest "climate strategies."
31. Regarding storytelling and ethnography that considers the question of method closely, see Van Dooren and Rose (2016) on "lively ethnography."
32. An essay by Sakakibara (2008) is a good illustration of why storytelling in the context of climate change can be productive. She presents Iñupiat storytelling as a mode of coping with an unpredictable environment, relocation, and the drowning of old homes and the making of new ones. Importantly, her work in the Arctic shows that stories not only impart skills or illustrate a sense of place but also become central to the process of adapting to climate change. In a similar vein, Whyte has made a call for "indigenous climate change studies" that offer a critical, decolonial approach through their consideration of climate change as "intensified colonialism" and how "ways of imagining the future guide our present actions" (2017, 154). Also see DeLoughrey (2019), who in her attempt to provincialize the Anthropocene turns to allegory in the arts, poetry, and literature of indigenous and postcolonial peoples in the Caribbean and Pacific islands.
33. The tenth-century Iraqi fable *The Case of the Animals versus Man before the King of the Jinn*, written by Ikhwan al-Safa and translated by Goodman and McGregor (2012), is an example of what Annu Jalais has described as "a 10th century Anthropocene talk by animals" (@AnnuJal, Twitter, August 15, 2020, https://twitter.com/AnnuJal/status/1294582506470047744). It consists of various animals coming together before a spirit king to complain of the dreadful treatment that humans have meted out to them. Also see Jalais (2018) on tiger stories and symbols in ancient Chinese cosmologies and their impact on understandings of "nature" and the "nonhuman."
34. See also the wonderful book by Despret (2016) that can serve as a model for undertaking interdisciplinary work on animals and new ways of telling stories about them. In the foreword to the book, Latour describes the method of the author as that of an "empirical philosopher's." The book, *What Would Animals Say If We Asked the Right Questions?*, runs through the English alphabet to ask provocative questions (e.g., "Q for queer: Are penguins coming out of the closet?") and then proceeds to answer them through evidence that is gathered from several different fields.

35. Corbett, too, consistently notes the "terror" of man-eating big cats, as do other colonial narrations. Pandian reads these accounts as a colonial discourse that recuperates the figure of the Oriental despot to characterize both the big cat and the preceding rulers in India. The terror is dispelled, in these stories, only through "the masculine intervention of the white hunter" (Pandian 2001, 87).
36. In their account of thinking with animals, Daston and Mitman ask the question succinctly: "In thinking with animals, how might we capture the agency of another being that cannot speak to reveal the transformative effects its actions have, both literally and figuratively, upon humans?" (2005, 5). See Rees (2017) for an excellent analysis of the question of animal agency, particularly in the history of science, that she ends by making the point that the age of the Anthropocene requires more empirical investigations into and demonstrations of the role played by nonhuman animals in the creation and destabilization of privilege of all forms. Also see Srinivasan (2017) on what it is like to be an octopus and Lynteris (2019) on how animals have historically come to be framed as "epidemic villains."
37. There is a growing body of rich and rather beautiful multispecies ethnographic work that opens up the complexity of human-animal relations in South Asia. Annu Jalais's (2011) *Forest of Tigers* brings out the deep historical and political connections between place, tigers, conservation, ecology, and development. Radhika Govindrajan's (2018) *Animal Intimacies* explores multispecies relatedness in Uttarakhand and makes a compelling case for embracing a critical anthropomorphism. Naisargi Dave (2014) on humanism and animal rights activism, Yamini Narayanan (2018) on cow protectionism, and Naveeda Khan (2014) on dogs and climate change disbelief in Bangladesh are demonstrative of an emergent ethnographic approach to nonhumans that allows the question of the animal to be centered in original ways.
38. But see Nadasdy (2004), who both undertakes an ethnography of the state and studies human relations with land and animals in Yukon, Canada. Also see West (2006) on the relationship between conservation and governance at different scales.
39. I follow Weston (2017, 7) in thinking of this as a relationship of "intimacy" due to the capaciousness of "intimacy" and its capacity to carry distinct meanings—of closeness and love but also distance and hatred—within it. Also see Parreñas (2018) on "affective encounters" between humans and orangutans.
40. Govindrajan similarly makes an important argument for "paying ethnographic attention—that is, sustained and careful attention—to what individual animals *do* over the course of their daily lives [as that] could yield valuable insights into their lives as empathetic, intentional, interpretive, and intelligent beings" (2018, 22; italics in the original).

CHAPTER ONE

1. Throughout this book I use "man-eater" to describe crooked cats when I am quoting someone else or referring to published/official/colonial accounts that use this term. I am conscious of the fact that "man-eater" is a problematic term due to its gendered connotations and long colonial history as well as the sorts of images it conjures up of India as a land peopled with fierce man-eating tigers. My utilization of "crooked cats" is an attempt to evade precisely all these associations and bring our attention to the manner in which these nonhuman animals are understood and discussed by those who live in their thrall. "Crooked cats" also captures, I hope, that mystifying query: What is it that makes some *seedha-saadha bagh* (simple, straightforward big cats) into something that is other and villainous? However, much like the phrase

"human-animal conflict," which I recognize as deeply problematic and attempt to move away from, "man-eater" is expedient to deploy at points in this text.

2. The distinguishing of different kinds of big cats by human populations that live in close proximity to them has been noted in other parts of the world too. In an important study that was one of the first to argue for combining social and biological research in the work of conservation, Marks (1984) distinguished three types of lions that the Bisa in Zambia note: ordinary lions, spiritual lions, and the imperial lion. Jalais (2011) too makes a distinction between the Sundarbans tiger and the cosmopolitan tiger. In both cases it is worth pointing out that the "ordinary" or local big cat is largely considered harmless and capable of living in harmony with humans.
3. The relocation of *adivasis* (a collective term that literally translates to "original inhabitants" and is widely used for communities classified as "tribes" in India) out of wildlife sanctuaries and national parks where they have resided for centuries remains one of the most fraught practices in India today (see Rangarajan and Shahabuddin 2006).
4. On the difficulties with counting tigers and the controversies over the traditional method of studying pugmarks, see Greenough (2003).
5. Wildlife Institute of India, *Leopard Census* (Dehradun: Wildlife Institute of India Publications, 2015).
6. See Nayantara Narayanan, "Why India's First-Ever Leopard Census Reveals Little about the Big Cats' Welfare," Scroll.in, September 9, 2015, https://scroll.in/article/754294/why-indias-first-ever-leopard-census-reveals-little-about-the-big-cats-welfare.
7. Vineet Upadhyay, "Over 140 Predators, Mainly Leopards, Declared Maneaters in Uttarakhand in 15 Years," *Times of India*, September 23, 2016, https://timesofindia.indiatimes.com/city/dehradun/Over-140-predators-mainly-leopards-declared-maneaters-in-Uttarakhand-in-15-years/articleshow/54469966.cms.
8. These claims are made consistently in both colonial and contemporary accounts. For instance, on a visit to India, the field biologist George Schaller said there is no such thing as a man-eater; rather, big cats attack humans purely in self-defense. As I make clear in the introduction, such incidents—accidental encounters or self-defense—have historically *not* been included in the ambit of what is a man-eater. Vishal Gulati, "Wild Animals Don't Want Trouble from Humans: Biologist George Schaller," India New England News, February 17, 2017, http://indianewengland.com/2017/02/wild-animals-dont-want-trouble-humans-biologist-george-schaller/.
9. It is worth noting that "man-eater" is a word found across Asia and Africa, such as in the phrase "the famous man-eaters of Tsavo." It is also, of course, the term that is found in government and conservationists' accounts in India today. In the Hindi language, *adamkhor* or *nar-bhakshi* is used, which I use too when referring to those sources. Both translate, roughly, into "man-eater," though the latter literally means "man-consumer."
10. Divisional forest officer to the chief wildlife warden, July 28, 2006, Chamoli District archive.
11. Some rough figures and studies are available from different parts of India. These are not comprehensive but give us some sense of the large scale of the big-cat translocations in India: "More than 150 leopards were relocated over two years (2001–2002) in Maharashtra. In North Bengal, at least twenty-five leopards were relocated to specific forested areas over five years. An average of fifty leopards trapped outside Gir National Park, Gujarat are relocated into the National Park each year" (Athreya 2006, 420).

12. Translocation is being practiced on not just big cats but also other nonhuman animals such as monkeys, with very similar results of increased conflict between humans and the "immigrant" animals. See Govindrajan (2018), who outlines this practice for Uttarakhand as well.
13. This is certainly the case with human-elephant conflict in India as well, with the state being accused of goading the elephants to kill villagers/adivasis (e.g., Ogra 2008).
14. Boomgaard reads these stories of no attacks on Europeans as an indication of the tiger as "an opportunistic predator who made a 'rational' choice between easy and difficult, unarmed and armed, weak and strong" (2001, 86).
15. The possibility that humans might have been reincarnated in the form of crooked cats was also sometimes brought up in the Himalaya, but it wasn't a strongly supported theory. Almost always it was agreed that the beast was a big cat. In the case of the man-eaters of Tsavo from East Africa, it has been noted that there was a strong belief that the lions were actually spirits of dead humans. As Patterson's notes from his travel diary in Tsavo in 1898 state, "[the lions'] methods then became so uncanny, and their man-stalking so well-timed and so certain of success, that the workmen firmly believed that they were not real animals at all, but devils in lions' shape . . . they were quite convinced that the angry spirits of two departed native chiefs had taken this form in order to protest against a railway being made through their country" ([1898] 2011, 13).
16. Rashkow is unclear on the motivations that inspired Hindu Indians to often risk their lives to protect animals under the British Raj but maintains that they go beyond the religious: "It is anachronistic and overtly instrumentalist to equate most cultural conservation of wildlife in India with a conscious environmentalist ethic in the contemporary sense, but whether because of religion or politics, Indians did offer de facto protection for numerous species, thus providing at least some limited validation of the ecological Indian hypothesis" (2015, 301).
17. Noah Sudarsky, "Catfight: How Mountain Lions Are Struggling to Survive," Salon, March 10, 2014, http://www.salon.com/2014/03/09/cat_fight_how_mountain_lions_are_struggling_to_survive_partner/.
18. Galhano Alves's article was published in 1999. In 2005 there was a national scandal when it was found that not a single tiger was left in the Sariska Tiger Reserve. This emptying out of tigers was largely ascribed to poaching and hunting, though not by the Gujjar community that lives inside the reserve.
19. *Natural World*, series 32, episode 1, "Leopards: 21st Century Cats," directed and written by Steve Gooder, presented by Rom Whitaker, aired May 17, 2013, on BBC Two, http://www.bbc.co.uk/programmes/b01sjtt3.
20. As Rangarajan notes in his account of the Gir lions, such learning is central to these big cats' capacity to survive: "My argument is that if they did not learn, the Gir lions could not have survived the last century" (2013, 126).
21. Of course, big cats are not the only nonhuman animals that are believed to have memory and the capacity for retribution. In India, snakes, especially the cobra, have been mythologized and popularized as particularly likely to extract revenge for past ills to oneself or one's kin. A series of Hindi films have been made around this theme, such as the 1976 blockbuster hit *Nagin*. Elephants, too, are believed to have strong memories, as recently fictionalized by Tania James in her 2016 novel *The Tusk That Did the Damage*, in which an elephant called "Gravedigger" witnesses the brutal death of his mother by a poacher. The novel is presented partly from Gravedigger's perspective as he plans his revenge on the poacher for killing his mother as well as for

all the other atrocities suffered by him at the hands of humans as a species. Similarly, see Tarquin Hall's (2001) *To the Elephant Graveyard*, which traces the hunt of a man-killing elephant in Assam and ruminates on the anger elephants—justifiably—have toward humans in India.

22. In the state of Rajasthan, I was told that tigers and leopards get angry at humans when they take away the cats' human kills. Those humans who pick up a dead human body that the big cat has been feasting on are also, therefore, marked out as the man-eater's prospective victims. See this news story on a man-eating leopard in Rajasthan's Alwar District that also states this belief: Salik Ahmad, "The Longest Night: Alwar Villagers Live in Shadow of 'Man-Eater' Leopard," *Hindustan Times*, February 24, 2017, http://www.hindustantimes.com/india-news/the-longest-night-alwar-villagers-live-in-shadow-of-man-eater-leopard/story-hmkAbX9UJxtxp0tQ62iujI.html.
23. Indeed, this is precisely what older hunters such as Corbett (1991a) claimed.
24. The public display of the corpse of a man-eater has a long history, and its present practice retains the state ceremonialism of past. It is customary for the hunter or hunters to pose with the corpse in all their hunting gear glory, displaying their guns, and flanked by state officials (also in uniform). In the mountains, there is an additional practice of parading the big cat's corpse on the front of a jeep. The man-eater is often adorned with a garland of marigold flowers, and a red vermilion mark is put to his or her forehead, both auspicious Hindu ritual practices for the dead. See the introduction and chapter 7.
25. For instance, see this story from Mongabay: Johan Augustin, "The Sundarbans: Frontlines of Climate Change for Tigers and People," Mongabay, January 13, 2020, https://india.mongabay.com/2020/01/the-sundarbans-frontlines-of-climate-change-for-tigers-and-people/.
26. Kai Schultz and Hari Kumar, "Bengal Tigers May Not Survive Climate Change," *New York Times*, May 6, 2019, https://www.nytimes.com/2019/05/06/science/tigers-climate-change-sundarbans.html.
27. For a write-up on this astonishing human-leopard landscape, see Hari Kunzru, "Life among the Leopards," *New York Times Style Magazine*, May 8, 2015, https://www.nytimes.com/2015/05/08/t-magazine/life-among-the-leopards-jawai-india.html#.

CHAPTER TWO

1. This game—of pretending the culprit has been caught even though it is only in the rarest of cases that we could know this as a fact—has gained particular importance with the passage of the Wildlife Protection Act (WPA) of 1972. The WPA completely bans and renders illegal the killing of any big cat in India other than those that are *proven* man-eaters. From 1972 onward, killing a tiger, leopard, or lion in India for which one has not obtained prior permission (in the form of a hunting permit) and that is not certainly a man-eater creates a peculiar set of complexities, including the need to play a complicated game of retrospective erasure—involving the disappearance of various matter ranging from the body of the big cat to photographs, and the silencing of accomplices and members of media—in order to paper over the illegal death of the innocent big cat.
2. Dicky Singh's entire account of the Ustad story is available on his blogging site: Dicky Singh, "T 24 or Ustaad Episode in Ranthambhore," *Aditya Dicky Singh* (blog), October 16, 2015, http://www.dickysingh.com/2015/10/16/t-24-or-ustaad-episode-in-ranthambhore/.

3. "Ustad Is Dangerous, Should Be in Captivity: Wildlife Expert," *Hindustan Times*, May 19, 2015, https://www.hindustantimes.com/india/ustad-is-dangerous-should-be-in-captivity-wildlife-expert/story-8PKIqlzNZtHYflebDXuFZI.html.
4. Gayatri Jayaraman, "Ustad: Man-Eater or Victim of Man-Animal Conflict?," *India Today*, issue dated June 8, 2015, updated May 29, 2015, https://www.indiatoday.in/magazine/cover-story/story/20150608-t24-ustad-tiger-forest-guard-rampal-saini-sajjangarh-biological-park-819774-2015-05-28.
5. Jayaraman, "Ustad: Man-Eater or Victim of Man-Animal Conflict?"
6. In this report by the National Tiger Conservation Authority (NTCA), for instance, this distinction between a "man-eater" and a "man-killer" is considered: NTCA, *Standard Operating Procedure to Deal with Emergency Arising due to Straying of Tigers in Human Dominated Landscapes* (Delhi: National Tiger Conservation Authority of India, January 2013), https://cdn.downtoearth.org.in/library/0.17541800_1541658521_final_sop_11_01_2013.pdf.
7. NTCA, *Standard Operating Procedure*, 2–3. Though leopards are not mentioned in the title, these SOPs cover leopards too, as the text of the document makes clear.
8. NTCA, *Standard Operating Procedure*, 18.
9. A short video clip that wonderfully describes this operation can be watched here: "Video: How a Group of Wildlife Enthusiasts Helped Capture a Rogue Leopard in Mumbai's Aarey Colony," Scroll.in, March 4, 2018, https://scroll.in/video/870682/video-how-a-group-of-wildlife-enthusiasts-helped-capture-a-rogue-leopard-in-mumbais-aarey-colony.
10. Seema Sharma, "Leopard Trapped in FRI: Was This the One That Killed Girl?," *Times of India*, March 20, 2015, http://timesofindia.indiatimes.com/city/dehradun/Leopard-trapped-in-FRI-Was-this-the-one-that-killed-girl/articleshow/46638320.cms.
11. Prashant Dayal, "India Puts Gujarat Lions on Trial after Three People Killed," BBC News, June 14, 2016, http://www.bbc.co.uk/news/world-asia-india-36526308.
12. According to the ethnobiologist Galhano Alves (1999a), there are nine rules that the Van Gujjar community follows when their members encounter a tiger in Sariska in Rajasthan. Of these nine rules there is a critical one that dictates the person must look straight into the eyes of the tiger and make sure to not take their eyes off those of the tiger.
13. An article with an example of this description can be found here: "NTCA Discusses Better Synergy with Ministries for Tiger Conservation," *Indian Express*, July 13, 2019, https://indianexpress.com/article/india/ntca-discusses-better-synergy-with-ministries-for-tiger-conservation-5865550/.
14. "Spotting the Killer," *Hindu*, September 7, 2013, updated June 2, 2016, http://www.thehindu.com/todays-paper/tp-features/tp-metroplus/spotting-the-killer/article5101910.ece.
15. An offense committed inside the core area of a tiger reserve attracts a mandatory prison term of three years, extendable to seven years, and a fine of ₹50,000, extendable to 2 lakhs of rupees. In the case of a subsequent conviction of this nature, there is an imprisonment term of at least seven years and a fine of 5 lakhs of rupees, which may extend to 50 lakhs of rupees.
16. Wildlife organizations have noted the difficulty of enforcing the WPA's penalties for nonofficials and poachers as well. However, my concern is not with the enforcement or the lack thereof but rather with the fear that this is, officially, an "illegal" act, which forest and district bureaucrats constantly mentioned nervously to me.
17. A report by the World Wildlife Fund (WWF) argues that anthropogenic climate change might wipe out half of India's wildlife by 2020, including the endangered

big cats. WWF, *Living Planet Report 2016: Risk and Resilience in a New Era* (Gland, Switzerland: WWW International, 2016), https://awsassets.panda.org/downloads/lpr_2016_full_report_low_res.pdf.

CHAPTER THREE

1. Pratyush Patra, "One Year On, Killer White Tiger Becomes Delhi Zoo's Biggest Celeb," *Times of India*, September 29, 2015, https://timesofindia.indiatimes.com/city/delhi/One-year-on-killer-white-tiger-becomes-Delhi-zoos-biggest-celeb/articleshow/49153374.cms.
2. "Man Killed by White Tiger Blamed; He Was Mentally Ill, Says Delhi Zoo," NDTV, first aired on September 24, 2014, YouTube video, 2:33, https://www.youtube.com/watch?v=j2VmYQTgWHE.
3. "How I Become a 'Murderer'—Story of White Tiger," *Allonas*, October 27, 2014, https://allonas.wordpress.com/2014/10/27/how-i-become-a-murderer-story-of-white-tiger/.
4. Somreet Bhattacharya, "Maqsood's Obsession with Tigers Led to His Death," *Times of India*, September 25, 2014, http://timesofindia.indiatimes.com/City/Delhi/His-obsession-with-tigers-led-him-to-his-death/articleshow/43358473.cms.
5. Aarti Sethi, "Remembering Maqsood Pardesi," *Ka□la*, September 27, 2014, https://kafila.online/2014/09/27/remembering-maqsood-pardesi/.
6. "Man Killed by White Tiger Blamed," NDTV, first aired on September 24, 2014.
7. The charisma I am referring to here is what Lorimer has termed "aesthetic charisma" or the visual appearance of a species—in, this case, a commodified form. He goes on to identify other forms of nonhuman charisma, including "ecological charisma" and "corporeal charisma" (Lorimer 2015, 40).
8. John Berger (2009, 33) notes that the emergence and sale of realistic animal toys, including soft toys, "coincid[e], more or less, with the establishment of public zoos." Soft toys are, in other words, enmeshed in the very particular historical processes of the commodification and display of wildlife.
9. See snippets of the celebration here, in this YouTube video posted by the *Navbharat Times* on July 20, 2017: https://www.youtube.com/watch?v=cSYyvgyJKn8.

CHAPTER FOUR

1. Ruth McD, "Demand Justice for Cecil the Lion in Zimbabwe," Care2, accessed January 22, 2016, http://www.thepetitionsite.com/821/738/351/demand-justice-for-cecil-the-lion-in-zimbambwe/.
2. For instance, my previous research was centered on the execution of the Mahatma Gandhi National Rural Employment Guarantee Act (MGNREGA), 2005, that legally enjoins the setting up of grievance redressal cells in districts and states (N. Mathur 2016). In most districts in Uttarakhand the grievance redressal cell became so rapidly flooded with petitions—or, in its language, "grievances"—that it couldn't cope, and in the end, they all had to be shut down. The shutting down of the grievance cell entailed, at its core, the closing of a register on "grievances" in the central district office—the MGNREGA "cell"—and thus foreclosed the space for any forms of petitioning around this gigantic welfare program. Most bureaucrats I encountered believed this was the right thing to do given what they consider "pathological petitioning" in India.
3. For an account of the wildlife conservationist regime that protects big cats and other such "endangered" animals in India, see the text of the Indian Wildlife (Protection) Act, 1972, which is available at http://nbaindia.org/uploaded/Biodiversityindia

/Legal/15.%20Wildlife%20(Protection)%20Act,%201972.pdf. Also see Rangarajan (2005). For a global history of conservationism see W. Adams (2004).

4. See Rees (2017) for a succinct summary of the core issues involved in debates on animal agency. On big cats and the question of their histories, memory, and capacity to remember and act—to be agentive—see Rangarajan (2013).
5. Nagrik Manch (Citizens Forum) of Chamoli District, Uttarakhand, to the district magistrate of Chamoli, petition, December 21, 2007.
6. On the history of the *dharna* including threats of suicide or forms of murder, see Singha, *A Despotism of Law* (1998), 86–90.
7. Up until the year 2000, present-day Uttarakhand used to be a part of the larger provincial state of Uttar Pradesh (UP). The mountain dwellers of Uttarakhand have an expressive way of distinguishing their lives from the lives of those in UP. They claim that "the mountains are at peace" (*pahar shanta hai*) in contrast to the wider history of communal and caste tensions in UP. This reputation of peaceful mountain persons (*paharis*) is one that is universally present among state agents of Uttarakhand as well.
8. This story, like many similar accounts of bagh murders in Uttarakhand, is not allowed to enter files and documents, as the actions described therein are direct contraventions of the Wildlife Protection Act, 1972. According to that statute and subsequent injunctions such as *Guidelines for Human-Leopard Conflict Management* (Ministry of Environment and Forests 2011), a leopard can only ever be captured or killed subsequent to the winning of a hunting permit for that specific leopard. This hunting permit can only be won after the accumulation of adequate evidence that the big cat in question is, indeed, a "man-eater." As there was no time for this cumbersome bureaucratic process, this murder was strictly kept off record. Concerned about more than the illegality of such actions, forest and district officials are careful about what details of leopards' deaths enter the records due to the fear of provoking the ire of conservationists in India.
9. Naturally, a WhatsApp arzee will remain a canny tool of communicating with the state for as long as its usage is low, as is the current situation in Uttarakhand.
10. Ellen Barry, "A Castle Receives a Weekly Delivery of Delhi's Secret Desires," *New York Times*, November 8, 2015, goo.gl/Wo8nQT.
11. Taneja (2013) traces this practice to a form of governance that was common in fourteenth-century Delhi, when royal guards were removed and subjects were allowed to enter the palace to directly petition the Tughlaq sultan.
12. Petitions in the district archives of Chamoli, Dehradun, and Tehri-Garhwal.

CHAPTER FIVE

1. On the question of the relationship between ethnography and literature, see Fassin (2014). Fassin notes that the relationship between ethnography and fiction is a "unique association of reality and truth. . . . If the fictional imagination lies in the power to invent a world with its characters, the ethnographic imagination implies the power to make sense of the world that subjects create by relating it to larger structures and events" (2014, 53).

CHAPTER SIX

1. Thanks to Malinowski for this famous passage from his *Argonauts of the Western Pacific*. As the reader will, no doubt, see, this is a somewhat contrary scenario of the Malinowskian site wherein he seeks to set the stage for a very different space and

time: "Imagine yourself suddenly set down surrounded by all your gear, alone on a tropical beach close to a native village, while the launch or dinghy which has brought you sails away out of sight" (Malinowski 2014, 3).

2. In these accounts, the artificial separation out of wilderness from human habitations, which has a longer history rooted in romanticism and the idea of nature, is undone by animals that transgress these boundaries.
3. The Sundarbans is perhaps the most famous region in India that boasts of records of "man-eaters" going more than 350 years back. There are many speculations on why the area is so very evil, with one proposal put forth that it is due to the salinity of the water in the region. As Madhusudan and Mishra (2005) note, however, this remains an unsubstantiated and unconvincing explanation.
4. A district is further divided into "development blocks" for the ease of administering developmental aid.
5. "Institute Campus," Forest Research Institute, Dehradun, accessed July 4, 2018, http://www.fri.res.in/the-institute/institute-campus/.
6. Maps of India, too, mimic such demarcations of human places from beastly ones with their clearly marked-out national parks, tiger reserves, and biodiversity zones. Such cartographic representations help aid the narrative that when a big cat is sighted in human-dominated landscapes that are not within the bounds of these officially sanctioned places, it is escaping from or straying into human zones.
7. Srivastava has argued that the Doon School in Dehradun "was an important site of construction of the 'modern' Indian citizen" (1998, 3). The school worked through its recruitment of the Indian elite into a British-style boarding school and by inculcating the virtues of modernity, masculinity, community, nation, and discipline into its students, who all went on to play a central role in newly independent India.
8. See this article for an example of the ways in which Corbett is constantly invoked by the hunters: Divya Gandhi and Raza Kazmi, "Why a Trophy Hunter, a School Teacher and a Businessman Are Hired to Shoot Man-Eaters," *Hindu*, December 7, 2018, https://www.thehindu.com/sci-tech/energy-and-environment/indias-new-age-shikaris/article25681773.ece.
9. As a rich literature has now argued, the hunting of man-eaters was a central means through which aristocrats and men of state in these imperial state formations exhibited a masculinist mastery over nature and attempted to promote perceptions of themselves as benign rulers. See MacKenzie (1988); Sramek (2006); Storey (1991); and Pandian (2001).
10. See the press release of the report issued by the Wildlife Conservation Society here: "Leopard Numbers in SGNP on the Rise," Wildlife Conservation Society-India, April 1, 2019, https://programs.wcs.org/india-beta/Newsroom/Press-Releases/ID/12751/Leopard-numbers-in-SGNP-on-the-rise.
11. For instance, the episode on cities in David Attenborough's *Planet Earth II* features the leopards extensively. See *Planet Earth II*, episode 6, "Cities," aired December 11, 2016, on BBC One, https://www.bbc.co.uk/programmes/b0861m8b.
12. See Luise White (2000) on the power of the transnational genre of African stories—what she terms "vampire stories"—to serve as a better, clearer, more analytical perspective on the colonial experience than other historical sources do.
13. Brockington (2009) has studied the interaction between celebrity and conservation, one that he argues has a long history but is getting accelerated of late due to the commodification and commercialization of conservation.

14. "Shimla City Census 2011 Data," Census 2011, accessed February 22, 2016, http://www.census2011.co.in/census/city/4-shimla.html. According to Himachal Pradesh Forest Department records, an average of thirty-four nonfatal attacks by leopards on people and three fatal attacks on humans per year have been reported between 2004 and 2015 (Wildlife Conservation Society report submitted to Himachal Pradesh Forest Department in March 2016).

CHAPTER SEVEN

1. As Ito notes, for the ultra-rationalist Singer it is language that is the primary mode of representing reason, "whereas an image is a more intuitive mode of representation, which has to be reflected upon by reason in order to know what the image really means" (2008, 129).
2. One of the first uses that camera traps were put to was the estimation of tiger populations. In 1991–1992, the Wildlife Conservation Society deployed camera traps for one year to study tigers in Nagarhole National Park in India. The conclusion of the study was that the camera trap was a huge improvement over the "demonstrably failure-prone and unvalidated pug-mark census method or its untested variants." The study went on to state that camera traps allow for "objective estimating" of size, density, survival, and other facets of "secretive animal species" such as tigers and leopards (Karanth 1995, 333).
3. Previously, a census was undertaken by field staff members such as beat guards who would be trained to identify pugmarks and were armed with a "pugmark tracking kit." On encountering a pugmark, they would pour plaster of paris in the impression on the ground and note specifics of the site and other information on the reverse side. These plaster casts would be collected for one area, and repetitions of the same tiger or leopard were removed collectively (Shaktawat 2018, 30). See Greenough (2003) for claims by leading tiger experts in India that the pugmark is a faulty mode of identifying big cats. In my experience in the Himalaya, however, it continues to be used extensively and is widely considered one of the most reliable tracking techniques.
4. Jeremy Hance, "Camera Traps Emerge as Key Tool in Wildlife Research," Yale Environment 360, December 5, 2011, https://e360.yale.edu/features/camera_traps_emerge_as_key_tool_in_wildlife_research.
5. Dave, too, centers the critical moment when the animal rights activists she has worked with see an animal such as a horse: "animal rights activists describe this critical moment as an intimate event in which the sight of a suffering animal, the locking of eyes between human and nonhuman, inaugurates a bond demanding from the person a life of responsibility" (2014, 434). In the cases I describe of an eye lock with a big cat, there is precisely a similar form of intimacy because it "occurs between two singular beings" (Dave, 434), but the gaze is interpreted differentially by individuals.
6. Quoted in Andres Guadamuz, "Can the Monkey Selfie Case Teach Us Anything about Copyright Law?," *WIPO Magazine*, February 2018, https://www.wipo.int/wipo_magazine/en/2018/01/article_0007.html; Jason Slotkin, "'Monkey Selfie' Lawsuit Ends with Settlement between PETA, Photographer," NPR, September 12, 2017, https://www.npr.org/sections/thetwo-way/2017/09/12/550417823/-animal-rights-advocates-photographer-compromise-over-ownership-of-monkey-selfie?t=1532948621013.
7. "PETA Statement: 'Monkey Selfie' Case Settled," PETA, September 11, 2017, https://www.peta.org/media/news-releases/peta-statement-monkey-selfie-case-settled/. Quoted in Slotkin, "'Monkey Selfie' Lawsuit."

8. Suzanne Monyak, "When the Law Recognizes Animals as People," *New Republic*, February 2, 2018, https://newrepublic.com/article/146870/law-recognizes-animals-people.
9. Kavita Upadhyay, "Animal Are Legal Entities with Rights, Duties and Liabilities of a Living Person: Uttarakhand HC," *Indian Express*, July 5, 2018, https://indianexpress.com/article/india/uttarakhand-high-court-declares-all-animals-as-legal-entities-5246002/. This judgment was ultimately overturned by the Supreme Court of India in 2019. Hence, it did not pass into law, but the point remains that there are now increasing calls for and instances of the conferral of legal personhood to non-humans, whether they are rivers or animals.
10. Julia Carrie Wong, "Monkey Selfie Photographer Says He's Broke: 'I'm Thinking of Dog Walking,'" *Guardian*, July 13, 2017, https://www.theguardian.com/environment/2017/jul/12/monkey-selfie-macaque-copyright-court-david-slater.
11. Trupthi Narayan, "Of Leopards and Lemons: Superstition Aids Wildlife Researchers in India," Mongabay, April 22, 2015, https://news.mongabay.com/2015/04/of-leopards-and-lemons-superstition-aids-wildlife-researchers-in-india/.
12. For instance, Amy Fitzmaurice, a conservationist who works for Chester Zoo, has experience with one tiger in Nepal who has destroyed two camera traps quite deliberately (personal correspondence).
13. This scenario constantly surfaces in written accounts, especially those from the colonial period. See, for instance, *The Man-Eating Leopard of Rudraprayag* (Corbett 1991b).
14. As when tranquilization happens in the wild, with trapped big cats too, large crowds tend to assemble to watch the animal. This adds further pressure on both the caged animal and the forest department and other officials/conservationists who are attempting to transport or calm down the big cat. People often jostle to take a picture of or, even worse, a selfie with the big cat, and this further exacerbates the situation.
15. Sara Malm, "Monkeys Rescue Leopard from Drowning in a Well after Alerting Indian Villagers to the Animal with Chattering and Jumping," *Daily Mail*, June 19, 2018, http://www.dailymail.co.uk/news/article-5860181/Monkeys-save-leopard-drowning-alerting-locals-chattering-jumping.html.
16. Mike Wright, "Vet Climbs Down 30ft Well to Rescue Stranded Leopard in India," *Telegraph*, December 15, 2017, https://www.telegraph.co.uk/news/2017/12/15/vet-climbs-30ft-rescue-stranded-leopard-india/.
17. Jake Polden, "Villagers Stage Dramatic Rescue after Using Just a Net and Ladder after a LEOPARD Gets Stuck Down a Well in India," *Daily Mail*, June 4, 2015, http://www.dailymail.co.uk/news/article-3110816/Leopard-rescued-villagers-lower-ladder-usher-safety.html.
18. Brian Clark Howard, "Watch Villagers Save Drowning Leopard in Dramatic Rescue," *National Geographic*, August 4, 2016, https://news.nationalgeographic.com/2016/08/drowning-leopard-rescued-well-india/.
19. "Epic India Leopard Rescue Photo Wins Award Five Years Later," BBC News, November 16, 2017, https://www.bbc.com/news/world-asia-india-41994292.
20. "Thirsty India Leopard Gets Head Stuck in Pot," BBC News, October 1, 2015, https://www.bbc.co.uk/news/world-asia-india-34409635.
21. Shayan Roy, "Would You Remove a Pot from the Head of This Leopard?," Buzzfeed, September 30, 2015, https://www.buzzfeed.com/shayanroy/who-turned-off-the-lights?utm_term=.rabYyyKVQK#.fybmwwYRXY.
22. "Leopard Kills Dog in Mumbai Apartment: CCTV Footage," Wild Films India, uploaded August 28, 2017, YouTube video, 1:04, https://www.youtube.com/watch?v=Hz0o2_i6pJg.

CHAPTER EIGHT

1. The biologist Svenning (2017) notes that post-1960s extinction of megafauna has the distinct characteristics of being anthropogenic; species disappear without an ecological replacement; and larger species tend to be poorly represented. In Svenning's long-term paleoecological account of seeing past worlds and imagining the future of megafauna, leopards in India are listed as having a somewhat hopeful prospect for thriving in the Anthropocene (2017, 80). This is an optimistic stance on what the future holds for big cats that is not entirely shared by *Crooked Cats*.
2. See, for instance, this story in the *Guardian*: Michael Safi, "Calvin Klein Fragrance Could Be Used to Lure Killer Tiger," *Guardian*, October 9, 2018, https://www.theguardian.com/world/2018/oct/09/calvin-klein-fragrance-could-be-used-lure-man-eating-tiger. Much of Avni's tale has been pieced together through a reliance on the extensive reporting that followed this celebrity big cat.
3. Krishna Thevar, "Was Avni a Man Eater? Expert Engaged by Maharashtra Has Doubts," *Economic Times*, November 9, 2018, https://economictimes.indiatimes.com/news/politics-and-nation/was-avni-a-man-eater-expert-engaged-by-maharashtra-has-doubts/articleshow/66559056.cms.
4. DNA Web Team, 'Avni killing-who are hunters Shafat Ali and Asghar Ali Khan?', DNA, November 4, 2018, https://www.dnaindia.com/india/photo-gallery-avni-killing-who-are-hunters-shafat-ali-and-asghar-ali-khan-2682651/maneka-lashes-out-2682654
5. Scroll Staff, "'Ghastly Murder': Maneka Gandhi Lashes Out at Maharashtra Government for Killing Tigress Avni," Scroll.in, November 5, 2018, https://scroll.in/latest/900895/ghastly-murder-maneka-gandhi-lashes-out-at-maharashtra-government-for-killing-tigress-avni.
6. Aaditya Thackeray (@AUThackeray), "Let's rename the Ministry of Forests as Ministry of Poaching. It's anyway a sham! #Avni," Twitter, November 3, 2018, https://twitter.com/AUThackeray/status/1058650103530053633?s=20.
7. Oliver Milman, "Mild Winter Spurs Bears to Emerge from Hibernation Earlier," *Guardian*, March 11, 2020, https://www.theguardian.com/world/2020/mar/11/mild-winter-bears-emerge-from-hibernation.
8. Tanmayee Tyagi, "Prowling Leopard Crates [*sic*] Panic in Greater Noida, Caught after Seven Hours," *Hindustan Times*, January 21, 2019, https://www.hindustantimes.com/india-news/leopard-enters-greater-noida-village-injures-boy/story-ZwAAxIwITOQS4Thvq2z3tI.html.
9. Ipsita Pati, "Camera Traps Set Up at DLF Golf Course in Gurgaon after 'Leopard Sighting,'" *Hindustan Times*, April 28, 2017, https://www.hindustantimes.com/gurugram/camera-traps-set-up-at-dlf-golf-course-in-gurugram-after-leopard-sighting/story-UIwwBmh7vMLGTvjZhDq7zH.html.

BIBLIOGRAPHY

Adams, Bill. 2020. "Digital Animals." *Philosopher* 108 (1) ("The Other Animals"). https://www.thephilosopher1923.org/adams.

Adams, W. M. 2004. *Against Extinction: The Story of Conservation*. London: Routledge.

Agrawal, Arun. 1995. "Dismantling the Divide between Indigenous and Scientific Knowledge." *Development and Change* 26 (3): 413–39.

Amrith, Sunil. 2018. *Unruly Waters: How Mountain Rivers and Monsoons Have Shaped South Asia's History*. London: Allen Lane.

Anderson, Kenneth. 2002. *The Call of the Man-Eater*. New Delhi: Rupa Publications.

Arts, Koen, René van der Wal, and William M. Adams. 2015. "Digital Technology and the Conservation of Nature." *Ambio* 44 (4): S661–73.

Athreya, V., M. Odden, J. D. C. Linnell, and K. U. Karanth. 2011. "Translocation as a Tool for Mitigating Conflict with Leopards in Human-Dominated Landscapes of India." *Conservation Biology* 25 (1): 133–41.

Athreya, V., M. Odden, J. D. C. Linnell, J. Krishnaswamy, and U. Karanth. 2013. "Big Cats in Our Backyards: Persistence of Large Carnivores in a Human Dominated Landscape in India." *PLOS ONE* 8 (3). https://doi.org/10.1371/journal.pone.0057872.

Athreya, V., S. Pimpale, A. S. Borkar, N. Surve, S. Chakravarty, M. Ghosalkar, A. Patwardhan, and J. D. C. Linnell. 2018. "Monsters or Gods? Narratives of Large Cat Worship in Western India." *Cat News* 67 (Spring): 23–26.

Athreya, Vidya. 2006. "Is Relocation a Viable Management Option for Unwanted Animals?—The Case of the Leopard in India." *Conservation and Society* 4 (3): 419–23.

Atkinson, E. T. (1881) 2002. *The Himalayan Gazetteer, or The Himalayan Districts of the North Western Province of India, Volume II*. Reprint, Delhi: Low Price Publication.

Barnes, Jessica, and Michael Dove. 2015. *Climate Cultures: Anthropological Perspectives on Climate Change*. New Haven, CT: Yale University Press.

Barua, Maan. 2014. "Bio-Geo-Graphy: Landscape, Dwelling, and the Political Ecology of Human-Elephant Relations." *Environment and Planning D: Society and Space* 32 (5): 915–34.

Barua, Maan. 2017. "Nonhuman Labour, Encounter Value, Spectacular Accumulation: The Geographies of a Lively Commodity." *Transactions of the Institute of British Geographers* 42 (2): 274–88.

Barua, Maan. 2018. "Animal Work: Metabolic, Ecological, Affective." Editor's Forum: Theorizing the Contemporary, *Fieldsights*, July 26, 2018. https://culanth.org/fieldsights/animal-work-metabolic-ecological-affective.

Benjamin, Walter. 1996. "The Task of the Translator." In *Walter Benjamin: Selected Writings, 1913–1926*, edited by Marcus Bullock and Michael W. Jennings, 253–63. London: Belknap Press of Harvard University Press.

Berger, John. 2009. *Why Look at Animals?* London: Penguin.

Bhan, Gautam, Teresa Caldeira, Kelly Gillespie, and AbdouMaliq Simone. 2020. "The Pandemic, Southern Urbanisms, and Collective Life." *Society and Space*, August 3, 2020. https://www.societyandspace.org/articles/the-pandemic-southern-urbanisms-and-collective-life.

Bhatt, S., S. Biswas, K. Karanth, B. Pandav, and S. Mondol. 2020. "Genetic Analyses Reveal Population Structure and Recent Decline in Leopards (*Panthera pardus fusca*) across the Indian Subcontinent." *PeerJ* 8. https://doi.org/10.7717/peerj.8482.

Bodenhorn, Barbara, and Olga Ulturgasheva. 2017. "Climate Strategies: Thinking through Arctic Examples." *Philosophical Transactions of the Royal Society A* 375. http://dx.doi.org/10.1098/rsta.2016.0363.

Bond, Ruskin. 2013. *Tigers for Dinner: Tall Tales by Jim Corbett's Khansama*. New Delhi: Rupa Publications.

Boomgaard, Peter. 2001. *Frontiers of Fear: Tigers and People in the Malay World, 1600–1950*. New Haven, CT: Yale University Press.

Booth, Martin. 1986. *Carpet Sahib: A Life of Jim Corbett*. Delhi: Oxford University Press.

Brittlebank, Kate. 1995. "Sakti and Barakat: The Power of Tipu's Tiger: An Examination of the Tiger Emblem of Tipu Sultan of Mysore." *Modern Asian Studies* 29 (2): 257–69.

Brockington, Dan. 2009. *Celebrity and the Environment: Fame, Wealth, and Power in Conservation*. London: Zed Books.

Brzozowska-Brywczyńska, Maja. 2007. "Monstrous/Cute: Notes on the Ambivalent Nature of Cuteness." In *Monsters and the Monstrous: Myths and Metaphors of Enduring Evil*, edited by Niall Scott, 213–28. Amsterdam: Rodopi Press.

Buden, Boris, Stefan Nowotny, Sherry Simon, Ashok Bery, and Michael Cronin. 2009. "Cultural Translation: An Introduction to the Problem, and Responses." *Translation Studies* 2 (2): 196–219.

Burton, Richard. 1931. *A Book of Man-Eaters*. London: Hutchinson.

Cahill, A. E., M. E. Aiello-Lammens, M. C. Fisher-Reid, X. Hua, C. J. Karanewsky, H. Yeong Ryu, G. C. Sbeglia, F. Spagnolo, J. B. Waldron, O. Warsi, and J. J. Wiens. 2012. "How Does Climate Change Cause Extinction?" *Proceedings of the Royal Society B* 280. http://dx.doi.org/10.1098/rspb.2012.1890.

Caputo, Philip. 2002. *Ghosts of Tsavo: Stalking the Mystery Lions of East Africa*. Washington, DC: National Geographic Society.

Cassidy, Rebecca. 2012. "Lives with Others: Climate Change and Human-Animal Relations." *Annual Review of Anthropology* 41 (1): 21–36.

Chakrabarty, Dipesh. 2009. "The Climate of History: Four Theses." *Critical Inquiry* 35 (2): 197–222.

Chandra, Vikram. 2006. *Sacred Games*. London: Faber & Faber.

Chua, Liana. 2018. "Too Cute to Cuddle? 'Witnessing Publics' and Interspecies Relations on the Social Media-scape of Orangutan Conservation." *Anthropological Quarterly* 91 (3): 873–903.

Chua, Liana, and Hannah Fair. 2019. "Anthropocene." In *Cambridge Encyclopedia of Anthropology*, edited by Felix Stein. University of Cambridge. https://www.anthroencyclopedia.com/entry/anthropocene.

Chua, Liana, and Nayanika Mathur. 2018. *Who Are "We"? Reimagining Alterity and Af□nity in Anthropology*. New York: Berghahn Books.

Cobb, Stephen. 1981. "The Leopard—Problem of an Overabundant, Threatened, Terrestrial Carnivore." In *Problems in Management of Locally Abundant Wild Mammals*, edited by Peter A. Jewell and Sidney Holt, 181–92. London: Academic Press.

Cons, Jason. 2018. "Staging Climate Security: Resilience and Heterodystopia in the Bangladesh Borderlands." *Cultural Anthropology* 33 (2): 266–94.

Corbett, Jim. 1991a. *Man-Eaters of Kumaon*. Oxford: Oxford University Press. First published 1944.

Corbett, Jim. 1991b. *The Man-Eating Leopard of Rudraprayag*. Delhi: Oxford University Press.

Corbett, Jim. 2007. *The Jim Corbett Omnibus*. Delhi: Oxford University Press.

Corsin Jimenez, Alberto, and Chloe Nahum-Claudel. 2019. "The Anthropology of Traps: Concrete Technologies and Theoretical Interfaces." *Journal of Material Culture* 24 (4): 383–400.

Crutzen, P. J. 2006. "The 'Anthropocene.'" In *Earth System Science in the Anthropocene*, edited by E. Ehlers and T. Krafft, 13–18. Berlin: Springer.

Das, Prasanta. 2009. "Jim Corbett's 'Green' Imperialism." *Economic and Political Weekly* 44 (15): 20–22.

Daston, Lorraine, and Gregg Mitman. 2005. "Introduction." In *Thinking with Animals: New Perspectives on Anthropomorphism*, edited by Lorraine Daston and Gregg Mitman, 1–14. New York: Columbia University Press.

Dave, Naisargi. 2014. "Witness: Humans, Animals, and the Politics of Becoming." *Cultural Anthropology* 29 (3): 433–56.

Deb Roy, Rohan. 2020. "White Ants, Empire and Entomo-Politics in South Asia." *The Historical Journal* 63 (2): 411–36.

De La Cadena, Marisol, and Mario Blaser. 2018. *A World of Many Worlds*. Durham, NC: Duke University Press.

DeLoughrey, Elizabeth M. 2019. *Allegories of the Anthropocene*. Durham, NC: Duke University Press.

Despret, Vinciane. 2016. *What Would Animals Say If We Asked the Right Questions?* Minneapolis: University of Minnesota Press.

De Waal, Frans. 2016. *Are We Smart Enough to Know How Smart Animals Are?* London: W. W. Norton.

Dirks, Nicholas B. 2001. *Castes of Mind: Colonialism and the Making of Modern India*. Princeton, NJ: Princeton University Press.

Divyabhanusinh. 2008. *The Story of Asia's Lions*. Mumbai: Marg Publications.

Doubleday, Kalli. 2018. "Human Tiger (Re)Negotiations: A Case Study from Sariska Tiger Reserve, India." *Society & Animals* 26 (2):148–70.

D'Souza, Rohan. 2015. "Nations without Borders: Climate Security and the South in the Epoch of the Anthropocene." *Strategic Analysis* 39 (6): 720–28.

Fassin, Didier. 2014. "True Life, Real Lives: Revisiting the Boundaries between Ethnography and Fiction." *American Ethnologist* 41 (1): 40–55.

Forrester, Katrina, and Sophie Smith. 2018. "History, Theory and the Environment." In *Nature, Action and the Future: Political Thought and the Environment*, edited by Katrina Forrester and Sophie Smith, 1–20. Cambridge: Cambridge University Press.

Fudge, Erica. 2002. *Animal*. London: Reaktion.

Galhano Alves, Joao Pedro. 1999a. "Men and Tigers in Sariska Tiger Reserve, India." *Cat News* 30 (Spring): 12–30.

Galhano Alves, Joao Pedro. 1999b. "Tigers and People: Strategies for Tiger Conservation in Sariska Tiger Reserve, India." *Cat News* 30 (Spring): 10–12.

Gell, Alfred. 1996. "Vogel's Net: Traps as Artworks and Artworks as Traps." *Journal of Material Culture* 1 (1): 15–38.

Ghosal, Sunetro. 2014. "Cats in the City: Narrative Analysis of the Interactions between People and Leopards in the Sanjay Gandhi National Park Landscape, Mumbai." Report submitted to the SGNP Forest Department. In Mumbaikars for SGNP 2014, 176–224.

Ghosal, Sunetro, and Darley Jose Kjosavik. 2015. "Living with Leopards: Negotiating Morality and Modernity in Western India." *Society and Natural Resources* 28 (10): 1092–107.

Ghosh, Amitav. 2016. *The Great Derangement: Climate Change and the Unthinkable*. New Delhi: Penguin.

Ghosh, Amitav. 2019. *Gun Island*. London: John Murray.

Giggs, Rebecca. 2020. *Fathoms: The World in the Whale*. New York: Simon & Schuster.

Godfrey-Smith, Peter. 2017. *Other Minds: The Octopus and the Evolution of Intelligent Life*. London: William Collins.

Goodman, Lenn Evan, and Richard J. A. McGregor, trans. 2012. *The Case of the Animals versus Man before the King of the Jinn: A Translation from the Epistles of the Brethren of Purity*. Oxford: Oxford University Press.

Gopalaswamy, Arjun, K. Ullas Karanth, Mohan Delampady, and Nils C. Stenseth. 2019. "How Sampling-Based Overdispersion Reveals India's Tiger Monitoring Orthodoxy." *Conservation Science and Practice* 1 (1): 1–11. https://conbio.onlinelibrary.wiley.com/doi/epdf/10.1111/csp2.128.

Govindrajan, Radhika. 2015. "'The Man-Eater Sent by God': Unruly Interspecies Intimacy in India's Central Himalayas." In "Unruly Environments," edited by Siddharta Krishnan, Christopher L. Pastore, and Samuel Temple, *RCC Perspectives* 3 (2015): 33–38.

Govindrajan, Radhika. 2018. *Animal Intimacies: Interspecies Relatedness in India's Central Himalayas*. Chicago: University of Chicago Press.

Greenough, Paul. 2003. "Pathogens, Pugmarks, and Political 'Emergency': The 1970s South Asian Debate on Nature." In *Nature in the Global South: Environmental Projects in South and Southeast Asia*, edited by Paul Greenough and Anna Lowenhaupt Tsing, 201–30. Durham, NC: Duke University Press.

Greenough, Paul. 2012. "Bio-Ironies of the Fractured Forest: India's Tiger Reserves." In *India's Environmental History*, vol. 2, *From Ancient Times to the Colonial Period*, edited by Mahesh Rangarajan and K. Sivaramakrishnan, 315–56. New Delhi: Permanent Black.

Hall, Tarquin. 2001. *To the Elephant Graveyard*. London: Grove Press.

Hamilton, P. H. 1981. *The Leopard (*Panthera pardus*) and the Cheetah (*Acinonyx jubatus *in Kenya: Ecology Status Conservation Management*. Report for the US Fish and Wildlife Service, the African Wildlife Leadership Foundation, and the Government of Kenya.

Haraway, Donna. 2015. "Anthropocene, Capitalocene, Plantationocene, Chthulucene: Making Kin." *Environmental Humanities* 11: 159–65.

Haraway, Donna. 2016. *Staying with the Trouble: Making Kin in the Chthulucene*. Durham, NC: Duke University Press.

Haraway, Donna J. 1990. *Primate Visions: Gender, Race, and Nature in the World of Modern Science*. London: Routledge.

Haraway, Donna J. 2008. *When Species Meet*. Minneapolis: University of Minnesota Press.

Haraway, Donna J. 2012. "Awash in Urine: DES and Premarin® in Multispecies Response-ability." *Women's Studies Quarterly* 40 (1/2): 301–16.

Harris, Daniel. 2000. *Cute, Quaint, Hungry, and Romantic: The Aesthetics of Consumerism*. Boston, MA: De Capo Press.

Hecht, Gabrielle. 2018a. "The African Anthropocene." Aeon, February 6, 2018. https://aeon.co/essays/if-we-talk-about-hurting-our-planet-who-exactly-is-the-we.

Hecht, Gabrielle. 2018b. "Interscalar Vehicles for an African Anthropocene: On Waste, Temporality, and Violence." *Cultural Anthropology* 33 (1): 109–41.

Heise, Ursula K. 2016. *Imagining Extinction: The Cultural Meanings of Endangered Species*. Chicago: University of Chicago Press.

Hetherington, Kregg. 2019. *Infrastructure, Environment, and Life in the Anthropocene*. Durham, NC: Duke University Press.

Hill, Catherine M. 2017. "Introduction: Complex Problems: Using a Biosocial Approach to Understanding Human-Wildlife Interactions." In *Understanding Con□icts about Wildlife: A Biosocial Approach*, edited by C. M. Hill, A. D. Webber, and N. E. C. Priston, 1–14. New York: Berghahn Books.

Hodges-Hill, E. 1992. *Man-Eater: Tales of Lion and Tiger Encounters*. Heathfield: Cockbird Press.

Howe, Cymene, and Anand Pandian. 2016. "Introduction: Lexicon for an Anthropocene Yet Unseen." Editors' Forum: Theorizing the Contemporary, *Fieldsights*, January 21, 2016. https://culanth.org/fieldsights/introduction-lexicon-for-an-anthropocene-yet-unseen.

Howe, Cymene, and Anand Pandian, eds. 2020. *Anthropocene Unseen: A Lexicon*. Santa Barbara, CA: Punctum Books. https://punctumbooks.com/titles/anthropocene-unseen-a-lexicon/.

Hughes, Julie E. 2013. *Animal Kingdoms: Hunting, the Environment, and Power in the Indian Princely States*. Cambridge, MA: Harvard University Press.

Hulme, Mike. 2009. *Why We Disagree about Climate Change: Understanding Controversy, Inaction and Opportunity*. Cambridge: Cambridge University Press.

Hussain, Shafqat. 2012. "Forms of Predation: Tiger and Markhor Hunting in Colonial Governance." *Modern Asian Studies* 46 (5): 1212–38.

Hutchins, Aaron. 2019. "To Kill a Polar Bear." *Macleans*. April 15, 2019. https://www.macleans.ca/to-kill-polar-bear/.

Ito, Mimei. 2008. "Seeing Animals, Speaking of Nature: Visual Culture and the Question of the Animal." *Theory, Culture & Society* 25 (4): 119–37.

Jalais, Annu. 2011. *Forest of Tigers: People, Politics & Environment in the Sundarbans*. New Delhi: Routledge.

Jalais, Annu. 2018. "Reworlding the Ancient Chinese Tiger in the Realm of the Asian Anthropocene." *International Communication of Chinese Culture* 5 (1): 121–44.

James, Tania. 2016. *The Tusk That Did the Damage*. London: Vintage.

Jobson, Ryan C. 2020. "The Case for Letting Anthropology Burn: Sociocultural Anthropology in 2019." *American Anthropologist* 122 (2): 259–71.

Kanwar, Pamela. 2004. *Imperial Simla: The Political Culture of the Raj*. Delhi: Oxford University Press.

Karanth, K. U., and R. Gopal. 2005. "An Ecology-Based Policy Framework for Human-Tiger Coexistence in India." In *People and Wildlife: Conflict or Co-existence?*, edited by R. Woodroffe, S. Thirgood, and A. Rabinowitz, 373–87. Cambridge: Cambridge University Press.

Karanth, K. Ullas. 1995. "Estimating Tiger *Panthera tigris* Populations from Camera-Trap Data Using Capture-Recapture Models." *Biological Conservation* 71 (3): 333–38.

Kashyap, Anurag, Neeraj Ghaywan, and Vikramaditya Motwane, dir. 2018. *Sacred Games*. Season 1. Aired July 5, 2018, on Netflix. Produced by Phantom Films.

Kelly, Ann H., Javier Lezaun, Ilana Lowy, Gustavo Correa Matta, Carolina de Oliviera Nogueira, and Elaine Teixeira Rabello. 2020. "Uncertainty in Times of Medical Emergency: Knowledge Gaps and Structural Ignorance during the Brazilian Zika Crisis." *Social Science & Medicine* 246. https://doi.org/10.1016/j.socscimed.2020.112787.

Khan, Naveeda. 2014. "Dogs and Humans and What Earth Can Be: Filaments of Muslim Ecological Thought." *HAU: Journal of Ethnographic Theory* 4 (3): 245–64.

Khan, Naveeda. 2015. "The Death of Nature in the Era of Global Warming." In *Wording the World: Veena Das and Her Interlocutors*, edited by Roma Chatterji, 288–99. New York: Fordham University Press.

King, Barbara J. 2014. *How Animals Grieve*. Chicago: University of Chicago Press.

Kingsolver, Barbara. 2012. *Flight Behaviour*. London: Harper Collins.

Kipling, Rudyard. 1894. "Mowgli's Brothers." *St. Nicholas Magazine*, vol. XXL (3): 195–206.

Kipling, Rudyard. 2018. *The Jungle Book*. London: Wordsworth.

Klein, Naomi. 2014. *This Changes Everything: Capitalism vs. the Climate*. New York: Simon & Schuster.

Kohn, Eduardo. 2013. *How Forests Think: Toward an Anthropology beyond the Human*. Berkeley: University of California Press.

Krishnan, Vidya. 2020. "The Callousness of India's COVID-19 Response." *Atlantic*, March 27, 2020. https://www.theatlantic.com/international/archive/2020/03/india-coronavirus-covid19-narendra-modi/608896/.

Landy, Frederic. 2017. "Urban Leopards Are Good Cartographers: Human-Nonhuman and Spatial Conflicts at Sanjay Gandhi National Park, Mumbai." In *Places of Nature in Ecologies of Urbanism*, edited by Anne Rademacher and K. Sivaramakrishnan, 67–86. Hong Kong: Hong Kong University Press.

Latour, Bruno. 2014. "Anthropology at the Time of the Anthropocene—A Personal View of What Is to Be Studied." Distinguished lecture delivered at the American Anthropological Association Annual Meeting, Washington, DC, December 2014.

Latour, Bruno. 2018. *Down to Earth: Politics in the New Climatic Regime*. Cambridge: Polity Press.

Linnell, J. D. C., R. Aanes, J. E. Swenson, J. Odden, and M. E. Smith. 1997. "Translocation of Carnivores as a Method for Managing Problem Animals: A Review." *Biodiversity and Conservation* 6 (9): 1245–57.

Lorimer, Jamie. 2015. *Wildlife in the Anthropocene: Conservation after Nature*. Minneapolis: University of Minnesota Press.

Lorimer, Jamie. 2017. "The Anthropo-scene: A Guide for the Perplexed Social Studies of Science." *Social Studies of Science* 47 (1): 117–42.

Luciano, Dana. 2015. "The Inhuman Anthropocene." *Avidly*, March 22, 2015. http://avidly.lareviewofbooks.org/2015/03/22/the-inhuman-anthropocene/.

Lynteris, Christos, ed. 2019. *Framing Animals as Epidemic Villains: Histories of Non-Human Disease Vectors*. New York: Palgrave Macmillan.

MacFarlane, Robert. 2019. *Underland: A Deep Time Journey*. London: Hamish Hamilton.

MacKenzie, John M. 1988. *The Empire of Nature: Hunting, Conservation, and British Imperialism*. Manchester: Manchester University Press.

Madhusudan, M. D., and Charudutt Mishra. 2005. "Why Big, Fierce Animals Are Threatened: Conserving Large Mammals in Densely Populated Landscapes." In *Battles over Nature: Science and the Politics of Conservation*, edited by Vasant Saberwal and Mahesh Rangarajan, 31–55. Delhi: Permanent Black.

Maggio, R. 2014. "The Anthropology of Storytelling and the Storytelling of Anthropology." *Journal of Comparative Research in Anthropology and Sociology* 5 (2): 89–106.

Malik, Aditya. 2016. *Tales of Justice and Rituals of Divine Embodiments: Oral Narratives from the Central Himalayas*. New York: Oxford University Press.

Malinowski, Bronislaw. 2014. *Argonauts of the Western Pacific*. New York: Routledge.

Malm, Andreas, and Alf Hornborg. 2014. "The Geology of Mankind? A Critique of the Anthropocene Narrative." *Anthropocene Review* 1 (1): 62–69.

Margulies, Jared. 2019. "Making the 'Man-Eater': Tiger Conservation as Necropolitics." *Political Geography* 69 (March): 150–61.

Margulies, Jared, and Kriti Karanth. 2018. "The Production of Human-Wildlife Conflict: A Political Animal Geography of Encounter." *Geoforum* 95 (October): 153–64.

Marks, Stuart A. 1984. *The Imperial Lion: Human Dimensions of Wildlife Management in Central Africa*. Boulder, CO: Westview Press.

Martin, Mark. 2011. *I'm with the Bears: Short Stories from a Damaged Planet*. London: Verso.

Mathur, Nayanika. 2014. "The Reign of Terror of the Big Cat: Bureaucracy and the Mediation of Social Times in the Indian Himalaya." *Journal of the Royal Anthropological Institute* 20 (S1): 148–65.

Mathur, Nayanika. 2015. "It's a Conspiracy Theory and Climate Change: Of Beastly Encounters and Cervine Disappearances in Himalayan India." *HAU: Journal of Ethnographic Theory* 5 (1): 87–111.

Mathur, Nayanika. 2016. *Paper Tiger: Law, Bureaucracy, and the Developmental State in Himalayan India*. Cambridge: Cambridge University Press.

Mathur, Nayanika. 2017. "The Task of the Climate Translator." *Economic and Political Weekly* 52 (31): 77–84.

Mathur, Nayanika. 2019. "Incursion." Forum on Volumetric Sovereignty. *Society and Space*, April 1, 2019. https://www.societyandspace.org/articles/incursion.

Mathur, Nayanika. 2020. "Telling the Story of the Pandemic." Somatosphere, May 11, 2020. http://somatosphere.net/forumpost/covid19-storytelling-pandemic/.

Mathur, Tapsi. 2018. "How Professionals Became Natives: Geography and Trans-Frontier Exploration in Colonial India." PhD thesis, University of Michigan.

Mawdsley, Emma. 1997. "Nonsecessionist Regionalism in India: The Uttarakhand Separate State Movement." *Environment and Planning A* 29 (12): 2217–35.

Mawdsley, Emma. 2004. "India's Middle Class and the Environment." *Development and Change* 35 (1): 79–103.

Ministry of Environment and Forests. 2011. *Guidelines for Human-Leopard Conflict Management*. Delhi: Government of India, April 2011.

Moezzi, M., K. B. Janda, and S. Rotmann. 2017. "Using Stories, Narratives, and Storytelling in Energy and Climate Change Research." *Energy Research & Social Science* 31 (September): 1–10.

Montgomery, Sy. 2015. *The Soul of an Octopus*. London: Simon & Schuster.

Moore, Jason. 2015. *Capitalism in the Web of Life: Ecology and the Accumulation of Capital*. London: Verso.

Moore, Jason, ed. 2016. *Anthropocene or Capitalocene? Nature, History, and the Crisis of Capitalism*. Oakland, CA: Kairos.

Morton, Timothy. 2013. *Hyperobjects: Philosophy and Ecology after the End of the World*. Minneapolis: University of Minnesota Press.

Mukherjee, S., and C. Mishra. 2001. "Predation by Leopard *Panthera pardus* in Majhatal Harsang Wildlife Sanctuary, W. Himalayas." *Journal of the Bombay Natural History Society* 98 (2): 267–68.

Multiple Mobilities Research Cluster (Miriam Ticktin, Radhika Subramaniam, Victoria Hattam, Laura Y. Liu, and Rafi Youatt). 2017. "Images Unwalled." *Anthropology Now* 9 (3): 24–37.

Mumbaikars for SGNP. 2014. *A Forest Department and Centre for Wildlife Studies Collaborative Project to Address Human-Leopard (*Panthera pardus*) Conflict in and around Sanjay Gandhi National Park (SGNP)*. Mumbai: Mumbaikars for SGNP. Available at https://www.slideshare.net/mumbaikaar/final-report-mumbaikarsforsgnpproject.

Nadasdy, Paul. 2004. *Hunters and Bureaucrats: Power, Knowledge, and Aboriginal-State Relations in the Southwest Yukon*. Toronto: UBC Press.

Narayanan, Yamini. 2018. "Cow Protection as 'Casteised Speciesism': Sacralisation, Commercialisation and Politicisation." *South Asia: Journal of South Asia Studies* 41 (2): 331–51.

Ngai, Sianne. 2012. *Our Aesthetic Categories: Zany, Cute, Interesting*. Cambridge, MA: Harvard University Press.

Odden, M., V. Athreya, S. Rattan, and J. D. C. Linnell. 2014. "Adaptable Neighbours: Movement Patterns of GPS-Collared Leopards in Human Dominated Landscapes in India." *PLOS ONE* 9 (11). https://doi.org/10.1371/journal.pone.0112044.

Ogra, M. V. 2008. "Human-Wildlife Conflict and Gender in Protected Area Borderlands: A Case Study of Costs, Perceptions, and Vulnerabilities from Uttarakhand (Uttaranchal), India." *Geoforum* 39 (3): 1408–22.

Packer, Craig, D. Scheel, and A. E. Pusey. 1990. "Why Lions Form Groups: Food Is Not Enough." *American Naturalist* 136 (1): 1–19.

Pandian, Anand S. 2001. "Predatory Care: The Imperial Hunt in Mughal and British India." *Journal of Historical Sociology* 14 (1): 79–107.

Paprocki, Kasia. 2019. "All That Is Solid Melts into the Bay: Anticipatory Ruination and Climate Change Adaptation." *Antipode* 51 (1): 295–315.

Parreñas, Juno Salazar. 2018. *Decolonizing Extinction: The Work of Care in Orangutan Rehabilitation*. Durham, NC: Duke University Press.

Patterson, John Henry. (1898) 2011. *The Man-Eaters of Tsavo and Other East African Adventures*. Reprint, Milton Keynes: Simon & Brown.

Philo, Chris, and C. Wilbert, eds. 2000. *Animal Spaces, Beastly Places: New Geographies of Human-Animal Relations*. London: Routledge.

Pooley, S., M. Barua, W. Beinart, A. Dickman, G. Holmes, J. Lorimer, A. J. Loveridge, D. W. Macdonald, G. Marvin, S. Redpath, C. Sillero-Zubiri, A. Zimmermann, and E. J. Milner-Gulland. 2017. "An Interdisciplinary Review of Current and Future Approaches to Improving Human-Predator Relations." *Conservation Biology* 31 (3): 513–23.

Power, Amanda. 2019. "Towards the Anthropocene: State-Formation and Environment in the Global Middle Ages." Paper presented at the Transnational and Global History Seminar: Scaling Global History, Nuffield College, Oxford, February 26, 2019.

Powers, Richard. 2018. *The Overstory*. London: William Heinemann.

Probyn, Elspeth. 2016. *Eating the Ocean*. Durham, NC: Duke University Press.

Pubby, V. 1988. *Shimla Then and Now*. New Delhi: Indus Publishing House.

Punwani, Jyoti. 2015. "Maharashtra's Beef Ban." *Economic and Political Weekly* 50 (11): 17–19.

Purdy, Jedediah. 2015. *After Nature: A Politics for the Anthropocene*. Cambridge, MA: Harvard University Press.

Rangarajan, Mahesh. 2005. *India's Wildlife History: An Introduction*. Ranikhet: Permanent Black.

Rangarajan, Mahesh. 2009. "Striving for a Balance: Nature, Power, Science and India's Indira Gandhi, 1917–1984." *Conservation and Society* 7 (4): 299–312.

Rangarajan, Mahesh. 2013. "Animals with Rich Histories: The Case of the Lions of Gir Forest, Gujarat, India." *History and Theory* 52 (4): 109–27.

Rangarajan, Mahesh, and Ghazala Shahabuddin. 2006. "Displacement and Relocation from Protected Areas: Towards a Biological and Historical Synthesis." *Conservation and Society* 4 (3): 359–78.

Rangarajan, Mahesh, and K. Sivaramakrishnan. 2011. *India's Environmental History: A Reader*. New Delhi: Permanent Black.

Rashkow, E. 2015. "Resistance to Hunting in Pre-Independence India: Religious Environmentalism, Ecological Nationalism or Cultural Conservation?" *Modern Asian Studies* 49 (2): 270–301.

Redpath, Stephen M., Saloni Bhatia, and Juliette Young. 2015. "Tilting at Wildlife: Reconsidering Human-Wildlife Conflict." *Oryx* 49 (2): 222–25.

Rees, Amanda. 2017. "Animal Agents? Historiography, Theory and the History of Science in the Anthropocene." *British Journal of the History of Science (BJHS): Themes* 2: 1–10.

Saberwal, Vasant K., James P. Gibbs, Ravi Chellam, and A. J. T. Johnsingh. 1994. "Lion-Human Conflict in the Gir Forest, India." *Conservation Biology* 8 (2): 501–7.

Saha, Jonathan. 2018. "Do Elephants Have Souls? Animal Subjectivities and Colonial Encounters." In *South Asian Governmentalities: Michel Foucault and the Question of Postcolonial Orderings*, edited by S. Legg and D. Heath, 159–77. South Asia in the Social Sciences. Delhi: Cambridge University Press.

Sakakibara, C. 2008. "'Our Home Is Drowning': Iñupiat Storytelling and Climate Change in Point Hope, Alaska." *Geographical Review* 98 (4): 456–75.

Salisbury, Joyce E. 2011. *The Beast Within: Animals in the Middle Ages*. Abingdon: Routledge.

Sankhala, K. 1993. *Return of the Tiger*. New Delhi: Lustre Press.

Seth, Vikram. 1999. *Beastly Tales: From Here and There*. London: Phoenix.

Shahabuddin, Ghazala. 2010. *Conservation at the Crossroads: Science, Society and the Future of India's Wildlife*. Ranikhet: Permanent Black.

Shahabuddin, Ghazala. 2014. "The 'Tiger Crisis' and the Response: Reclaiming the Wilderness in Sariska Tiger Reserve, Rajasthan." In *Shifting Grounds: People, Animals, and Mobility in India's Environmental History*, edited by Mahesh Rangarajan and K. Sivaramakrishnan, 252–69. New Delhi: Oxford University Press.

Shaktawat, Daulat Singh. 2018. *My Encounter with the Big Cat and Other Adventures in Ranthambore*. Delhi: Niyogi.

Shell, Jacob. 2015. *Transportation and Revolt: Pigeons, Mules, Canals, and the Vanishing Geographies of Subversive Mobility*. Cambridge, MA: MIT Press.

Shresth, Swati. 2015. *The Colonial Hunt: Metropole, Colony, and Wildlife in India, 1850–1950*. Nehru Memorial Museum and Library Occasional Paper. Perspectives in Indian Development, New Series 50. New Delhi: Nehru Memorial Museum and Library.

Singer, Peter. 1995. *Animal Liberation*. London: Pimlico.

Singha, Radhika. 1998. *A Despotism of Law: Crime and Justice in Early Colonial India*. Delhi: Oxford University Press.

Skinner, Quentin. 2018. "Afterword: Climate Change in the Light of the Past." In *Nature, Action and the Future: Political Thought and the Environment*, edited by Katrina Forrester and Sophie Smith, 221–30. Cambridge: Cambridge University Press.

Sondhi, Sanjay, Vidya Athreya, Anchal Sondhi, Arun Prasad, Amit Verma, and Neha Verma. 2016. *Human Attacks by Leopards in Uttarakhand, India: An Assessment Based on Perceptions of Affected People and Stakeholders*. Dehradun: Titli Trust.

Sramek, Joseph. 2006. "'Face Him like a Briton': Tiger Hunting, Imperialism, and British Masculinity in Colonial India, 1800–1875." *Victorian Studies* 48 (4): 659–80.

Srinivasan, Amia. 2017. "The Sucker, The Sucker: What's It Like to Be an Octopus?" *London Review of Books* 39 (17): 23–25.

Srivastava, Sanjay. 1998. *Constructing Post-Colonial India: National Character and the Doon School*. London: Routledge.

Storey, William K. 1991. "Big Cats and Imperialism: Lion and Tiger Hunting in Kenya and Northern India, 1898–1930." *Journal of World History* 2 (2): 135–73.

Surve, Nikit. 2015. *Ecology of Leopard in Sanjay Gandhi National Park, Maharashtra with Special Reference to Its Abundance, Prey Selection and Food Habits*. Report submitted to SGNP and Maharashtra Forest Department, Mumbai. https://sgnp.maharashtra.gov.in/Site/Upload/Pdf/Ecology_of_leopard_in_SGNP_2015-Nikit_Surve.pdf.

Svenning, Jens-Christian. 2017. "Future Megafaunas: A Historical Perspective on the Potential for a Wilder Anthropocene." In *Arts of Living on a Damaged Planet*, edited by Anna Tsing, Heather Swanson, Elaine Gan, and Nils Bubandt, 67–86. Minneapolis: University of Minnesota Press.

Taneja, Anand Vivek. 2013. "Jinnealogy: Everyday Life and Islamic Theology in Post-Partition Delhi." *HAU: Journal of Ethnographic Theory* 3 (3): 139–65.

Telesca, Jennifer E. 2020. *Red Gold: The Managed Extinction of the Giant Bluefin Tuna*. Minneapolis: University of Minnesota Press.

Thomas, Julia Adeney. 2014. "History and Biology in the Anthropocene: Problems of Scale, Problems of Value." *American Historical Review* 119 (5): 1587–607.

Thomas, Julia Adeney. 2019. "Why the 'Anthropocene' Is Not 'Climate Change' and Why It Matters." Asia Global Online, January 10, 2019. https://www.asiaglobalonline.hku.hk/anthropocene-climate-change/.

Todd, Zoe. 2015. "Indigenizing the Anthropocene." In *Art in the Anthropocene: Encounters among Aesthetics, Politics, Environment and Epistemology*, edited by Heather Davis and Etienne Turpin, 241–54. London: Open Humanities Press.

Travers, Robert. 2019. "Indian Petitioning and Colonial State-Formation in Eighteenth-Century Bengal." *Modern Asian Studies* 53 (1): 89–122.

Tsing, Anna L. 2015. *The Mushroom at the End of the World: On the Possibility of Life in Capitalist Ruins*. Princeton, NJ: Princeton University Press.

Tsing, Anna L., Andrew S. Mathews, and Nils Bubandt. 2019. "Patchy Anthropocene: Landscape Structure, Multispecies History, and the Retooling of Anthropology." *Current Anthropology* 60 (20): S186–S197.

Turnbull, Jonathon, Adam Searle, and William M. Adams. 2020. "Quarantine Urban Ecologies." Editors' Forum: Covid-19, *Fieldsights*, May 19, 2020. https://culanth.org/fieldsights/quarantine-urban-ecologies.

United Nations Framework Convention on Climate Change. 2011. *Fact Sheet: Climate Change Science—the Status of Climate Change Science Today*. February 2011. https://unfccc.int/files/press/backgrounders/application/pdf/press_factsh_science.pdf.

Urban, Mark C. 2015. "Accelerating Extinction Risk from Climate Change." *Science* 348 (6234): 571–73.

Van Dooren, T., and D. B. Rose. 2016. "Lively Ethnography—Storying Animist Worlds." *Environmental Humanities* 8 (1): 77–94.

Velten, Hannah. 2013. *Beastly London: A History of Animals in the City*. London: Reaktion.

West, Paige. 2005. "Translation, Value, and Space: Theorizing an Ethnographic and Engaged Environmental Anthropology." *American Anthropologist* 107 (4): 632–42.

West, Paige. 2006. *Conservation Is Our Government Now: The Politics of Ecology in Papua New Guinea*. Durham, NC: Duke University Press.

Weston, Kath. 2017. *Animate Planet: Making Visceral Sense of Living in a High-Tech Ecologically Damaged World*. Durham, NC: Duke University Press.

White, Luise. 2000. *Speaking with Vampires: Rumor and History in Colonial Africa*. Berkeley: University of California Press.

Whitehead, Hal, and Luke Rendell. 2015. *The Cultural Lives of Whales and Dolphins*. Chicago: University of Chicago Press.

Whyte, Kyle. 2017. "Indigenous Climate Change Studies: Indigenizing Futures, Decolonizing the Anthropocene." *English Language Notes* 55 (1–2): 153–62.

Wittenberg-Cox, Avivah. 2020. "What Do Countries with the Best Coronavirus Responses Have in Common? Women Leaders." *Forbes*, April 13, 2020. https://www.forbes.com/sites/avivahwittenbergcox/2020/04/13/what-do-countries-with-the-best-coronavirus-reponses-have-in-common-women-leaders/.

Wolch, J. R., and J. Emel, eds. 1998. *Animal Geographies: Place, Politics, and Identity in the Nature-Culture Borderlands*. London: Verso.

World Wildlife Fund. n.d. *Solving Conflicts between Asian Big Cats and Humans: A Portfolio of Conservation Action*. Gland, Switzerland: Global Species Program, WWF International. Accessed April 12, 2017. https://wwfeu.awsassets.panda.org/downloads/abchwcinfdocfromthewwfglobalspeciesprogramme.pdf.

Yong, Ed. 2020. "How the Pandemic Defeated America." *Atlantic*, September 2020. https://www.theatlantic.com/magazine/archive/2020/09/coronavirus-american-failure/614191/.

Yusoff, Kathryn. 2018. *A Billion Black Anthropocenes or None*. Minneapolis: University of Minnesota Press.

Zeiderman, Austin. 2016. "Adaptive Publics: Building Climate Constituencies in Bogotá." *Public Culture* 28 (2): 389–413.

INDEX

Note: page numbers in italics indicate figures.

ABOUT THE AUTHOR

Nayanika Mathur is associate professor in anthropology and South Asian studies as well as Fellow of Wolfson College at the University of Oxford. She is the author of *Paper Tiger: Law, Bureaucracy and the Developmental State in Himalayan India*.